MOTORING

OTHER BOOKS BY JOHN A. JAKLE AND KEITH A. SCULLE

The Gas Station in America (1994)

The Motel in America (1996), with Jefferson S. Rogers

Fast Food: Roadside Restaurants in the Automobile Age (1999)

Lots of Parking: Land Use in a Car Culture (2004)

Signs in America's Auto Age: Signatures of Landscape and Place (2004)

motoring

JOHN A. JAKLE AND KEITH A. SCULLE

University of Georgia Press ◆ Athens and London

▼ in association with the Center for American Places at Columbia College Chicago ●

Motoring: The Highway Experience in America
is part of the series *Center Books on American Places,*
George F. Thompson, series founder and director.
For more information about the Center for American
Places, please go online: www.americanplaces.org.

© 2008 by the University of Georgia Press
Athens, Georgia 30602
Photographs © 2008 by John A. Jakle and Keith A. Sculle
All rights reserved.
Designed by Mindy Basinger Hill
Set in 10/14 point Minion Pro
   by Graphic Composition, Inc., Bogart, Georgia
Printed and bound by Maple Press
The paper in this book meets the guidelines for
permanence and durability of the Committee on
Production Guidelines for Book Longevity of the
Council on Library Resources.

Printed in the United States of America

12   11   10   09   08   C   5   4   3   2   1

Library of Congress Cataloging-in-Publication Data

Jakle, John A.
Motoring : the highway experience in America / John A. Jakle and Keith A. Sculle.
     p. cm. — (Center books on American places)
   Includes bibliographical references and index.
   ISBN-13: 978-0-8203-3028-0 (hard cover : alk. paper)
   ISBN-10: 0-8203-3028-0 (hard cover : alk. paper)
   1. Automobile travel—United States—History.
2. Automobile driving—United States.
3. Roads—United States.
I. Sculle, Keith A. II. Title.
   GV1021.J33 2008
   917.304—dc22   2007022330

British Library Cataloging-in-Publication Data available

"Allons! the road is before us!"

"Allons! Whoever you are, come travel with me!"

WALT WHITMAN, "Song of the Open Road"

CONTENTS

ACKNOWLEDGMENTS

We thank the many people who furnished information used in writing this book. Jessica Rowecroft, Charleston, Massachusetts, kindly provided a copy and granted use of her unpublished paper, "The Truck Stops Here! The History and Physical Development of the Truck Stop Industry." The people who provided information from the collections they oversee include Dianne Brooks, National Safety Council Library, Washington, D.C.; Edward O. Handy, Barnstable Historical Society, Barnstable, Massachusetts; Craig Ordner, Railroad and Heritage Museum, Temple, Texas; Beverly Reid, historian, Town of North Elba, Village of Lake Placid, New York; Carol Saunders, Hyannis Public Library Association, Hyannis, Massachusetts; and Mary Sicchio, special collections librarian, Cape Cod Community College Library, Cape Cod, Massachusetts.

"I am the motor. I have clipped the wings of Time, and broken through the barriers of Space." So mused the editor of *The Highwayman,* a publicity magazine published by New Jersey's highway department, in 1922.[1] Written in a biblical style, the article continued, "I have opened the gates of cities, that those who dwell therein may go as on wings to . . . open spaces and find again the sun and wind and the stars they had forgot." While "in the marts of day," the article assured, "your ear has heard my whirring in a thousand streets. . . . The wheels of industry spin faster, the work of the world is done in shorter hours." Then came the important pitch, a plea for a certain kind of auto-oriented religious faith: "I have given much, and one thing have I asked—roads. Flowing roads for my spinning wheels; roads to reach into the humble corners, and stretch even to the far places of the earth."

Above the roadbed and usually behind an internal combustion engine (mounted on a chassis with wheels, of course), sat a driver, a person at first called an automobilist (or sometimes an autoist) but then more popularly a motorist. In romantically praising America's new auto age, early commentators might emphasize the prized machine and the enabling roadway, thus slighting the motorist as consummate traveler. The editor of an industry trade journal found it easy to treat motorists mainly as backers of ever more cars and ever more road improvements. However, in this book, an assessment of America's first half century of automobility, we seek to give motorists their full due. Our emphasis is motoring, a concept we define as that experience by which drivers, machines, and highways became integrally linked.

In recent decades, the nation's automobile dependence has faced increasing criticism. The motor car is increasingly blamed for urban sprawl, energy waste, and many forms of environmental degradation and is fully implicated in many social problems involving race, class, age, and gender differences. As the wisdom of America's passionate embrace of automobility has come into serious question, reassessing how Americans became so dependent on automobiles seems more important than ever. How did we position ourselves to be so dominated? This book does not offer outright celebration of the automobile's triumph. We tell of those who questioned the new technology as we deal with some of the negative aspects of auto ownership and use. But why did their voices go unheeded? We assess the cultural predispositions that led Americans to reject earlier modes of travel. We explore the rise of the various vested interests that vigorously promoted automobility. Why did their arguments prove so persuasive?

Motoring, the human/machine response to the road, offers important insight into American culture. The driver, the motor car, the highway, and indeed the passing landscape largely made convenient for automobiles speak of values central to being American and provide important metaphors for comprehending life in the United States. Every day, we speak in terms of "getting ahead," "keeping to the straight and narrow," and "going the distance." Motoring at first suggested a wanderlust where grass always seemed greener over the distant hill, a kind of independence, a freedom to get places not only quickly but essentially under one's own direction. Motoring spoke of mobility not just geographical in nature but social as well. Motoring became the travel response not only to what Americans came to call the highway but also to what Americans called the open road, a place of important opportunity.

The highway is a distinctive kind of place.[2] Highways are engineered paths that facilitate rapid movement by motor vehicles, function clearly reflected in form. There is the roadway, variously surfaced, leveled, embanked, widened or constricted, and linked with other roads to form networks of interconnectivity. There are the cars, motor trucks, and other vehicles in motion or at rest along highway margins. There are the signs that regulate moving and stopping, and of course there are drivers, who, cocooned in their vehicles, respond variously to the rules encoded in signs. There is the roadside, highway margins variously connected to the road, the car, and the driver. Finally, there is the landscape beyond, the encompassing context for highway travel seen as connected (or disconnected, as the case might be) from the road itself.

The highway is a kind of place experience. It is first and foremost a corridor for movement experienced sequentially. It involves departures and arrivals variously articulated in sequences of locomotion. Highways imply passage. On the highway—the great connector—places of origin combine with places of destination to define the journey as trip. Trip taking "places" motorists in a nether circumstance not fixed as "at home" or "at work" (places where people fully belong) but in a region of transience, a state of being neither here nor there but in between. Being "on the road" carries liberating implications, a separation from the tight conformities of home and work where one is well known. The highway is a place where strangers engage one another superficially, relating but readily disconnecting, with social engagements that tend to be transitory and anonymous.

Travel—even the commute to work or trip to shop—carries implications of release. Especially liberating, however, is leisure travel. Breaking everyday routines in the pursuit of touristic pleasure is perhaps the highway's ultimate liberating prospect. Totally divorced from home and work, the tourist rejuvenates through the vicarious consumption of place—not only touristic places specially packaged to be consumed as attractions but also the place of passage that the highway itself represents. The highway sequences the motorist's experience as sightseer (or the seer of sites). The motorist becomes an observer of a world flowing past. Life is experienced rather like a sequence of pictures rapidly emerging but also rapidly occluding. We believe that today's automobile world is substantially rooted in such exhilaration.

No motorist—least of all the habitual commuter—moves all the time at levels of heightened awareness. The highway provides novel opportunities to observe and to know, but the modern highway, smoothed and fully standardized, along with today's comfortable cars, can also lull the mind. Travel is monotonous where highways are overly level, overly straight, and divorced from surroundings by wide rights-of-way and limited access. Traveler attention tends to be deflected from roadside margins in high-speed driving, and getting there can dissolve into categories of blindness, the passing scene registering only as intermittent display. The highway as forward trajectory, reinforced by the sidelong blur of the lateral roadside, can become hypnotic, an invitation to reverie divorced from immediacy. It is but one way in which contemporary Americans function in relative social isolation. Given the amount of time the typical American spends driving a car, however, it is an important way.

The modern American roadside has been structured in ways that fully reflect the cognitive realities of motoring. First, roadside architecture is convenient to the motorist through driveways and parking lots that come easily into view as extensions of the highway itself. Second, buildings and signs loom in exaggerated forms to awaken motorists to immediate opportunities. Indeed, many roadside buildings are themselves signlike, configured by shape, bright coloring, and nighttime lighting to beckon drivers just as advertising signs communicate. Lining the nation's highways are easily identified places defined at the scale of the retail store. They scream for attention. Whether in a commercial strip or clustered at a freeway interchange, the message is the same: "Stop here!" The motorist receives heightened images to collect and access in objectifying the world, not just houses and barns and such other features of traditional landscape but also gasoline stations, motels, and fast food restaurants, modern phenomena directly related to motoring.

Automobility virtually transformed American geography during the early twentieth century—the traditional city, for example, gave way to highway reorientation. The early champions of automobility hardly expected this development. Cities grew outward along major axes of auto movement, rural roads made into commercial strips to provide framework for residential subdivisions, shopping centers, office and industrial parks, and every other kind of real estate development. In the new suburbia, the automobile became a necessity as urban opportunities came to be loosely strung out along highway corridors far distant from traditional city centers. In older inner cities, built originally for pedestrians and riders of mass transit, land became increasingly oriented toward auto use, with widened streets, expressways, and parking lots that spread things out there as well in one or another variation of the suburbanizing impulse. What was at first, therefore, the playful world of the automobile tourist—the promised world of enhanced freedom in leisure movement—became the mundane world of everyday life.

The highway as an ideal came to define much of modern America's political agenda. Treated as sacrosanct was the Highway Trust Fund generated through the collecting of federal gasoline taxes, a perpetual-motion machine for building roads. The more people drove, the greater the investment in highways; the more highways, the more people drove. American foreign policy acted to secure petroleum supplies, with the nation's military twice sent to war in the Persian Gulf area in recent years. The world of motoring is very much a political expression, a creation of government. Construction standards, road markings, and speed limits, among other safety rules, are administered by the government. Although the American highway may symbolize freedom in geographical and social mobility, with implications for autonomy and individual prerogative, it is in fact a creature of government intervention, perhaps the nation's strongest expression of community purpose. How Americans first came to embrace the automobile—with all of its implications for individual prerogative—still substantially obscures that reality.

At least three generations have matured in the nation's auto age, and motoring has very much come to influence popular culture. A sense of nostalgia readily attaches to aspects of America's motoring past, especially to the relics of automobiling—not just old cars but old roadside architecture and relic stretches of highway as well. The "open road" has been much explored in literature and cinema and of course in music. America has always been a place in flux, with each generation adopting new technologies and new ways of thinking and doing. Language used to anticipate the future reflects the highway's centrality. Thus, the "superhighway" of the Internet, for example, describes possibilities inherent in electronic communication, an analogy fully comprehensible in a society of highly mobile auto-mobilists.

In the pages that follow, we explore the rise of motoring in American life, focus-ing on 1900 to 1960. Although we necessarily consider many of the people directly responsible for the automobile's development, the growth of the nation's auto and related industries, and indeed the growth of the nation's vast highway infrastruc-ture, we focus on the role of the common motorist. We see this approach as setting this book apart from others. We focus on Americans as consumers of motorized travel experiences. We emphasize tourist travel, the source of motoring's early exhilaration, which energized much of what came after. We do not neglect other kinds of motoring, such as commuting and the journey to shop. But touring and the delights of visual landscape encounter grounded America's infatuation with a motorized transport system. Highways may have been justified on grounds of military defense or economic prosperity, as we outline, but the growing numbers of motorists, initially as tourists, made highway building not just politically fea-sible but compelling. Americans did not have the automobile imposed on them.

The book is divided into twelve chapters. In chapter 1 we place the rise of motor-ing in historical context. In chapters 2, 3, and 4, we outline the rise of the nation's modern road system as it evolved first through "named" highways, encouraged by private highway associations, and then through full intervention of federally subsi-dized state highway departments. Motoring, especially early on, was rarely without problems. Garages, our emphasis in chapter 5, loomed large as places to solve those problems. Out of the garage evolved the gasoline station, to be joined by an array of other roadside service establishments. In chapter 6, we focus on roadside tour-ist attractions as places of recreation and entertainment—not tourist destinations per se, but intervening temptations packaged along the roadside to snare tourist dollars. We return to the theme of highway building in chapter 7 to treat America's brief flirtation with parkway aesthetics: landscaped highways largely sanitized of marginal commercial intent. In chapter 8, we consider the nation's freeways and toll roads, where the beauty of landscaping largely gave way to the functionalism of civil engineering. Of course, cars were not the only motorized vehicles in the nation's fast lane. Truck traffic now dominates the freeways in many localities. In chapter 9, we consider trucking primarily as it affected the highway experiences of early twentieth-century motorists—for example, through the institution of the truck stop. In chapter 10, we assess the importance of motor bus travel. Unfortu-nately, space does not permit us to embrace the motorcycle and the novel world of the biker. Nor does it permit us to focus on the use of recreational vehicles. In chapter 11, we continue the story of America's evolving roadside services. If the gasoline station evolved from the garage, then the modern convenience store evolved in part from the gasoline station. But the convenience store is much more than just a place to buy gas. Today, one finds goods and services formerly available separately on the roadside very much bundled together at single locations. What might this development portend for the future? Chapter 12 offers concluding synthesis and speculation regarding what the nation's motoring heritage might yet bring to the United States.

Motoring changed people's lives. The highway experience clearly assumed a significance in American life that even the most ardent promoters of the automobile did not anticipate a century or so ago. Of course, the highway experience came to mean different things to different people and to different kinds of people. American women participated fully in motoring but usually did so in ways different from men, at least initially, when men fancied themselves as drivers and mechanics and women more as passengers. The open road—the heart and soul of motoring as an ideal—beckoned African Americans just as it did whites. If African Americans could not own the best houses or houses in the best neighborhoods, they could own the best motor cars, and many did, relying on black-owned and -operated motels and restaurants when they motored away from home. Teenagers came to embrace the automobile, perhaps as a means of escaping parental control, nurturing a subculture built around car-oriented pastimes from cruising to drag racing. For all Americans, irrespective of gender, race, or age, motoring came to offer empowerment through mobility, both geographical and social. Speed and convenience figured especially prominently. Motoring assumed a kind of centrality in American life, an influence that forcefully played out in the reconfiguring of landscape and place: the highway as open road became a kind of cultural imperative.

motoring

AN INTRODUCTION

Motoring is a somewhat slippery if not peculiar word. It derives, of course, from the stem word *motor,* which, like many words of modern implication, has changed meaning as its applications have changed. At the beginning of the twentieth century, motors were invariably devices that changed electrical energy into mechanical energy. Motors, for example, powered electric cars. What powered other autos were more appropriately called engines: steam engines (their boilers fired with kerosene) and, of course, internal combustion gasoline engines.[1] By 1920, however, the term *motor* had come to reference numerous kinds of power sources in cars and indeed had become shorthand for motor cars pure and simple. The word *motoring,* for its part, became a broad qualifier referring to the use of motorized vehicles. A *motorist,* in turn, was one who motored.[2] Motoring, therefore, referred to a kind of experience obtained through auto use—what motorists experienced when, for example, they were caught in congested traffic (figure 1.1). America was evolving as an auto-altered world, with the motorist at the center.

Inventing the Automobile

The idea that road vehicles might move under their own power took a long time to reach perfection. For example, in 1805, Oliver Evans introduced the Orukter Amphibolos, a wagon that could float but that also, more importantly, moved under steam power: a belt from a steam engine was attached to either an axle or a paddle wheel as need arose.[3] In the 1870s, when another "steam wagon" threatened the quietude of Wisconsin's rural roads, the state's legislature offered a cash prize to the first person to build a self-propelled machine capable of quietly moving at a minimum of 5 miles per hour "at least 200 miles in a continuous line."[4] The offer lapsed without takers. Not until 1891 did the auto age begin in America: F. W. Lambert initiated a small, lightweight gasoline-powered "tri-cycle" on the streets of Ohio City, Ohio.[5] Of course, others claimed to have been first, including bicycle

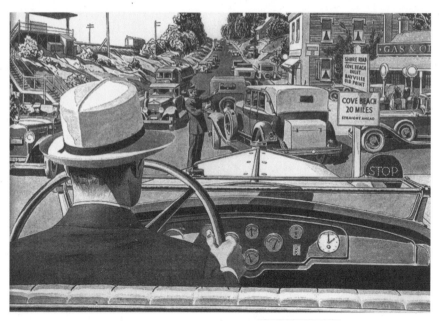

Figure 1.1. Advertisement for Tarvia Asphalt. *American City* 43 (September 1930): 180.

mechanics Charles and Frank Duryea, whose four-wheeled, bicycle-like "motor buggy" took to the streets of Springfield, Massachusetts, that same year. Also early off the mark was Charles Brady King of Detroit, whose "quadricycle" anticipated by three months the success of Henry Ford's first vehicle.

Not every auto pioneer embraced the gasoline engine. Ransom E. Olds experimented first with steam but then switched to the internal combustion engine for his Oldsmobile, the first American car manufactured in any quantity, starting in 1897. Conversely, Albert Pope, manufacturer of the Columbia Bicycle (America's best-selling brand), experimented successfully with internal combustion but turned to the manufacture of battery-driven electric cars instead. Francis and Freelan Stanley perfected their steam car in 1897, as did the White Brothers in 1901. A gasoline/electric hybrid car reached the market as early as 1910, but rather than generating power for the car's battery, as in today's hybrids, its gasoline engine merely kicked in when battery power was exhausted.[6]

The zeal with which Americans experimented with motorized vehicles might be credited to basic American values such as the Puritan notion of perfectibility. America's optimism contrasted greatly with Europe's retarding fatalism. Americans solved problems, observers argued, while Europeans abided problems.[7] But if such was the case, why did most of the key technological breakthroughs leading to the modern motor car's evolution derive largely from Europe? Nicholas Otto's

1876 compression-stroke engine and Wilhelm Maybach's 1892 atomizing carburetor revolutionized gasoline engines. And the 1892 Daimler-Benz Mercedes revolutionized car design by placing the engine up front and connecting it to the rear wheels by a driveshaft. (Previous vehicles had featured engines located under the seat and connected to the front wheels by either gears or belts.) The Daimler-Benz Mercedes had four cylinders rather than one or two, and the car was low slung, so that passengers sat between rather than above the wheels.[8]

From the beginning, European cars were heavy and low to the ground, following the Système Panhard, a carriage-making tradition developed in France. They were high powered, with gear ratios calculated to rapid acceleration. American cars, by contrast, owed much to the bicycle. As "motor buggies," they were very light in weight and low powered. Like a bicycle, motorists rode on rather than in them, very high up. As American motor vehicles grew in size and power, they came to have more in common with horse-drawn wagons and were often called motor carriages. Also called high-wheelers, at least by auto historians, American vehicles offered greater road clearance than did European motor cars, as dictated by America's still primitive roadways. American cars had gear ratios calculated more to pulling out of mud than to fast acceleration. Between 1898 and 1916, 123 manufacturers produced high-wheelers in seventy-four cities and towns across nineteen states.[9]

In the first years of the twentieth century, the most popular cars on the American market were expensive European models suitable only for city and town use. These cars were either imported or built in the United States under license. For example, Steinway and Sons, manufacturers of fine pianos, produced and marketed the Mercedes. American cars, while retaining high clearance, came to be engineered more like European cars, carrying four passengers plus the driver (figure 1.2). In some cars, the driver sat on the left, while in others he or she sat on the right, although left-hand drive became standard in the United States during the 1910s. Control of acceleration, shifting, and braking also were not at first standardized, with every car equipped with its own complex of foot pedals and hand switches, most of which were mounted on the steering column.

Elite Car Ownership

Before 1908, when Henry Ford introduced the Model T, the vast majority of American carmakers produced expensive cars for an elite market. The automakers themselves liked to be seen driving such cars when they visited their favorite country clubs or other prestigious places. The four-thousand-dollar price tag on the Stevens-Duryea Model Y was very high considering that it took the average wage earner seven years to earn that amount. Cars were not only expensive to

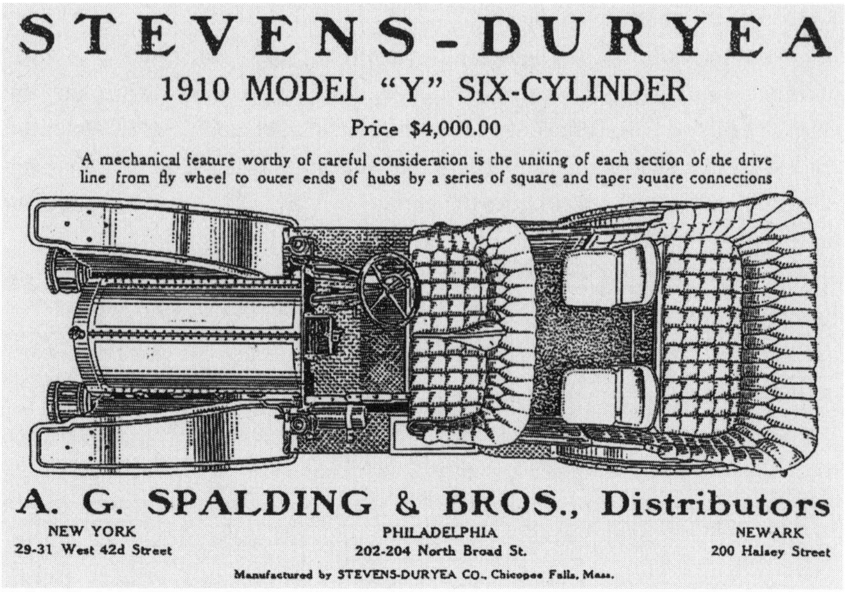

Figure 1.2. Advertisement for the Stevens-Duryea 1910 Model Y Six-Cylinder. *Automobile Club of America Journal* 1 (November 13, 1909): 659.

buy but also costly to operate. Even a relatively inexpensive two-door runabout that might cost only six hundred dollars, when operated over a single summer's driving season, would require several sets of tires (not including inner tubes and valve stems). Such repairs alone could run upward of half the value of the car. A car owner could expect to pay at least fifty dollars for gasoline and five dollars for lubricating oil.[10] Unless a garage was available (and a small private garage could be built for around five hundred dollars), the owner had to pay for car storage, at least during the winter months.

The very wealthy tended to employ professional drivers just as they did with for their horses and carriages. The word *chauffeur,* like the word *automobile,* was of French origin. The verb *chauffer* meant "to stoke up or fire up," as was done to steam engines and presumably gasoline engines.[11] Early cars, even European models, were notoriously unreliable, and mechanical expertise rather than driving skill brought the chauffeur to the fore. Auto repair was potentially dirty work, the kind of thing the wealthy traditionally hired others to do. Only now sophisticated technology was involved, and paradoxically, chauffeurs, through control of that technology, became empowered as employees. Nonetheless, owning an expensive car and being driven around in it fully advertised one's position in society irrespective of growing chauffeur independence and even insolence.

Motor Racing

Motoring became a sport, especially through embrace of speed. Speed, especially rapid acceleration, involved a mix of sensations. Muscles tensed as one's skeletal frame eased backward, and the face and stomach flattened. Vision focused forward, with peripheral vision a blur. Implicit was heightened awareness of one's surroundings, exhilarating for the change of pace yet somewhat fearsome for the enhanced risk. In racing, the challenge was what counted, whether two or more machines dashed toward a finish line or whether a car and driver merely competed against the clock. Motor racing, like horse racing, became a popular spectator sport. Human muscle and wit pitted against a machine and drivers and machines pitted against each other offered clear spectacle. Spectators did not have to participate directly in motoring to be enthused by it.

The first publicly sanctioned motor competition in the United States, sponsored by the *Chicago Times-Herald*, was held in the fall of 1895. However, completing the race took several attempts, car breakdowns eliminating all competitors on several occasions before a finish line could be reached. The ultimate winner, driving a German-made Benz, took nine hours and twenty-two minutes to drive round-trip between Chicago's near South Side and suburban Waukegan north of the city. He averaged only six miles per hour.[12] W. K. Vanderbilt Jr., whose fortune came largely from railroading, established the Vanderbilt Cup, the first annual race of national note, on Long Island in 1905. The winner of the first contest averaged 52 miles per hour over 268 miles of public road. Traditionally, New York City's elites partied through the night and then about two in the morning drove out to the race for its daybreak start. As one journalist remembered, "The sight of thousands of cars slinking in the dark into positions along the course, with their searchlights cutting soft, triangular swathes in the murky, dust-laden air, is a picture that many an old race lover still carries in his mind."[13]

Such racing venues were endurance runs rather than what came to be called speed races. Although such racing proved the driver's skill and stamina, it mainly tested car reliability. When the Detroit factory where Olds produced the Oldsmobile burned to the ground, only a single car survived. Olds ordered the vehicle driven overland to the Second Annual New York City Auto Show of 1901. The stunt made the car the show's prime attraction and greatly facilitated Olds in financing a new factory. At the tiller was Roy Chapin, a recent graduate of the University of Michigan's College of Engineering, who later became the driving force behind Hudson Motor Cars. Chapin personified the man willing to strip off his coat and white collar and work alongside the car mechanics who, as skilled craftsmen, assembled the automobiles on Detroit's early factory floors. The first endurance run promoted as such, a race from New York City to Buffalo that coincided with the 1901 Pan-American Exposition, was organized by the Buffalo automobile club. It was cut short at Rochester when news arrived that President William McKinley has been assassinated at the fairgrounds. The most celebrated of these runs (or tours) was that promoted by Charles J. Gidden between 1905 and 1913.[14]

Speed races were usually conducted on oval racetracks. Automakers very quickly came to appreciate these tracks as venues for demonstrating car reliability and for experimenting with technical innovation. Auto pioneers Alexander Winton and Henry Ford solidified their reputations through racing. At a track in Grosse Pointe, Detroit's first elite suburb, Ford won a dramatic ten-mile race against Winton in 1901. At the same track, bicycling legend Barney Oldfield set numerous world speed records in Ford's experimental 999, built in 1902. With the opening of the Indianapolis Speedway in 1909 and the launch of the five-hundred-mile Memorial Day race in 1911, formula motor racing came fully into its own. Indianapolis was Detroit's principal competitor as a car-manufacturing city. The first Indy 500 was won by an Indianapolis-made Marmon Wasp in six hours and forty-three minutes, with an average speed of 74.6 miles per hour.[15]

Motor racing declined in popularity during the 1920s as manufacturers went on to develop their own test tracks and to market car attributes other than speed and mechanical dependability. However, emphasis on midget-car and stock-car racing in the 1930s (the latter perhaps an outgrowth of Prohibition and the fast cars used by bootleggers) helped sustain the sport. Today, stock car racing, overseen by the National Association for Stock Car Auto Racing (NASCAR), is the second-most-popular spectator sport in the United States behind professional football. The rise of the hot rod also spoke forcefully of the love of speed and competition. Customizing (to produce cars that not only ran fast but looked fast) spread from its origins in southern California. Fast motoring thus permeated America's middling classes, becoming part of the American vernacular.[16]

Making Automobiles

In 1900, about four thousand motor cars were sold in the United States, 22 percent of them gasoline powered, 38 percent electric powered, and 40 percent steam powered. Operating costs for electric cars, however, were about three cents per mile, in contrast to one cent per mile for cars that ran on gasoline or, as with steam cars, kerosene.[17] Makers of steam-powered and electric cars turned to internal combustion engines or quit the business. Most makers of gasoline cars, however, grudgingly paid a royalty to the Electric Vehicle Company (and later the Association of Licensed Automobile Manufacturers), which held a patent for cars with internal combustion engines. The patent, filed in 1879 by George B. Selden, had been kept alive through the filing of numerous amendments. In 1911, Henry Ford challenged the patent in the courts, taking the position that the Selden design, which was never actually built, had not included Nicholas Otto's version of the internal combustion engine. The victory not only saved the automakers money but also in a sense liberated them.[18]

Between 1902 and 1907, 287 companies were either created or reoriented (in whole or in part) to the manufacture of cars, their total capitalization coming to about $25 million.[19] Established firms that turned to manufacturing automobiles included Winton Motor Carriage of Cleveland, previously a maker of bicycles; Peerless Manufacturing, also of Cleveland, previously a maker of clothes wringers; and the partnership of Heintz, Pierce, and Munshauer of Buffalo (renamed Pierce Arrow), previously manufacturers of a range of products including refrigerators and, of all things, bird cages. International Harvester (today's Navistar) was created in 1902 through the merger of McCormick, Deering, and several other farm-implement firms. The company placed a two-cylinder, air-cooled motor buggy on the market, the profile of which looked very much like that of a surrey. The company also offered a motorized spring wagon (with removable rear seats to open up haulage space) from which a line of trucks emerged.[20] Studebaker Brothers, the nation's largest wagon maker, also moved into the automotive field, first as a supplier of auto bodies to other manufacturers and then as a maker of an electric runabout. In 1910, Studebaker took over Detroit's Everitt-Metzger-Flanders car factory and began converting its South Bend, Indiana, works to car and truck production.[21]

In 1919, the United States had 230 companies assembling passenger cars and 372 assembling trucks. Factories were spread across thirty-two states and represented capitalization in the range of $275 million. More than a thousand additional firms produced car bodies, parts, and accessories, with a total capitalization of $337 million. The automakers and their suppliers employed six hundred thousand workers, who received salaries and wages worth $611 million annually. In addition, the nation had more than twenty-seven thousand auto dealers: they employed some 230,000 people and were capitalized at an estimated $184 million. More than 5.5 million motor vehicles were registered in the United States, their value estimated at $5 billion.[22] The auto industry clearly had moved beyond the pioneering stage of craft shop manufacture. Standardized interchangeable parts, moving assembly-line production, and the accompanying deskilling of labor had quickly come to the fore. The Ford Motor Company led the way.

Ford became something of an industry unto itself, alone employing more than 150,000 workers by 1923. Two thousand additional firms either produced parts directly for Ford or supplied Ford customers with add-on accessories.[23] Ford's first venture into corporate capitalism had proven disappointing. The Detroit Automobile Company, established in 1899, built several dozen cars, defaulted, and reorganized as the Henry Ford Company, only to default again. When Ford departed the firm, investors brought in Henry M. Leland, owner of Detroit's highest-quality machine shop, and changed the company's name to the Cadillac Automobile Company. Cadillac quickly distinguished itself as the maker of carefully crafted, high-quality, but very expensive motor cars. When the new General Motors absorbed Cadillac several years later, Leland left to found Lincoln. In an irony of history, Ford took over Lincoln in the 1920s, its quality auto line offering Edsel Ford, Henry's son, the opportunity to bring styling to the fore at his father's company. In championing practical, inexpensive cars for the common person ("I will build a car of the multitudes"), the senior Ford rigidly ignored the marketing implications of car styling.

Henry Ford's quest for a "people's car" began with the four-cylinder Model N, which, following still another corporate reorganization, a new Ford Motor Company introduced in 1906 for $600. Then in 1908 came the Model T. The company constantly worked to reduce production costs through mass-production strategies, and the price of the Model T fell to just $290 in 1913. In that year, Ford sold 189,000 cars; orders for another 100,000 remained unfilled.[24] A removable cylinder head permitted easy access to pistons, cylinders, and valves. Indeed, all interior parts of the motor could be reached either from the top or from the bottom, in the latter instance through the removal of a bottom plate from the crankcase. No tearing down was required to make motor repairs, and anyone reasonably handy with tools could do it. Ford used the highest-quality materials—for example, vanadium alloy steel—not just in the motor but on every moving metal part throughout the car. Compared to other cars of the era, the Model T was remarkably easy to drive. A special feature was its spur planetary transmission, which produced not only ease of operation but smooth and silent running.[25]

Also unique was the car's suspension. Axles and wheels were engineered to allow each wheel a degree of independence (figure 1.3). No useless spinning of wheels ever occurred, and the car rarely got hung up. The car's high-torque engine, necessary because the transmission had only two forward speeds, could pull the vehicle up the steepest hills and out of the muddiest quagmires. The car's frame was high off the ground, giving the car something of a awkward silhouette but guaranteeing more-than-adequate clearance on uneven roads. There were three body styles: the two-passenger Runabout, the five-passenger Touring Car, and the six-passenger Town Car.[26] Cars originally came painted black, although eventually a limited array of colors could be ordered. Ford sold a highly standardized product and left the flourishing accessory business largely to others. To improve the car's

Figure 1.3. Ford's Model T. The original caption read, "It is no rare occasion for Ford cars to twist and bend their axle and spring construction into every conceivable shape while touring over rough country roads." "Remarkable Photograph Shows Ford Flexibility," *Ford Times* 6 (December 1912): 102.

ride, Model T owners could buy spring and shock absorber kits. To improve its looks, they could add nickel and chrome trim.

No other American car ever made such an impact. "It democratized mobility, opened up the suburbs, brought the farmer to town, emptied the churches on Sunday . . . and moved courtship off the front porch and into the back seat," was one assessment.[27] It was "everyman's car: sturdy, thrifty, and powerful," was another. The Model T offered less affluent Americans a "definite toe-hold on the running board of life."[28] Americans idolized the car and idolized Henry Ford for providing it. A poem, "My Sturdy Ford," written by a Ford owner in Oklahoma, read in part,

I grasp the wheel of my Model T—
    A sturdy little car—
And through the city's crowded streets
    Speed on to fields afar.
It goes with ease where big cars go,
    It trails through mud and sand;
At little cost it serves me well—
    My Ford is simply grand![29]

Some fifteen million Model Ts were sold during the nineteen years of its production. By 1913, Ford had seven thousand sales agents throughout the United States, and nearly every town with a population greater than two thousand had a Ford dealership. The company then turned its focus on even smaller places, so that by 1930, 38 percent of its sales and service outlets were located in places smaller than one thousand people. Through the 1920s, Ford cars dominated rural America, enabling the company to correctly claim that every third car in the nation was a Ford.[30]

To make the Model T, Ford built a new plant in Detroit's Highland Park suburb, engaging Albert Kahn, the nation's leading industrial architect, to design the facility. In 1907, Kahn had pioneered the use of steel-reinforced poured concrete, creating for Packard multistory factory buildings with work floors largely uninterrupted by supporting columns. No journalist visited Detroit without seeing an auto plant. A visit to Highland Park was like a visit to the future. Wrote one journalist, "From the interior of the mammoth building and the great yards come the incessant noise of manufacture . . . the soft purr of countless pulleys on miles of shafting, the dull hum of rapidly moving machinery mingled with the harsh crash of monster hammers."[31] In 1913, the plant employed more than fifteen thousand workers, with another seven hundred in the front office. It produced two hundred thousand cars.[32]

Ford's River Rouge plant, opened in suburban Dearborn in the 1930s, was even larger. At its peak of production, just prior to World War II, it employed 110,000 workers in more than eleven million square feet of factory space spread over two thousand acres.[33] Henry and Edsel Ford integrated production vertically: they controlled sources of raw material (iron, coal, rubber, silicates, and so on), delivered those materials to the Rouge plant using the company's ships and railroad, and produced all of the steel, glass, rubber, and other materials needed at the plant. Rouge produced engines, frames, bodies, and indeed nearly everything required for complete car assembly. At Rouge, the company not only manufactured the Model A, the Model T's replacement, but more importantly perfected what scholars came to call Fordism: industrial processes fully rationalized by machine and consequently substantially dehumanized.

At Ford's original Mack Avenue plant, Ford workers had been scrutinized, their tasks broken down into fundamental movements in accordance with the study of time and motion as popularized in the nineteenth century by F. W. Taylor and thus called Taylorism. The Highland Park plant was then equipped with machines that speeded these movements and thereby minimized human effort as much as possible. The skilled laborer, a craftsman who was expensive to employ, was thus replaced by the unskilled machine tender at low wage. At Highland Park, fundamental tasks were arrayed in logical order and more importantly arrayed through the device of moving assembly lines. The worker no longer went to the task; rather, the task came to the worker. Visitors observed "long rows of automatic machinery, each machine manned by an expert engaged producing just one article day after day until he had attained a perfection unbelievable." For example, one worker had the job of sitting and "squawk[ing] horns."[34] Of course, such routinized work was fatiguing, if only in its monotony. Many workers rebelled, and the turnover at Highland Park and at Detroit's other auto plants, which quickly copied Ford's assembly-line methods, was very high. Even after Ford offered factory workers the extraordinary wage of five dollars per day, heroic efforts at labor recruiting were still required. To Detroit came the dispossessed of several continents, people often desperate for work—white and then black tenant farmers and sharecroppers from the American South, peasants from villages in eastern and southern Europe.

General Motors (GM) challenged and then superseded Ford's dominance of the American car market. William Durant, a successful carriage maker from Flint, Michigan, sought, in partnership with J. P. Morgan, to create an auto manufacturing monopoly patterned after the trusts that controlled the nation's petroleum and steel industries. Although the scheme faltered, Durant organized GM as a vast holding company. His motto, "A car for every purse," was reflected in a variety of auto nameplates the company purchased or created over the years, including Cadillac, Buick, Oldsmobile, and Oakland (later Pontiac). Ford's low prices had given the company great success in attracting first-time buyers, and, given the Model T's durability, Ford also dominated the sale of used cars. By 1927, however, GM had surged ahead, controlling more than 40 percent of the market.[35] But Durant's buying spree (involving such brands as Cartercar, Elmore, Ewing, Marquette, Randolph, Reliance, Scripps-Booth, and Sheridan) kept GM close to insolvency. Forced out of the company's presidency, Durant left to found still another car syndicate, Republic Motors, based in Flint. To this new endeavor Durant attracted celebrated Swiss car racer Louis Chevrolet, around whose persona he launched the Chevrolet Motor Company. Durant also bought up GM stock, the value of which remained depressed, and quickly gained a majority holding. He retook the helm at GM, bringing with him the Chevrolet nameplate.

GM once again teetered on the brink of insolvency, but this time rescue came through an infusion of money from the Du Pont family when Pierre Du Pont took over corporate management. GM partnered with Du Pont Chemical to perfect highly resilient polychrome lacquers, the so-called Ducar paints. GM cars were the first to come in a wide variety of colors. Alfred P. Sloan Jr., groomed by Du Pont as his successor, would shape General Motors into an industrial giant. Sloan had come to GM when it purchased Hyatt Roller Bearing and made it the centerpiece of

GM's parts and accessories subsidiary, United Motors.[36] Sloan reduced the number of GM nameplates and minimized the market overlap of those retained. He sought a hierarchy of brand names that closely conformed to the pyramid-shaped distribution of America's social classes—broad at the bottom and narrow at the top.

Key was Chevrolet. General Motors could not meet Ford's prices. However, the Chevrolet offered car buyers an important opportunity to move beyond the bare necessities of motoring. The car's standard equipment included an easy-to-use gearshift transmission, four-wheel hydraulic brakes, balloon tires, and shock absorbers. Sloan also introduced annual model changes that hinged less on mechanical improvement and more on styling. Such "built-in obsolescence" came to be widely criticized. However, style change, when coupled with GM's revolutionary installment-buying program (through the newly created General Motors Acceptance Corporation), greatly stimulated car sales. Customers who purchased cars with loans tended to buy more expensive vehicles than did people who saved up their money in advance.[37] Sloan's success in redirecting American car-buying habits forced Henry Ford to upgrade his cars and, as Edsel had encouraged all along, to push styling rather than engineering to the front.

Chrysler (recently Daimler-Chrysler) was formed in 1923 around the persona of Walter Chrysler. With 10 percent of the market, the firm became America's third-largest car producer in 1928, displacing Hudson.[38] Chrysler had "retired" from General Motors in 1919, joining Maxwell-Chalmers, a firm that, through absorption of various companies, manufactured a full line of vehicles, including Briscoe, Chalmers, and Graham motor cars and the Graham and Sampson trucks. When it was introduced, the Chrysler car was essentially the Maxwell reengineered and renamed. Acquisition of Dodge Brothers in 1925 greatly strengthened the firm. John and Horace Dodge, owners of a Detroit machine shop, had previously supplied Ford Motor with engines and car bodies and held an equity interest in Ford. Walter Chrysler eliminated all but the Chrysler and Dodge car brands but then added Plymouth and De Soto; the Graham truck became the Dodge truck.

The economic recession that followed World War I greatly reduced the number of car companies. Eighty-eight firms were in production in 1921, compared to only fifty-nine three years later.[39] Nameplates also declined precipitously in number, with forty-nine canceled in 1923 alone and thirty-six the following year.[40] The Great Depression of the 1930s only added to the trauma. In addition to GM, Ford, and Chrysler, only Hudson, Nash, Packard, Studebaker, and Willy-Overland survived. The military contracts of World War II revitalized the survivors, however. Detroit's Packard, for example, manufactured aircraft engines, while Toledo's Willys-Overland made jeeps. After the war, the various "independents," as they were called, operated at distinct disadvantage, lacking economies of large-scale production through vertical integration. Packard, the creation of Henry Joy, had always excelled in engine manufacture and of course final car assembly. However, almost every other aspect of production was contracted out to suppliers. Joined briefly by upstart Kaiser-Fraser after World War II, the independents slowly succumbed. Nash and Hudson merged to form American Motors which, in turn, bought out Willys-Overland. In 1987, Chrysler absorbed American Motors, largely for its Jeep brand.

The auto industry quickly became an industrial giant. In 1929, it already consumed 85 percent of the rubber produced in the United States, 67 percent of the plate glass, 27 percent of the lead, and 19 percent of the iron and steel. It consumed 15 percent of the country's copper, tin, and zinc.[41] The number of workers employed in making, selling, and servicing motor vehicles stood at an estimated 1.5 million.[42] Throughout the twentieth century, car registrations and gasoline consumption increased steadily. Some 45 million motor vehicles were registered in the United States in 1950; by 2000, that number had grown to 221 million.[43]

Middle-Class Car Ownership

The editors of the *Literary Digest* reported in 1922 that they had found the typical car buyer.

He is a married man 33 years old.

He has a bank account and carries life insurance.

He buys a $1,400 car and pays $700 down.

He pays the balance at the rate of $100 a month.

He owns real estate in which his equity is $500.

He has personal property worth about $2,000.

He has bought cars before.

He also bought his previous car on the time payment plan.

They concluded, "The clearly evident fact is that the passenger automobile has become so important a factor in American life that thousands of families of moderate means are entirely willing to make serious sacrifices of other things in order to be able to possess them."[44] Sociologists Robert and Helen Lynd reached exactly the same conclusion in their classic study of Muncie, Indiana, which they dubbed "Middletown." People, they reported, would rather go without new clothes or even adequate food than lose their cars.[45] The car had become a measure of family worth. Indeed, the automobile was increasingly referred to as the "family car." Families not infrequently started in the privacy of automobiles, something that reflected liberalization of America's sexual mores. Of course, cars also offered everyday convenience in daily life and errand running. Cars especially affected farm life, reducing isolation. Cars also were plentiful in small towns. Although only 9 percent of the American population lived in towns of fewer than five thousand people, that population owned more than 20 percent of the nation's automobiles.[46]

Automobiles not only increased mobility, making travel more convenient, but did so with increased reliability. In 1927, the average life of a motor car was 7.04 years. An estimated 75 percent of all cars sold in any given year would still be operating 4.75 years later. Fifty percent would be functioning at the end of 6.95 years, and 25 percent at the end of 9.2 years.[47] In terms of the aggregate number of miles traveled each year, preference for motoring soared after 1925. Car ownership not only began to replace travel previously undertaken by rail (especially mass transit) but encouraged new travel that previously might not have been undertaken at all, especially vacation travel. Car use remained remarkably constant during the depression of the 1930s, but gas rationing during World War II curtailed motoring, diverting people back to the railroads and to the nation's motor buses.

Women as Motorists

Although automobiles were increasingly justified in terms of family use, American motorists were usually thought of as being male, the car identified as primarily a masculine concern. Early motor cars were considered too technically complicated and physically demanding for most women to operate. Initially, starting a gasoline engine was physically taxing, and carelessness could easily result in serious bodily injury.[48] Women of means were advised to hire chauffeurs or drive electric cars. Indeed, the market for electric automobiles, sustained largely by women, collapsed soon after GM's Charles Kettering perfected the electric starter (dubbed the "ladies aid") for the 1911 Cadillac.

Mechanical breakdown, including punctured tires, caused problems for all motorists. But was the average woman capable of overcoming such difficulty single-handed? Yes, argued one early autoist, Minna Irving, writing enthusiastically about her motoring adventures. With her car had come a tool set: a wheel cap wrench; a set of S-shaped wrenches; two monkey wrenches, one large and one small; a pair of pliers; an oil syringe; a hammer; a steel chisel; a small screwdriver; a tire lever jack; and a tire pump. To this assortment she added a hacksaw, copper wire insulator tape, both high- and low-tension wire, spare nuts and bolts with spring washers, gaskets for valve caps, and spare spark plugs. She always carried lubricating oil but had found kerosene best at loosening sticky valves. "Though my palms grew cal-

Women are Better Drivers than Men
Says American Automobile Association
The Pictures Prove it

IN FACT THE SKILL THEY SHOW IN
DRIVING A CAR IS ALMOST MIRACULOUS —

Figure 1.4. Cartoon Celebrating the Woman Motorist. Courtesy
Columbus (Ohio) Dispatch; reproduced in *Hoosier Motorist* 14
(October 1925): 9.

loused from handling tools and grasping the wheel, joy sparked in my eyes, roses bloomed on my cheeks, and vigorous health rounded out my form," she confided. She truly relished driving at a "reckless pace." But mainly she loved the smell of gasoline.[49]

Car use substantially changed the woman's role in American family life. As one sociologist summarized, "The car helped loosen family ties, reduce parental authority over children, introduce women to new opportunities for recreation, romance, and work outside the home; and, in general, expand social contacts between the sexes."[50] A 1925 cartoon from the *Hoosier Motorist* anticipated such scholarly observation (figure 1.4). At first, however, women recognized the automobile's recreational potential. Automobility especially broke the isolation of the suburban home, located as it was at a distance from most urban amenities. With a car, homemakers could enjoy an "undreamed of circle of social activities," argued Hilda Ward in 1907. But motoring, especially in open country, was to be especially treasured. "There is not unalloyed joy in motoring through crowded city streets, with narrow-minded policemen in unexpected places," she observed. "But, coursing over the wide stretches of macadam road in small settlements, motorists find much to attract them in the way of pretty scenery, adequate hotels, country clubs, handsome residences."[51] Out in the early suburbs, the wife/mother became the family chauffeuse, every day dropping her husband at the commuter railroad station and her children at school. By no means, however, did women make their mark on motoring only as housewives. Until banned by the male establishment, Joan Newton Cuneo competed in early Gidden Cup and other road races.[52] In 1909, Alice H. Ramsey, sponsored by Maxwell-Briscoe Cars, became the first woman to drive coast to coast.[53]

The feminine penchant for comfort and style, observers said, had really affected motoring. As one journalist asserted, "Man made the automobile; woman tamed it." She explained, "Leather would have done for man; for himself he never would have demanded velvet and tapestried upholsterings, but woman wanted something more effeminate, and there followed deep, soft cushions, beveled windows, plated heaters, softly shaded dome lights."[54] Perhaps Henry Ford epitomized the male position, scorning "knickknacks" on cars and espousing the idea that catering to feminine desire for ornamentation was a corrupt automotive virtue.[55]

Auto Styling

Between 1929 and 1932, as new car sales declined along with the economy, a new industrial design profession held out hope that if the companies embraced modernist style vocabulary, customer demand could be renewed. Car appearance came to reflect aerodynamic principles, especially the teardrop shape worked out first in dirigibles and then in airplane design. The Chrysler and De Soto "Airflows" were innovative not just in appearance but in chassis layout and engine placement: the passenger compartment was moved forward so that the rear seat was no longer located over the real axle and the engine was moved forward and placed squarely between the front wheels. The result was an extremely smooth ride. Critics, however, claimed that Airflow styling produced cars that looked like inverted bathtubs.

At the end of World War II, Hudson, Nash, Packard, and Studebaker moved quickly to get new models onto the market ahead of GM, Ford, and Chrysler. The new Studebaker, designed by Raymond Loewy, adopted the look of a jet fighter, complete with bullet-shaped nose. To their misfortune, each of these companies chose to continue the teardrop shape that had seemed before the war to offer a template for a secure design future. However, market-dominant GM, particularly late to retool, moved off in a somewhat different direction, making the streamline modern style of the 1930s quickly passé.

From 1929 to 1959, GM styling was under the direction of Harley Earl, who, before Alfred Sloan brought him to Detroit, had flourished in customizing cars in Los Angeles, most notably for Hollywood movie stars. At first called the Arts and Color Section, Earl's office helped give visual expression to GM's annual model changes. Over time, GM cars were lengthened and lowered, making silhouettes more expressive of speed. Design conceits included wraparound windshields, rocket-exhaust taillights, and fenders with exaggerated tail fins. Appearance was fully adopted as a sales tool. Earl's design philosophy, which carried definite sexual overtones, was "to go all the way and then back off."[56] During the 1950s, General Motors, followed closely by Ford and Chrysler, began to raise horsepower, creating a generation of "muscle cars." With allusions to racing, model names such as Grand Prix and Trans-Am sought to capture the "adventurous, youthful (or young-at-heart) driver."[57]

Designers also paid close attention to car interiors (figure 1.5). After all, motoring was experienced from the inside of cars. Ergonomics (the study of the human body engaged in physical activity) joined style as a concern. If architecture was "static controlled environment," then the motor car was "mobile controlled environment."[58] With buildings a sense of security might be foremost, but with motor

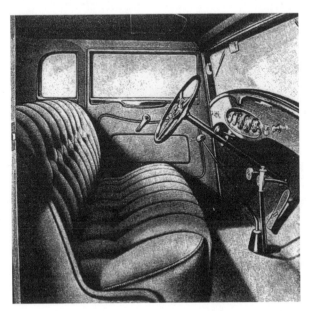

Figure 1.5. Interior of a 1932 Studebaker Coupe. The original caption read, "The lounge seat—widest in motordom—is adequate to carry even three in comfort and instruments are so designed as to afford the greatest ease of driving." *Studebaker Wheel*, January 1932, 11.

cars empowerment was what mattered. Special consideration was given to what motorists saw immediately in front of them, especially the dashboard, with its array of dials and knobs. After World War II, when jet aircraft so influenced external car styling, dashboards came to simulate cockpit panels, with numerous gauges, most of them offering superfluous information, such as engine revolutions per minute. The automakers had much reduced the physical exertion of driving through automatic shifting, power-assisted steering, and power-assisted braking, for example. No longer was the typical car the least bit difficult to control. With the fancy new dashboards, however, automakers moved to suggest at least a semblance of difficulty.

Enclosed car bodies, of course, had also radically changed motoring. Now cocooned in metal and glass, motorists found themselves farther removed from the road and the roadside. No longer was the force of wind directly in one's face, nor outside smells and outside noises quite so evident. When the car radio arrived, allowing motorists to surround themselves with a curtain of sound, psychological separation from things outside only increased. Studebaker was among the first manufacturers to make radios standard equipment. Studebaker radios featured "automatic volume control" and "split-hair tuning," the controls for which were compactly and neatly built into the instrument panel, as one advertisement asserted, "to harmonize with the driving instruments." "Baseball games, stock reports and news reviews are yours every day—and every evening you may have your favorite musical or feature program literally 'at your window.'"[59] Soundproofed auto bodies, air-conditioning, reclining bucket seats, and stereophonic sound ultimately made American automobiles into virtual mobile sound studios.[60] Listening to sound tracks easily replaced looking at the passing scene as motoring entertainment.

Touring

The taking of trips first made motoring an American obsession. Early trip taking involved at least three kinds of travel: the commute, the short outing, and the longer vacation trip. As a form of relaxation, motor travel was nurtured as a kind of art form. The intrigue of adventure, the pleasure of being liberated from normal routines, and the sense of being in command of one's vehicle conspired to endear Americans to motoring, despite the poor roads, lack of services, and often less than fully dependable automobiles. But adversity or at least its overcoming could be looked at positively. Adversity provided opportunity, after all, to prove one's mettle. The word *travel* derives from the same Latin root as the word *travail*, another term borrowed from the French. In English, it referred to toil, exertion, or strenuous work.[61]

At first, motoring was thought stimulating even for the commuter driving to work. In 1912, journalist Karl Grenville Baker saw the auto commuter as a "healthy, outdoor freedom-loving fellow, who objects to living in the octopus city where he labors. He loves the country, green growing things, gardens, flowers, and the song of the birds. He is a man who leaves his business cares in his office, shut tight in his desk while he goes to his home in the suburbs and really lives for a few hours out of the twenty-four." Unlike the harried railroad commuter, he was not tied to train timetables. He was free in spirit the minute he left work, the drive home potentially one of "adventurous relaxation free from a jostling crowd."[62] C. Bailey Sanderson, also writing in *Suburban Life*, emphasized the trip away from home. "To come out of the house after a good breakfast; to slip into the comfortable, leather-cushioned seat—no stuffy, stiff train seat with a chance of having an obnoxious partner—to feel the engine throbbing and purring underneath, and the round of the wheel fitting like an old friend into your hands; and then to catch your breath, as the fresh breeze strikes you and sets your heart to throbbing and your very hair to tingling, while the brown, green-bordered roads spin by. I tell you, man, that's living!"[63] But which came first, buying a suburban house or buying a car? Buying the one usually led to buying the other (figure 1.6).

Cars initially served mainly for pleasure, not for commuting. An auto was a recreational thing. A family might pack a picnic lunch and, either alone in or caravan with others, motor out of town. Notorious was the "Sunday driver" out on a lark who leisurely puttered along, backing up traffic (figure 1.7). Touring was primarily a warm-weather proposition, although hardy adventurers might sally forth even in the winter. Romanticized one author, "There is exhilaration in the onward rush through the biting wind. There is health and healing in the pure clean cold. There is tonic in the sweep of the crystal clean air, keen as a whetted scimiter [*sic*], and whipped home by the added impetus of flight of a fast moving motor-car."[64] Of course, open cars in cold weather required heavy coats, hats, gloves, blankets, and even hot-water foot warmers. An enclosed car helped but was hardly adequate. Not until the 1920s did manufacturers begin to include heaters as standard equipment in cars. These devices were electrical-coil heaters operated off a car's battery, hot-air heaters using gases from the exhaust system, or hot-water heaters connected to the radiator.

The long vacation trip made auto ownership into something truly special. The car gave Americans opportunity to more fully discover America, observers argued. Auto owners needed only encouragement. Thus in 1917, the *American Motorist,*

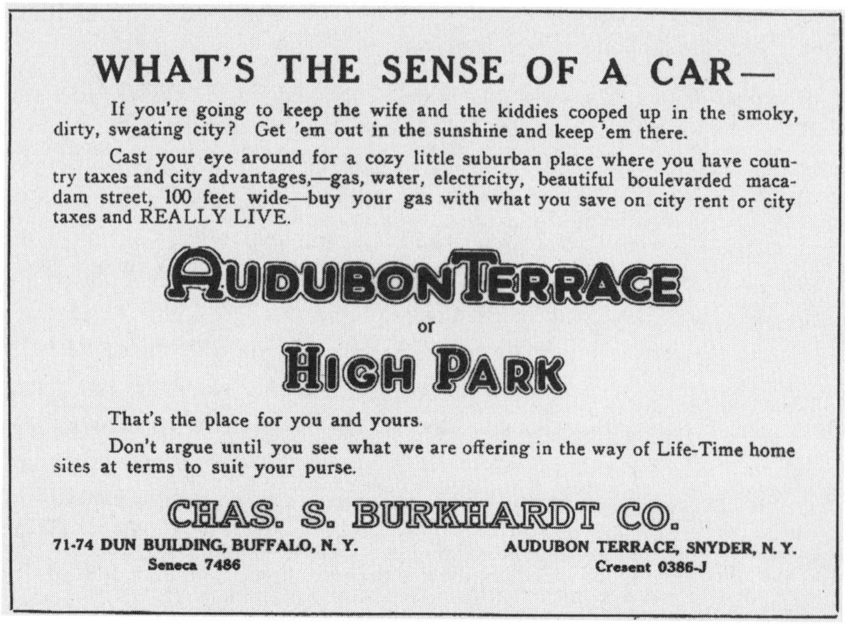

Figure 1.6. Advertisement for a Buffalo, New York, Realtor. *Buffalo Motorist* 16 (May 1923): 39.

Figure 1.7. The Thornton Family of Homer, Illinois, on an Afternoon Outing in Indiana, 1916. The note on the back of the snapshot reads, "Out looking at the hills in Parke County near Turkey Run, August 1916." Authors' collection.

the magazine of the American Automobile Association, published the "Motorist's Creed," which read in part,

I believe the Gasoline Engine is one of mankind's greatest blessings.

I believe that nothing is doing or can do more to broaden the outlook of the people and educate them to a proper knowledge of their country and its greatness than the Automobile.

I believe that my physical welfare and my mental growth call for frequent journeyings into new territory, with the resultant meeting of new people and the absorption of new ideas.

I believe the Automobile promotes joy and dispels gloom, increases health, banishes disease and stimulates mental and moral growth.[65]

Such sentiment fit with the "See America First" campaign that accompanied Europe's closure to American tourists with outbreak of World War I. The automobile offered a viable alternative. Americans now could wander their own roads to explore strange localities and discover just how many different kinds of people made up their nation. Wrote one advocate, "The man behind the steering-wheel has become the lord of distances. His horizon has immeasurably widened, the highway is made panoramic and belongs to him, and the satisfaction of living has sensibly increased."[66]

Arthur Jerome Eddy responded even earlier to the siren call. Eddy left Chicago on August 1, 1901, for New York City "on" (not in) a two-seat, 8½-horsepower gas buggy. He returned on September 29, having motored twenty-nine hundred miles. It rained nearly the entire distance out, putting the roads into terrible condition. He was obliged "to travel hour after hour on the hill-climbing gear," traveling only between five and eight miles an hour. But he kept right on, "taking the mud as it came." He learned as he went along: "I found in practice that it was better to take the soft deep mud in the center of the road than to try for the heavy sticky ruts at the side."[67] Seven years later, when M. Worth Colwell went "motor-mountaineering" across Pennsylvania, automobiles and roads were much improved. "We would gaze across the hill and nooks and vales in wonder and remain lost in silent admiration," he reported, "until a bump in the road would bring us back to our senses." "Almost no gateways are barred to the modern machine," he concluded, "and the motorist can go when and where he liketh, and is the freest of all travelers."[68]

Horatio Nelson Jackson is credited with being the first person to motor coast to coast, doing so in a two-cylinder Winton in the summer of 1903. He required sixty-three days, twelve hours, and forty minutes. However, he lost much time idling in towns along the way, waiting for replacement parts and fresh tires to arrive by train from distant cities. In 1906, another car, following a similar route from San Francisco to New York City, took fifteen days. By 1916, those who drove straight through could make the trip nonstop in only five days, approximately the time necessary to make the same journey by rail.[69] With the way uncertain, the Jackson party had been forced several times to double back in search of the correct route, but in 1916 the way was well marked. Jackson's trip across the Great Basin east of the Sierras had been particularly difficult. Deep ruts constantly lifted one of the wheels off the ground. "The tough sage brush not only stripped off the canvas under the engine and the paint from the car body, but completely wore away, as well, the tough wooden handle of a shovel strapped underneath," Jackson remembered. "The steep sides of many ravines were climbed by 'jumping' the car by fly-wheel momentum."[70]

Young Edsel Ford motored from Detroit to San Francisco in 1915, part of a car caravan that included a Cadillac, a Stutz, and, of course, a Ford. The *Ford Times* reported, "From the rolling level pastoral scenes of prosperous farms and gardens, through the busy streets of towns and cities, past magnificent factories, representing the greatest accomplishments in industrial life, on to the climb of gigantic mountain peaks, through their passes and canyons, down and over the desert to the sunny skies of golden California, [it was] a trip of unparalleled attractiveness . . . and a significant object lesson as to the extent, greatness and majesty of our land."[71] Of course, Ford dealers were available all along the way to assist Edsel's party.

Nonetheless, before driving long distances even in the 1920s, motorists were advised to make extensive preparations. "Go over the car carefully," suggested one traveler, basing his comments on firsthand experience. As for the engine, the valves needed to be ground, the carbon cleaned out, and the bearings tightened. A new fan belt was a must. The crankcase needed to be drained and filled anew with oil, as did the transmission. New plugs and fuses were essential. The generator, starter, and springs needed to be checked.[72] Long-distance motoring required extra equipment, although some of the advice offered was questionable. West of Denver, advised the *American Motorist,* "you should carry a coil of chicken wire 12 inches wide, about 150 feet long, to be used to get out of deep sand and mud."[73] But even reasoned advice could produce a lengthy list of things to take along.[74]

By the late 1920s, touring across the country, though still sometimes difficult, had become more predictable. Motorists drove faster and thus farther. Indeed, many vacationing motorists found the length of a day's drive—three hundred or four hundred miles—the primary source of pride. Two journalists, Jan and Cora Gordon, motored and then wrote a book about their experiences, which they summarized as, "Thirty-five miles an hour from daybreak to sunset, piling impression onto impression at as rapid a speed as possible so that in the memory nothing remains but the few objects of nature's facetiousness which are usually photo-graphed in the tourist folders—the rock like an Indian's face, the waterfall in seven stories, the boulder which is shaped like a frog, and so on."[75] Pennants and flags flew from tourist cars announcing states and cities of origin or intended destina-tions. "The flags added an air of gaiety to the road," the Gordons wrote, adding a "boyish spirit" of cheer and "pleasant transient good will."[76] Auto tourism had come of age, with soft drinks, balsam pillows, hot dogs, and rubber snakes readily available at the roadside. Garages and gas stations, campgrounds and cabin courts, and highway-oriented eateries had popped up nearly everywhere.[77] Motorists on vacation flooded the nation's roads, especially in summer months (figure 1.8). In 1927, twenty-nine million Americans (more than a third of the nation's population) took pleasure trips by car each year, spending an estimated half billion dollars.[78]

As important as pleasure driving was, the automobile had also become quite indispensable to everyday life. For many Americans, commuting and running er-rands by car had become habitual. The special delights of motoring might remain important to recreational travelers, but even tourists, as the Gordons suggested, could turn motoring very much into a routine. Nonetheless, the family car re-mained an important status symbol, and not owning a car carried a clear social stigma. Without automobility, a person was clearly disadvantaged. As one jour-nalist observed, "Once a person had bought a car, it is very rare for that owner, thereafter, no matter what his or her means, to be without some kind of car. The motorcar has firmly established itself as an absolute necessity."[79]

Unintended Consequences

Motoring was not without its downside. Auto safety quickly became, as it remains, a very serious issue. The first recorded traffic death involving a motor car occurred in New York City in 1899, when an unfortunate passenger stepped off of a streetcar into the path of an oncoming taxicab that had swerved to avoid hitting a truck.[80] In 1920 the *Literary Digest* reported that 4,684 people had been killed in motor vehicle accidents in the state of New York during the previous five years, a total that exceeded the number of New Yorkers killed in World War I.[81] In 1927, motor accidents took 26,618 lives nationwide and injured 798,618 people. In other words, someone was killed or injured in a traffic accident every thirty-nine seconds. Sixty percent of these casualties were pedestrians hit by cars.[82] The statistics worsened. In 1965, thirteen million traffic accidents took place, with forty-nine thousand fa-talities.[83] During the twentieth century, an estimated fifteen million Americans were killed in traffic accidents.[84]

Hupmobile
The car of The American Family

Touring Car or Roadster, with regular equipment . . . $1050

With electric starting and lighting, demountable rims, over-size tires and tire carrier, $1200. Prices f. o. b. Detroit.
In Canada — Touring Car or Roadster, with regular equipment, $1200. With electric starting and lighting, demountable rims, over-size tires and tire carrier, $1380. Prices f. o. b. Windsor.

40,000 Owner-Salesmen

Wonderful stories have come to us from dealers everywhere of the number of sales made as the result of friendly interest shown by Hup owners.

Some weeks ago we instructed Hup salesmen visiting all parts of the country to make a detailed report on this point.

These reports, covering every State in the Union, are now in our hands; and they reveal an astonishing and gratifying condition.

Out of 1500 dealers more than 90 per cent testify that the Hup owner is by far the most important factor in making new sales.

"I will have to admit it," says one big distributor, "even if it deprives me of some of the credit for this season's splendid business."

It seems to us that nothing we might say to you about the Hup could possibly inspire you with greater confidence in the car than this attitude of Hup owners.

We do not mean to imply that other owners of other cars do not feel kindly toward those cars.

But we do believe that such wholesale and unanimous enthusiasm as this is unique.

We do believe that it is unusual for people of all sorts and conditions to go out of their way to help the Hup dealer make sales.

We are certain that they could not so commit themselves if they did not feel sure of what the Hup is and what the Hup will do.

We consider it proof positive of our repeated assertion that the root of Hup popularity is continuous service at a lesser cost.

It shows us that, almost to a man, Hup owners back us in our belief that the Hupmobile is the best car of its class in the world.

And we confidently refer you to the Hup owner and the Hup dealer in your home town.

Hupp Motor Car Company, 1243 Milwaukee Ave., Detroit, Mich.

Figure 1.8. Advertisement for Hupmobile Touring Car. *Literary Digest* 48 (June 20, 1914): 1519.

Slower to come into public awareness was the automobile's health and environmental implications. Writing in 1929, journalist Silas Bent tried to coin a new term, *autotosis*. He wrote of a new disease whose symptoms included headaches, dizziness, and "that tired feeling." The cause was "modified carbon-monoxide poisoning from breathing air tainted with the exhaust from automobiles."[85] Well recognized were seasickness and even airsickness. Why not carsickness? The smell of auto exhaust, especially in cities, was apparent to everyone. Although the ordinary person might not think in the chemical terms of noxious hydrocarbons, carbon dioxide, nitrous oxide, and the like, by the 1950s something clearly was accumulating over cities such as Los Angeles. It was visible and it burned the eyes. It was called smog.

◆ ▼ ●

The American love of the automobile remains very much a search for self-affirmation. Motoring came to suggest a special kind of freedom, the freedom to go, see, and do. Cars were important; they could be owned as prized possessions. But important also were the improved roads that smoothed the way, enabling motorists to self-fulfill. Improved automobiles and improved highways went hand in hand, advances in the one encouraging advances in the other. Although automobility has contributed to a range of serious social and ecological dysfunctions, its promise in America remains one of empowering the individual through enhanced geographical and social mobility. Romantically, motoring's core attraction was what many Americans came to refer to as the call of the open road. An extraordinary amount of verse has been published, especially in motor magazines, taking the open road as a theme. As one motorist penned,

> The steady pulse of a balanced six,
>   The purr of a mighty twin,
> The living surge of a straight line eight,
>   On a mixture clear and thin;
> The looming hill and the rush of gas
>   When the motor takes its load,
> Are the clear sharp notes that sounds the call.
>   The call of the open road.[86]

And another mused,

> Give me the road, the open road, and that will do for me.
> With the motor's drone and the fragrant breeze, and feeling that I'm free,
> For the city's din has a little way of tingeing thought with blue,
> But roads have arms, it always seems, that stretch right out to you.[87]

Of course, Walt Whitman first celebrated the open road in letters long before the coming of the automobile. In 1923, D. H. Lawrence reformulated the Whitman view in automotive terms.

> He drove an automobile with a fierce headlight, along the track of a fixed idea, through the darkness of this world. And he saw everything that way. Just as a motorist does in the night.
>
> I, seeing Walt go by in his great fierce poetic machine, think to myself: what a funny world that fellow sees!
>
> ONE DIRECTION! Toots Walt in the car, whizzing along. . . .
>
> ONE DIRECTION! whoops America, and sets off also in an automobile.[88]

america's good roads search

Together, the car and highway came to constitute a modern transportation system, a development initially brought about through the popularity of motoring. In 1900, the United States had some 2.5 million miles of rural road, but less than 160,000 miles could be said to be improved above the level of dirt track. Very little of this mileage—only a few hundred miles—were hard surfaced and/or adequately drained.[1] Farm-to-market roads served local populations and were not meant to offer clear sailing to recreational motorists wishing to travel long distances quickly (figure 2.1). By 1920, however, an estimated 20,000 miles of rural highway had been hard surfaced and thus was suitable, on a sustained basis, for the rapid movement of both motor cars and motor trucks.[2]

As President Woodrow Wilson emphasized in a 1916 "good roads" speech, improved highways could serve even higher purposes than pleasure tripping. The nation certainly needed to thank auto owners, pleasure trippers, and the auto clubs and highway associations that serviced them, since they had diligently lobbied for highway improvement. Nonetheless, good roads were not for them alone: "The highway is not intended, first of all, and chief for all, for the pleasure vehicle. It is not intended for the mere traveler." Highways were needed to exploit fully the nation's resources, facilitating the farmer in moving produce, better enabling the manufacturer and the wholesaler to assemble materials and distribute finished products, and helping retailers attract customers. Good roads would also break down provincialism, binding the nation closer together politically. "Wherever you have a good road you have tied a thong between that community and the nation to which it belongs," he concluded.[3]

Wilson was by no means the first American president to speak out on behalf of highway improvement. In 1903, Theodore Roosevelt had written, "The faculty, the art, the habit of road building marks in a nation those solid, stable qualities, which tell for permanent greatness."[4] For Roosevelt, the highway's economic implications loomed large, especially in the nation's rural districts, which had escaped

Figure 2.1. Toot 'N' Be Darned, Novelty Postcard, c. 1910. Authors' collection.

the benefits of largely city-centered modern development. He therefore advised citizens not to judge the highway's potential on the basis of mere motoring. Good roads would benefit everyone, not just society's elites. "Arrogant and insulting as some of the owners of automobiles are," confided one journalist in 1907, "still they do not represent the greater part of the class now interested in the running of motor cars."[5] Motor vehicles would soon carry ordinary people between centers of population, just as the railroads did. Trucks would be used like freight cars to connect even the most isolated farms with the cities; the only difference would be that delivery was door to door.

Automobile Clubs

The good roads movement was rooted initially in bicycling, popularized in the United States beginning in the 1870s. Albert Pope, a bicycle manufacturer and later an automaker, was the sport's most vigorous advocate. Pope sponsored riding schools, subsidized cycling clubs, and most importantly promoted the League of American Wheelmen, founded in 1880. The league, with a membership cresting at some 150,000, lobbied state, county, and township governments for improved roads, particularly around Boston and New York City, where the bulk of the organization's members resided. The league led a petition effort that resulted in Congress's 1893 establishment of the Office of Road Inquiry (ORI) in the Department of Agriculture.[6] *Good Roads* magazine, launched by the league's National Good

Roads Association, became a major advocate for improved highways after motoring replaced cycling as the nation's most popular on-road sport. The league was a precursor to the many automobile clubs organized in the United States beginning about 1900.

At first, automobile clubs were very much like other clubs. They began as social organizations rather than as commercial enterprises and, like the private clubs that promoted yachting, tennis, golf, and other sports, auto clubs initially promoted motoring very much as a recreational pursuit. The Automobile Club of America (ACA) sustained an elite social agenda for New York City's well-to-do and well-connected, maintaining an elaborate headquarters building in midtown Manhattan that included the city's first large parking garage. Club members, especially those who resided on Manhattan's affluent Upper East Side, could conveniently store cars there, have them serviced, and, on request, have them delivered quickly to their town house doors. Those who commuted to midtown offices from Long Island, Westchester County, and other elite suburban areas stored vehicles at the garage during working hours. The ACA sponsored outings and endurance runs and marked tour routes in and out of Manhattan as well as long-distance highways, including one between New York City and Boston.

The Automobile Club of Buffalo sought to be a "car owner's organization along broad democratic lines." It would "take in every man who runs a machine."[7] The club maintained quarters in a downtown Buffalo hotel and after 1911 in a suburban clubhouse, where members could swim; play tennis, croquet, and baseball; and even trap shoot, providing motorists with a destination and an added excuse for pleasure driving. The club also marked rural highways, including the B-P (Buffalo to Pittsburgh) Trail. After 1920, it provided members with emergency road service, including free towing (figure 2.2). And like other auto clubs, it provided travel advice backed by free road maps and travel guides that rated hotels and restaurants. The organization merged with other clubs, opened numerous branches, and eventually changed its name to the Automobile Club of Western New York, which became the nation's largest auto club before World War II.[8]

Through the 1920s, per capita auto ownership had its highest U.S. rates in Detroit and Los Angeles. Detroit, the Motor City, led the world in the manufacture of motor cars. Los Angeles, also a boom city, enjoyed good weather year-round, itself an important invitation to motoring and car ownership. The Automobile Club of Michigan also became a large commercial enterprise and surpassed the Automobile Club of Western New York as the nation's largest after World War II. The Michigan group operated one of the nation's largest automobile insurance businesses through a subsidiary, the Detroit Inter-Insurance Exchange. The club initially maintained facilities in the Pontchartrain Hotel, a celebrated downtown

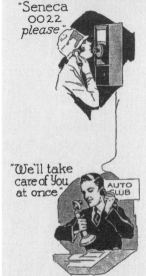

DON'T BE SELFISH!

Let your friends enjoy this Club's
Free Emergency Road Service

GET THEM TO JOIN NOW!

Members of the Automobile Club of Buffalo have FREE Emergency Road Service at their command day or night throughout the city. Very often this service in a single instance is worth more to the member than the cost of membership for an entire year.

Beyond the confines of Buffalo similar service is available for our members day or night nearly everywhere in the UNITED STATES AND CANADA. Thousands of Service Stations officially appointed to serve the AAA membership in every emergency are "on the job" promptly.

During the past year, our members used this Free Service in places as far distant as Owen Sound, Maine, Florida, and Texas. We have thousands of grateful letters.

Get a friend to sign this coupon.
You'll be doing him a real favor.

Date ....

Automobile Club of Buffalo,
Lafayette Hotel, Buffalo, N. Y.

Please present my name to your Membership Committee, as I would like to join the club, and thus become entitled to Free Emergency Road Service, Gasoline Price-Reducing Coupons, and all other privileges. My check for $13.50, cost of membership dues, herewith.

Name ....

Address ....

License Number ....

Figure 2.2. Advertisement for the Automobile Club of Buffalo. *Buffalo Motorist* 29 (April 1928): 14; courtesy the Automobile Club of Western and Central New York.

meeting place for the city's pioneer automakers, including Henry Ford.[9] Another large organization, the Los Angeles–based Southern California Automobile Association, early on placed signs and emergency telephones along California's main highways, erecting colorful "mission-bell" signposts directing motorists along the Camino Real, the state's premier tourist route. Like its Buffalo and Detroit counterparts, the Los Angeles club undertook a vigorous lobbying effort on behalf of good roads.

Auto clubs in the United States, most of them small, local organizations, were affiliated through the American Automobile Association (AAA), founded in 1902. The AAA advertised itself as America's national association of automobilists, but motorists joined through local auto club affiliates. Over its first half century, the AAA grew to include some one thousand touring organizations with a combined membership of more than 3.5 million motorists.[10] Triple-A functioned as a central clearinghouse for road and travel information.

AAA issued its first statewide map (for New York) in 1911.[11] It was the work of A. L. Westgard, the association's widely publicized "pathfinder," who drove the nation's highways checking distances and noting road conditions for map and guidebook purposes. After 1920, the AAA's Washington, D.C., headquarters issued most of the road maps and tour directories distributed by its affiliates. Very important to early auto tourism were the multivolume *Automobile Blue Books,* published annually, with each volume covering the roads of a different section of the country (figure 2.3). Routes were described in detail, with explicit directions for road intersections and local landmarks. To keep to a route, motorists had only to read the printed instructions. Wording was crisp and to the point: "From hotel entrance go east down hill past sawmill on the left. Turn right." Each *Blue Book* also contained maps of cities and large towns and advertising appropriate to the travel services available in those places.

By 1952, AAA affiliates distributed roughly five million folded paper maps, two million softbound tour books, and thirty million strip maps.[12] Introduced in the 1930s, the tour books, with volumes for various sections of the United States and Canada, came initially in two series, one that described tourist attractions and one that described hotels, motels, and restaurants recommended by the AAA. Each year, inspectors fanned out across the nation to rate lodging and eating places. Facilities that met standards could subscribe to AAA listing and thus display the AAA sign as a symbol of quality. The strip maps, which replaced the *Blue Books,* provided only some of the detail previously written out. They came on narrow sheets of paper that could be bound together in loose-leaf fashion to constitute personalized trip plans. The AAA provided its members with updated reports on road conditions, especially in regard to detours associated with road construction.

Figure 2.3. Advertisement for the *Blue Book* Holder. *Official Automobile Blue Book* (Chicago: Automobile Blue Book, 1923), 2.

Automobiles and their drivers at first generated substantial antagonism, especially among the nation's farmers. Noisy machines frightened horses, and runaway teams could injure both people and property. Farmers were known to spread glass, throw logs across roads, and even dig ditches across rights-of-way in attempts to discourage motoring. Most farmers did not oppose improved roads as such. Wagon roads had, after all, traditionally provided market connection. However, many rural Americans worried about the increase in taxes necessary to build and sustain auto roads, which likely would primarily serve wealthy city people. Farmers resisted the idea that their roads would become speedways for sporting enthusiasts.[13]

Some localities briefly outlawed automobiles altogether. More typical, however, were laws designed only to impede motoring. New York State's notorious Bailey Law of 1902 restricted motorists to eight miles per hour within a half-mile radius of the main post office of every city and town, with penalties of more than six months' imprisonment for repeat violators. Speed slower than eight miles per hour was mandated whenever and wherever a motorist passed a person riding or driving a horse or a pedestrian walking along a public right-of-way.[14] A later law established fifteen miles per hour as the "normal" speed for motor vehicles but required drivers, when requested, to stop and remain stationary "so long as may be necessary to allow . . . horses or domestic animals to pass."[15] The automobile clubs lobbied not only for the liberalization of restrictive traffic laws but also for the adoption of standardized traffic regulations among counties within states and among states nationwide. The clubs most strenuously opposed laws calculated to entrap motorists rather than to regulate motoring. For example, motorists who arrived at the principal downtown intersection in Trinidad, Colorado, were required to come to a complete stop and to signal with their horns just how they intended to proceed (one honk for one direction, two for another, and so on). A justice of the peace sat nearby, ready to fine unwary out-of-towners.[16]

Congress and Good Roads

The federal government was slow in coming to the cause of highway improvement. At first, the federal role was limited to information gathering. As its name suggested, the ORI made inquiries about road building and road maintenance. The agency sought to determine which construction techniques and materials were best used under various road-making conditions and then to prepare advisory reports to be disseminated through state agricultural colleges and their local agricultural extension offices. Partnering with the National Good Roads Association, the ORI sponsored "good roads trains" on the Illinois Central and other railroads, each train carrying road-making equipment for display and demonstration.[17] The ORI also established road standards for communities participating in the U.S. Postal Service's rural free delivery program. The ORI was briefly renamed the Office of Public Road Inquiry before being absorbed into the newly formed Office of Public Roads (OPR) in 1905.

Unlike the Office of Public Road Inquiry, the OPR had its own recurring budget line, thereby amplifying, in and of itself, the federal government's commitment to highways. The OPR established two test tracks, a mile-long brick pavement at Jacksonville, Florida, and a half-mile macadam pavement on the grounds of the U.S. Weather Bureau's installation at Mount Weather, Virginia.[18] The agency's charge clearly reflected the political climate of early twentieth-century progressivism, the optimistic belief that social reform could resolve ills created, in the words of one historian, by the "country's unsteady movement toward an urban industrial culture."[19] Progressive reform focused not only on rooting out political corruption but also, and perhaps more importantly, on promoting honest and efficient public administration.

Congress faced steadily increasing pressure to do more for highways. The first National Road Convention was held in Buffalo in 1908, and the first Federal Aid Convention took place in Washington, D.C., in 1912, both sponsored by the AAA. From the latter meeting came a joint Senate and House committee to decide whether federal monies might be used to match state funds for highway improvement. In a tentative first step toward improving roads, money was appropriated in 1912 to upgrade selected postal roads in various localities nationwide. In 1914, the American Association of State Highway Officials was formed under the auspices of the AAA and the American Highway Association (AHA), an organization serving road builders. Members of the American Association of State Highway Officials, in cooperation with officials from the Bureau of Public Roads (the latest name of the OPR), drafted a bill for congressional approval, an activity that culminated in the Federal Highway Act of 1916.

State Highways and County Roads

New Jersey was the nation's highway leader, creating the first state highway department in 1889. At the same time, the state legislature permitted county governments to issue bonds to sustain local road construction. Massachusetts followed in 1893 with a state highway commission charged with providing townships and cities with free road construction and maintenance advice. Connecticut and California established highway programs in 1895, followed by Vermont, Maryland, and

New York. By 1910, twenty-six states had highway construction and maintenance departments.[20] Even so, most highway work, even in those states, remained in the hands of authorities at the county or township levels.

Road improvement in some states was severely hampered by extreme localization. Arkansas, for example, was divided into highway districts, with road taxes collected within a given district spent there. In many localities, road money was siphoned off to pay officials inflated salaries.[21] In addition, politics, even of the progressive kind, dictated that tax dollars be spent evenly across each political jurisdiction. It was a democratic ideal. Consequently, almost all localities tended to have some improved roads, but they did not usually produce connected or integrated road networks. Dane County, Wisconsin (with the city of Madison at its center), was a classic case. In 1917, short sections of hard-surfaced road had been completed in every township, but few of the pieces connected to facilitate long-distance motoring (figure 2.4). In many localities, corvée labor (roadwork in lieu of taxes) rather than tax money actually sustained road maintenance. In 1915, Pennsylvania's new highway department hired contractors to lay brick pavement along sections of the old National Road near Uniontown. But throughout the remainder of the state, road improvement remained largely in the hands of local labor gangs under corvée obligation or in the hands of good roads volunteers (figure 2.5).[22]

Following the 1903 convention of the National Good Roads Association, held in St. Louis, the Illinois Legislature authorized a highway commission that initially sought, as in most other states, to advise local governments. The state had roughly one hundred thousand miles of designated wagon road and approximately 11,500 local road officials whose combined annual salaries exceeded six hundred thousand dollars. Less than thirty-five hundred miles of the state's rural roads were hard surfaced (most with macadam), and less than four thousand miles were properly drained with tile or ditching.[23] A convict labor law allowed the state's board of prisons to furnish the highway commission with crushed rock to be distributed free to counties and townships. In 1914, Illinois put into place an aid program under which the state offered to cover half of each county's road improvement costs for no more than 15 percent of each county's road mileage.[24]

Some Illinois localities moved aggressively to take advantage of the state program, while others responded not at all; as a result, the quality of rural roads remained uneven across the state. Motorists traveling between Chicago and St. Louis thus could expect to find some of the nation's best and some of the nation's worst roads. Vermilion County in east-central Illinois was one of the more aggressive players. In June 1916, the governor helped dedicate a new concrete road there, the result of a local $1.5 million bond issue matched by state funding. Planners

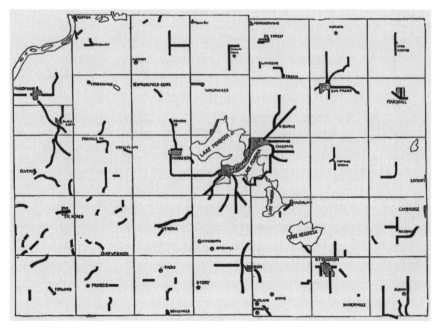

Figure 2.4. Improved Roads of Dane County, Wisconsin, 1917. *Dependable Roads* 3 (June 1917): 10.

Figure 2.5. Good Roads Day, Caernarvon Township, Berks County, Pennsylvania, 1914. *Good Roads* 11 (May 6, 1916): 209.

intended to construct a countywide network of hard-surfaced thoroughfares, 141 miles with concrete and 28 miles with brick. After the state highway commissioner's speech, "The Farmer and the Road Question," a parade of more than five hundred automobiles made its way through Danville.[25] In 1918, Illinois voters approved a $60 million bond issue to underwrite a four-thousand-mile statewide network of hard-surfaced trunk roads connecting all of the state's county seats. Bonds were to be retired through auto licensing fees, thereby shifting the burden of road improvement from the general taxpayer to the motorist.[26]

Highway Associations

With the federal government as well as various state governments slow to respond to the growing popular demand for better roads, numerous highway associations organized.[27] Business leaders launched these private (and for the most part nonprofit) ventures to seize the advantages road improvement could bring both to themselves and to their localities. The group would choose a name of some distinction and mark and advertise a route that would funnel as many motorists as possible through supporting communities. Most associations lobbied governments to make road improvements specifically along the designated route and in many cases physically improved the road, mainly through volunteer labor with volunteered equipment. For a decade after 1915, motorists driving long distances relied heavily on these trails, as they were called. Route markings, usually color-coded bands, were painted on power poles or otherwise posted along road margins, with each highway association choosing its own distinctive logo (figure 2.6).

More than three hundred different named highways appeared on highway maps during the early 1920s (figures 2.7 and 2.8). Most were mainly "paper trails," labeled on the maps but not marked or signposted on the ground. Rand McNally maps were especially misleading in that regard. The firm's "Blazed Trail" program used map labeling to suggest or promote highway marking as much as report it.[28] Most motorists appreciated the convenience that the markings offered, as they eliminated the need to follow maps, guidebook directions, or advice offered by locals. Keeping the way was easy, as one only had to follow the "stripes." As Emily Post noted when crossing the country in 1916, "In the Middle West, automobile associations or highway commissioners do magnificent work. Roads are splendidly sign posted."[29]

Perhaps the earliest proposal for a named automobile highway came from members of the Daughters of the American Revolution, which suggested in 1909 that the route of the old Santa Fe Trail be posted to the west from Kansas City. This idea led to a proposed "Old Trails Road" that would also include the Boone's Lick Road

TRAIL MARKINGS

2 LINCOLN HIGHWAY — RED. WHITE. BLUE — L

17 ELIZA-BETH-PHILLIPS-BURG WAY — RED

48 BRIDGE TON WAY — BLUE

4 YELLOW STONE TRAIL — METAL SIGN — YELLOWSTONE TRAIL

18 THOUSAND ISLANDS TRAIL — BLUE

49 CUMBER LAND-SHE NANDOAH VALLEY PK — BLACK ON WHITE — C S V

6 NAT'L. OLDTRAILS ROAD — RED. WHITE. BLUE

19 CHICAGO-BUFFALO HIGHWAY — RED

53 WHITE HORSE TRAIL — YELLOW

9 WM. PENN HIGHWAY — RED AND WHITE BLUE KEYSTONE — WM PENN HY

23 CAPE MAY WAY — BLACK LETTERS ON WHITE — CAPE MAY

50 BUFFALO PITTSBGH HIGHWAY — BLACK ITS WHITE — B P BUFFALO PITTSBGH

10 ALTOONA CUMBER-LAND TRAIL — BLUE

28 CAPITOL TRAIL — BLACK ON WHITE — CAPITOL TRAIL

52 WASH-HARRIS-BURG ROUTE — BLACK-ON WHITE — W H

11 LAKES-TO-SEA HIGHWAY — YELLOW

31 RAHWAY-TRENTON-CAMDEN-SALEM — BROWN

65 ANCHOR LINE — BLACK ON WHITE

12 HORSE SHOE TRAIL — WHITE ON ORANGE

37 KEY STONE TRAIL — BLACK ON WHITE

67 SOUTH-ERN TIER ROUTE — RED

13 BALTI-MORE PIKE — BLACK ON YELLOW

38 SUSQUE-HANNA TRAIL — BLUE

70 GAP WAY — BLACK ON WHITE — W GAP Y

15 POWDER WAY — BLACK ON WHITE

40 LAKE-HOPAT-CONG ROUTE — RED

83 VICTORY HIGH WAY — METAL SIGN

16 PIKES-PEAK "O" TO "O" HIGHWAY — RED WHITE — PP

47 SALEM—CAPE MAY ROUTE — YELLOW

97 MIDLAND TRAIL — ORANGE BLACK ORANGE

Figure 2.6. Logos of Selected Named Highways in Pennsylvania. Gulf Oil, *Blazed Trails of Pennsylvania* [road map], c. 1920.

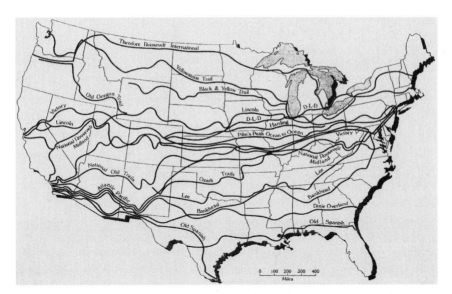

Figure 2.7. Major East-West Named Highways, c. 1925. John A. Jakle, "Pioneer Roads: America's Early Twentieth-Century Named Highways," *Material Culture* 32 (Summer 2000): 4.

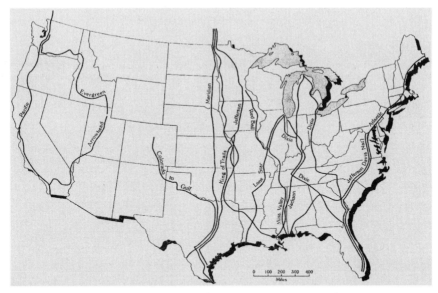

Figure 2.8. Major North-South Named Highways, c. 1925. John A. Jakle, "Pioneer Roads: America's Early Twentieth-Century Named Highways," *Material Culture* 32 (Summer 2000): 5.

between St. Louis and Kansas City and the route of the old National Road (and its extensions) east from St. Louis to Baltimore and Washington, D.C. (see figure 2.7).[30] The effort ultimately resulted in the National Old Trails Highway Association. Another early road was the Yellowstone Trail, the idea for which originated with the Twin Cities–Aberdeen-Yellowstone Park Trail Association organized at Lemmon, South Dakota, in October 1912.[31] The Yellowstone Trail eventually was marked from Boston to Portland, Oregon (see figure 2.7). Nonetheless, the first widely publicized and actually marked named highway was the Lincoln Highway, which captured the American imagination, largely because the effort was supported by many of the nation's leading automakers.

Carl Graham Fisher, founder of Indianapolis's Prest-O-Lite, proposed in 1912 a "Coast to Coast Rock Highway" to be financed through corporate contributions. Within a month he had pledges of nearly a million dollars. The idea quickly evolved into the Lincoln Highway Association and a plan to mark a 3,389-mile route honoring the memory of Abraham Lincoln from New York City through Gettysburg, Pennsylvania, to San Francisco (see figure 2.7).[32] When Henry B. Joy, founder of Packard, assumed leadership of the organization, Fisher, who had invested heavily in Florida real estate, turned his attention to the Dixie Highway. The Lincoln Highway, along with all of the other imitators that quickly followed, was widely celebrated as a national unifying force (figure 2.9). Motoring, even just for pleasure, would bring people together as never before, proponents of the highways argued. Thus journalist Newton Fuessle offered hyperbolic praise for the Lincoln Highway, which he described as "teaching patriotism, sewing up the remaining ragged edges of sectionalism, revealing and interpreting America to its people, giving swifter feet to commerce, gathering up the country's loose ends of desultory and disjointed good roads ardor and binding them into one highly organized, proficient unit of dynamic, result-getting force, electric with zeal . . . quickening American neighborliness, democracy, progress, and civilization."[33]

Auto tourist Effie Gladding, driving east from Stockton, California, praised the Lincoln Highway as motoring reality. "We were now to traverse the Lincoln Highway," she reminisced, "and were to be guided by the red, white, and blue marks; sometimes painted on telephone poles, sometimes put up by way of advertising over garage doors or swinging on hotel signboards; sometimes painted on little stakes, little croquet goals, scattered along over the great spaces of the desert."[34] Roy Chapin, president of Hudson, joined Joy in vigorously promoting the Lincoln Highway, eventually becoming the association's head. Chapin drove the road in 1915 and reassured Americans that auto travel, even in the West, was safe, although it remained "something of a sporting proposition." What could be seen

Figure 2.9. Highway Travel and National Unity. *Concrete Highway* 9 (November 1925): 263.

along the road in the East was certainly picturesque (figure 2.10). But the West was absolutely spectacular and exhilarating (figure 2.11). "The delights of eastern touring fade into insignificance," he wrote, "when, after hours of travel over desolate, salt-encrusted plains, treeless, motionless save for the silently shifting dunes and the occasional ghostly sand-whirl which flits across his horizon, or the gleam and shimmer of cool and sparkling lakes seen in mirage, one dips down into some fertile, smiling river valley, and follows the course of the rippling stream through irrigated gardens."[35]

Supporters of the Lincoln Highway included General Motors, Willy-Overland, U.S. Royal, and Goodyear. These companies provided funds to build portions of the road—for example, across the desert landscape west of Salt Lake City. "Ideal miles" (or "ideal sections") were proposed, one for every state through which the

Figure 2.10. The Lincoln Highway in Pennsylvania, Postcard, c. 1915. Authors' collection.

Figure 2.11. The Lincoln Highway in Wyoming, Postcard, c. 1915. Authors' collection.

highway ran. The ideal section at the state line separating Indiana and Illinois was more than a mile long with concrete paving laid forty feet wide and ten inches thick to accommodate four lanes of heavy traffic. And landscaping and lighting were added.[36] The Lincoln Highway Association was especially adept at attracting state and federal funds for work on the road, and by 1923, the states had received an estimated $50 million in federal grants.[37]

The National Old Trails Highway was marked in 1915 between Washington, D.C., and Los Angeles, with an extension (later dropped) to San Francisco (figure 2.7). In the mid-1920s, the National Old Trails Monument Fund was launched to finance memorials to America's pioneer women. Harry S. Truman, then president of the Kansas City–based organization, coordinated the fund-raising through chambers of commerce, civic clubs, men's service organizations, various women's clubs, and church groups. Twelve "Madonna of the Trail" monuments were eventually placed, one in each of the states traversed by the highway: Truman drove the road to help select the sites. Arline Moss, chair of the National Old Trails Committee of the Daughters of the American Revolution, waxed poetic in praise of the monuments:

> May all who pass within the
>   Shadow of my Form, pause
> A while, and Understand the Faith,
>   the Ideals, and the real Inner
> Beauty of Soul of those Mothers
>   of Old, as they Passed Down the
> Great Homing Trail of the Nation.[38]

Whereas the Lincoln Highway was promoted with the nation's future in mind, the National Old Trails Highway was promoted more as a backward look in time, a glimpse at the nation's heroic past made attractive to auto tourists.

In the East, where the National Old Trails Highway followed the historic National Road, it possessed, said travel writer R. H. Johnston, "a distinctive individuality." The road's macadam surface, at least across Pennsylvania, varied from sixty to eighty feet in width and was closely paralleled by telegraph and telephone lines (figure 2.10). It was so well defined that no motorist could possibly lose the way, according to Johnson.[39] Arrayed along the road were old taverns and other structures from the previous century. Across Ohio, the road still utilized the old S-shaped bridges suitable for horse-drawn wagons but very dangerous to speeding motorists. In the West, especially beyond Santa Fe, where there was hardly any "old trail" to follow, the search for history differed substantially. Roads in New Mexico, Winifred Dixon observed, were "here today and gone tomorrow, cut off in their flower by a washout or a sandstorm, or simply collapsing because they weary of standing up."[40] Keeping the way was fully reminiscent of the difficulties once encountered by the West's heroic pioneers. Victor Eubank accompanied an "auto train," a caravan of cars motoring east from Los Angeles under the auspices of a tour company. Near Laguna, New Mexico, they halted for the night with the cars drawn up on the lee of a hill to protect them from a biting wind, rather like the circling of covered wagons.[41]

The Pikes Peak Ocean to Ocean Highway was also marked between New York City and Los Angeles. Organized in 1919, the Pikes Peak association co-opted the phrase "ocean to ocean" from the Lincoln Highway's early planning. Promoters also dubbed the road the "Appian Way of America" in further asserting its potential importance. Because the road passed through General John Pershing's hometown of Laclede, Missouri, it was also promoted as the "Pershing Transport Route," a designation that tied it into the U.S. Army's post–World War I experimentation with long-distance truck convoys, a project that benefited from the full involvement of another future president, Dwight Eisenhower, whose administration would launch the system of limited-access interstate highways during the 1950s.

Like other named highways, the Pikes Peak Ocean to Ocean Highway stitched together sections of already improved road and sought to promote additional improvements to close the gaps between those segments. Towns along the proposed route competed by promoting road bonds and, equally important, by recruiting construction volunteers—for example, through the sponsoring of periodical "road dragging days." A feature article in *Modern Highway,* "How Sparks (Kan.) Won the Pikes Peak Highway," lauded the town's forty-eight volunteers: seventeen teams, six trucks, and five tractors labored for two days to improve twenty miles of road. The article celebrated the "friendly smiles on the faces of the men engaged in the work. They feel good to be doing something for the common weal. The bonds which hold humanity together to induce them to do grand things, the unselfish thing, are being exerted very strongly now."[42] The local people were intent on opening up their area to automobile convenience as a matter of civic pride.

The Pikes Peak Ocean to Ocean Highway Association was sustained by membership subscriptions (a few dollars annually from individuals, more from businesses) and community subscriptions that reached as high as tens of thousands of dollars, with the amounts assigned by a formula based on a community's population, the volume of its bank deposits, and the length of the road in the area.[43] Paint trucks went out early each spring to repair, extend, and improve road markings. The association held an annual national convention plus annual state conventions, where enthusiasm for road improvement was kept at high level. The association printed and distributed free maps and brochures that described the road and advertised the highway in national newspapers. The association unrelentingly lobbied for a "365-day road" along the highway's intended route, sending lobbyists, primed at annual meetings, to the legislatures of each of the states traversed. Local clubs or chapters were responsible for advocating road improvement in their townships and counties. Indeed, many local highway officials used the clubs to muster political support for local road improvement generally. The association also promoted annual "relay runs," car convoys sent out in the summer months that publicized the highway.

As road improvements were completed, especially when hard-surfaced sections were put into service, the association organized dedication ceremonies. When the new concrete road was opened between St. Joseph, Missouri, and Wathena, Kansas, the celebration included a chicken dinner served by the women's auxiliary of the local American Legion and entertainment by the Kansas University Footwarmers Orchestra, the Wathena Boy Scout Orchestra, and Platt's Ukulele Girls. Agnes Neudorff and Mrs. Ralph Pettis sang, and dancing followed. L. A. Libel, president of the Farmers State Bank, spoke from a platform in the Odd Fellows Grove.[44]

The Pikes Peak Ocean to Ocean Highway shared much right of way across the West with other named highways. Motorists frequently confronted a jumble of colors and logos along road margins. Telephone poles, for example, might be striped from top to bottom with competing highway association insignias. Introduced in Wisconsin, the practice of numbering rather than naming routes made for less confusion.

The better publicized of the north-south trails included the Jackson Highway, which was marked between Chicago and New Orleans by way of Indianapolis, Louisville, and Nashville (with a branch initially connecting Birmingham, Montgomery, and Mobile as well) (see figure 2.8). Members of the Alabama Daughters of 1812 had initiated the route to honor Andrew Jackson but realized that they could not only celebrate the past but also "advocate and by example push a policy of 'road education.'"[45] Alma Rittenberry, the highway's principal enthusiast, argued, "We need in the South the influx of our neighbors above the Mason and Dixie [sic] line. I am a Southern woman with a Southern woman's pride, but facts compel me to admit that the curse of the South is its poverty and illiteracy, the main cause being inaccessibility." "These transcontinental highways, with their interconnecting roads reaching out through the counties," she continued, "will help do away with this handicap with which the South is burdened and open up to our neighbors rich lands and glorious climate."[46]

But the Dixie Highway generated the most excitement in the South. Requests for information on routes to Florida had begun to pour into the Hoosier Motor Club in Indianapolis. W. S. Galbraith, the club secretary, thought it might be time to mark a road south. Through Carl Fisher, Galbraith enlisted the support of several state governors, traveling to enlist further support in various cities for what he dubbed a "Hoosierland-Dixie Highway." Rebuffed in Atlanta, he was embraced in Chattanooga, and that city's chamber of commerce and automobile club took up the cause. The Dixie Highway Association was organized in 1915, and the Dixie Highway—actually a road network—was marked the following year. Its northern end had two main stems, from Chicago to Chattanooga and Detroit to Chattanooga, while the southern branch continued across Georgia and down Florida's east coast to Miami (figure 2.8). Additional branches were later added, with one running through the center of the Florida peninsula and the West and East Michigan Pikes converging at the Straits of Mackinac. Laying out the Lincoln Highway, Joy had insisted on a single route, a "shortest distance" track between New York and San Francisco. Fisher had disagreed, arguing that a named highway ought involve multiple corridors as well as numerous feeder lines. With the Dixie Highway, Fisher got his way.[47]

Most of these named highways have now been forgotten. It may be difficult to imagine just how important they were before Congress fully energized the federal highway program. Without the named highways, however, motorists who ventured overland for long distances would have been essentially on their own, as Eugene Brown, an early highway enthusiast, illustrated:

> Hello, my friend, can you direct us
> How to get to Kent?
> I know we took this road before
> And it seems to me we went
> A mile or so beyond the school—
> And then, I just forget;
> We want to take the shortest road,
> I ought to know it yet.

He ended in parody:

> And one old geezer took a stick
> And marked the whole thing out,
> Right there, by Jingo, in the dirt.
> It took an hour about.
> And there we sat and fumed and fussed
> And just before we start,
> Up comes a kid, 'bout ten years old,
> A country lad, but smart,
> And blurts right out,

"What road you want?
To Kent? Why yes, I know where;
See the Trail Mark on the post?
Follow that, it goes straight there."[48]

Federal Aid for State Highways

As vigorous as some highway associations proved—the Lincoln Highway Association, for example, built roads—the taxing power of government would be necessary to build and maintain a highway system of any scale. As the nation's highway associations lobbied to increase government spending, they lobbied themselves out of existence. The Federal Highway Act of 1916 provided $75 million in federal aid for state highway construction to be distributed over the ensuing five years, plus $10 million for national forest roads over the next ten years. Only states with highway departments that met stringent standards were eligible for the subsidy, however. Eight states scrambled to create highway departments, while all but two other states immediately set about bringing their preexisting programs up to snuff. The act did not mandate that states create an interconnected system of highways. State highway departments were allowed to choose which roads would be improved, including widely scattered segments when that approach proved politically advantageous. Federal participation was not to exceed 50 percent of the total costs of road construction provided that overall costs per mile did not exceed ten thousand dollars.[49]

In 1918, just as the guns of war fell silent, the federal government transferred to the states $140 million worth of surplus war equipment, including some twenty-seven thousand motor vehicles.[50] Ties between the military and road building, however, involved much more than surplus trucks. During the war, railroad capacity had proven inadequate, and war materiel had backed up behind the Atlantic ports. Truck convoys involving eighteen thousand vehicles had been pressed into service under the aegis of the federal government's Council for Defense—specifically, its Transport Committee, headed by Chapin. Wartime trucking, however, had literally torn up the roads of the Northeast, especially along the Lincoln Highway. Future military preparedness clearly would require federal government involvement in highway building—a system of national "defense highways."

The Federal Highway Act of 1921 appropriated $75 million for state highway construction for 1922 alone. Funds would henceforth be allocated in annual appropriations. From 1921 through 1932, the federal government allocated an average of about $100 million annually.[51] This legislation mandated an integrated nationwide highway system, requiring states to designate interstate (primary) and intercounty (secondary) roads not to exceed 7 percent of their total rural road mileage.

Only such designated roads would be eligible for matching federal aid. Moreover, matching funds could be used only for new construction, leaving the states responsible for highway maintenance and repairs. The work of the private highway associations was all but ended. The new federal highways were to be numbered, not named, since numbers were easier to post and easier for motorists to read. The Bureau of Public Roads refused to assign any single numeral to any one formerly named highway. Thus the Lincoln Highway came to carry the number 30 across much of the Midwest and East and a variety of numbers, including 50, in the West. The Pikes Peak Ocean to Ocean Road became, east to west, U.S. 22, 36, 24, 50, 89, 91, 6, and 66. It was perhaps inappropriate for government to sustain private interests such as the highway associations represented.

◆ ▼ ●

The first two decades of the twentieth century marked an era of transition during which both a new automobile technology and an accommodating system of highways rapidly evolved. The former would remain very much the domain of private, albeit corporate, initiative. The latter would become very much the domain of government. The automobile clubs and the highway associations built up public sentiment favorable to long-distance motoring on improved roads. The highway associations also gave roads personalities, associating them in the public mind with names, color schemes, logos, regional hype, heritage association, and most importantly ease of travel. These associations gave the American road a sense of place, packaging the highway experience to the benefit of localities linearly arrayed in mutual reinforcement. Along these trajectories, which became distinctive places in themselves, American motorists were encouraged to pursue novel travel experiences. The open road became an invitation.

What changes would the numbered highways bring? As the *New York Times* editorialized in 1925, "The Traveler may shed tears as he drives the Lincoln Highway or dream dreams as he speeds over the Jefferson Highway, but how can he get a 'kick' out of 46 or 55 or 33 or 21! The roads of America would still be on paper if the pleas that were made ten years or more ago had been made in behalf of a numerical code."[52] Perhaps it would not be the same; nonetheless, times had already changed. Private enterprise might launch good roads enthusiasm and bring some accomplishments, but in the final analysis, public roads were just that—public. Government ultimately needed to play the commanding role in bringing to the nation a coordinated system of improved highways. The result would be an interstate highway program built around the federal government's taxation of gasoline at the pump and the use of those revenues to build highways through mandated state highway programs.

detour ahead

REBUILDING AMERICA'S ROADS

Even before World War I, motorists frequently found themselves stopped, diverted, and not infrequently misdirected by seemingly ubiquitous detours. The cause, of course, was highway construction—the motorist's immediate convenience postponed for a larger public good, convenient motoring for everyone in the future. Motorists almost invariably spoke of detours in derogatory terms (figure 3.1). Each motorist felt as if he or she had been personally singled out for abuse.

A highway network, like any kind of interconnected system, was only as good as its weakest link. And for most early motorists, the weakest links in the routes they traveled were invariably highway sections undergoing improvement. In Connecticut in 1927, 120 detours totaled one hundred miles of extra driving.[1] Most diversions were short—a few hundred feet—but even in these instances, traffic was often forced to a crawl or stopped altogether to accommodate trucks and other construction equipment. Numerous diversions measured in miles and sometimes in the tens of miles, however. In Pennsylvania in 1928, for example, the average length of detour was 2.6 miles per construction zone. Detours totaled 819 miles longer than the rights-of-way for which they substituted, and each detour inconvenienced an average of 825 vehicles per day. The typical detour obstruction lasted 120 calendar days.[2]

Although highway departments and contractors might have good intentions, motorists found detours to be more ad hoc than carefully planned and rarely adequately signed. The detour routes themselves tended to be anything but improved. Travel diarist Vernon McGill and his wife found themselves near Las Animas, Colorado, after dark when they came upon a barrier and a "Road Closed" sign where a new bridge was only partially completed. They found a narrow track down a steep bank that would have been hazardous enough in broad daylight but seemed only to invite disaster at night. The path led down to a nearly dry riverbed and then up the steep bank to the other side. His wife went ahead with a flashlight and pointed the way. McGill put the car in first gear and, with a "tight grip on the brakes," started down into the "Stygian darkness," partly skidding and partly sliding to the

Figure 3.1. The Detour: Necessity or Nuisance? *American Motorist* 9 (August 1917): 44.

river. In the darkness beyond, however, they found miles of new gravel road and eventually safe harbor for the night.[3]

Highway department engineers and their road-building contractors were not really villains. Indeed, they could be seen as popular heroes, the great expediters of the motor era, a sentiment captured in verse by C. Wiles Hallock.

> O, brothers of the open road,
>> Be mindful, in your motors,
> Of this, our common gift, bestowed
>> By less enleisured voters.
> Be mindful how these thorofares,
>> Were made to serve all comers—
> The meek and humble millionaires,
>> The plutocratic plumbers.
> O, brothers, when you motor out,
>> In double fours or flivvers,
> To lamp the landscape round about
>> And agitate your livers,
> The while your gas-consumer flies,
>> O'er beaten trails and by-ways—
> O, breathe a prayer and bless the guys
>> That built the bloomin' highways.[4]

Earth, Gravel, and Macadam Roads

In today's world of high-speed driving, it is difficult to think of earth (or dirt) and gravel roads as anything but unimproved. Nonetheless, today's rural roads, even in the most isolated areas, tend to be evenly graded, well drained, and appropriately signed—important improvements, indeed. At the beginning of the twentieth

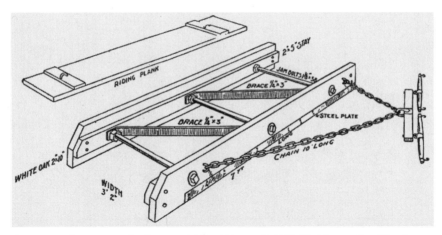

Figure 3.2. Advertisement for Commercial Road Drag to Be Pulled by Horses. *Good Roads* 8 (December 1907): 70.

century, however, such was not the case even in rural areas close to towns and cities. Little more than reserved rights-of-way left open for public travel, most of America's rural roads were notoriously primitive and usually amounted to little more than dusty tracks that dissolved into mud in wet weather. Long-distance movement of people and goods had long been diverted to the railroads, and the nation's rural roads accordingly suffered from substantial neglect.

Most county and township road commissions created improved earth roads, primarily by scraping the surface to eliminate ruts and smooth road crowns (figure 3.2). Road officials usually contracted with local farmers to "patrol" and, as necessary, drag county roads, with work beginning after the spring thaw and continuing throughout the summer, especially following heavy rains. Farmers usually used their own teams and their own road drags. Corvée labor was also used seasonally to fill potholes, clean ditches, and do other hand work with hoes, rakes, and shovels. After county and township road programs became better funded, especially through state aid programs, government-owned equipment, operated by government employees, became increasingly common. Road building, conversely, was contracted out to commercial construction companies, often locally owned businesses. New machines came quickly to fore, especially mechanized graders and rollers. Trucks—in particular, dump trucks—replaced horse-drawn wagons, and tractor-pulled steam- and subsequently gasoline-powered road scrapers superseded horse-drawn road drags.

When added to a dirt road, gravel provided not only a surface more readily smoothed through dragging or scraping but also a surface that shed water, substantially eliminating the mud problem in wet weather. It was best to slightly excavate a road, leaving dirt shoulders with which to contain and stabilize the gravel,

Figure 3.3. Steam Shovel at Work East of Erie, Pennsylvania. *Good Roads* 10 (August 7, 1915): 79.

making the gravel a fill rather than a mere appliqué. Ideally, gravel was laid down thicker at the center and then "feathered" out to a road's edges, thus creating a high road crown that aided drainage. By 1910, steam shovels had come to dominate excavation (figure 3.3).

A whole new alignment was created when West Virginia improved the Franklin-Petersburg Pike along the Potomac River. The old road was not only in poor condition but had steep grades. "In places it followed the bed of the river itself until, coming to a sharp bluff, it would turn in toward the bank and after making a climb of 10 to 12 percent for several hundred feet would pitch down again," reported the state's senior highway engineer. In times of high water it was flooded to a depth of between two and ten feet. Gravel had to be transported thirty miles from the closest railroad siding, as did a steam shovel, which was broken down into pieces and reassembled at the construction site. Following an approach that was unusual for the time, the state constructed a whole new highway nearly eight miles long between 1918 and 1920, moving eighty thousand cubic yards of material. "Rip rap and rubble walls [protected] the embankment from the stream," continued the engineer. These barriers were "constructed from excavation material, the percentage of rock running in places as high as 80 percent. In addition the road has been surfaced with gravel 8 in. thick at the sides and 12 in. thick at the center, and under the maintenance of a regular patrolman is kept in excellent condition."[5] The project also involved construction of several substantial concrete bridges and extensively used culvert pipe.

Local experiments that resulted in success often spread regionally. Throughout much of the American South, red clay, popularly called gumbo or buckshot, was especially plastic and thus very sticky when wet. Fire was widely used to dry out and harden the clay, and the burning of wood along rights-of-way produced "burnt roads." After excavating a few inches of surface clay, construction crews dug shallow furrows from ditch to ditch across the road. Workers then laid down cordwood longitudinally to form a series of flues, and threw another layer of wood irregularly across this flooring. Clay excavated from the road was then layered above, with still more wood placed atop. The Office of Public Roads recommended one cord of wood for each eight linear feet of roadbed twelve feet wide.[6] The process produced a covering of burnt clay that when rolled after firing formed a compacted road pack six to eight inches thick.

In the Chesapeake Bay area and along the Gulf coasts of Louisiana and Texas, shell roads were popular. Oyster shell obtained from shuckeries or canneries, clamshell dug from river banks, and "reef shell" obtained offshore with suction or dipper dredges was used. According to one engineer, "The shell is dumped from wagons and spread with shovels and hoes. Spreading with a grading machine is unsatisfactory, as it makes a lumpy road. Rolling is useless, as the particles of shell are flat, or nearly so, and break up under the roller instead of wedging and compacting."[7] Among the more unusual road-improvement practices was the use of straw. Following grading, six or eight inches of straw was applied to the center of a roadbed—about twenty rack loads of straw per mile.[8] The straw, worked into the road by traffic, dampened dust, which most people agreed was rural America's biggest road problem next to mud.

Macadam, named for its developer, John Louden McAdam, a Scottish road builder, provided many localities in the United States with their first hard roads. Technically, the term designated any road surface where broken or crushed stone was mechanically locked into place by rolling: a bond of stone screening was "worked into the voids and flushed and 'set' with water."[9] When bituminous oils replaced water, terms such as *plain macadam* and *water-bound macadam* came into use to designate the original type. Macadam was used on the National Road in the early nineteenth century. There and on other well-constructed roadways of the period, several layers of macadam totaling eight inches or more in thickness were separated by crushed stone with drains running through them. The development of the mechanical stone crusher and the steamroller about 1860 greatly facilitated macadam road construction.

Paving with Asphalt

The use of bituminous oils in creating macadam pavements led road builders to rely increasingly on petroleum-based materials. The term *asphalt* denotes black to dark brown cementlike material that liquefies when heated. "Native asphalt" occurs in natural deposits, and before 1900, most of the asphalt used for road paving in the United States was of this type and was imported from Trinidad. America's first asphalt paving was laid down in front of city hall in Newark, New Jersey, in 1870.[10] When widespread auto use vastly increased the demand for gasoline, refiners were left with large petroleum residues, including what came to be called "petroleum asphalt." The U.S. government soon issued a number of patents for asphalt paving materials that variously combined petroleum residue with crushed stone of various consistencies. Asphalt plants began long-distance shipment to road construction sites in steam-coil heated railroad tank cars. Prominent among the various brand names were Warrenite, Aimesite, Asphaltoilene, and Tarvia. In 1910, F. J. Warren, the developer of Warrenite, sued the city of Topeka, Kansas, for patent infringement. The asphalt pavement laid in that city, which came to be called the Topeka mix, used half-inch stone aggregate. Since Warren's product used stone up to two inches in size, the court concluded that it was a different product, and the suit was dismissed.[11] Thereafter, road contractors were free to concoct their own mixes and no longer relied solely on commercial products.

Asphalt surfaces were laid using both "cold-mix" and "hot-mix" methods. In cold-mix construction, crushed stone was spread and bladed to create a smooth subgrade two to three inches deep. Hot asphaltic bitumen was applied from a wagon or a truck through a pressure distributor. Smaller stone aggregate was then spread and bladed, a second application of bitumen was made, and a final layer of gravel was applied. Rolled and swept by broom, the road was immediately opened to traffic, using passing cars and trucks to compact the accumulated material. A premixed cold bituminous top or cap was then applied after several weeks. The mixture was shoveled and raked into place by hand and rolled with a three-wheeled ten-ton roller. Washed sand was then spread on the surface to prevent traffic from peeling away the uncured asphalt.[12] In hot-mix construction, hot asphaltic concrete, obtained either from a distance or mixed at a construction site in a portable mixer, was laid down from a wagon or truck and smoothed by hand (figure 3.4). The road was then rolled and portland cement was usually swept onto the surface and the rolling repeated.[13] Finishing machines riding on secured steel side forms set to grade became common only after 1925. Yet even after these machines became widespread, both cold-mix and hot-mix paving continued to involve substantial hand labor.

Various terms evolved to differentiate types of asphaltic mix or of paving applications. A few, such as *tarmac, road mix,* and *blacktop,* became generic terms designating asphaltic pavements. Technically, tarmac involved tar and crushed-stone mixtures laid down in two courses, a binder course 1½ inch thick and a ½-inch

Figure 3.4. Advertisement for Dolarway Paving Showing the Finishing Coat Being Laid on a New Asphalt Pavement. *American Motorist* 4 (August 1912): 620.

wearing course.[14] Road mix designated a cap of crushed stone and sand to which liquid asphalt had been applied. The liquid would penetrate down several inches.[15] A synonymous term was *oil mix*. Blacktopping referred to any road surface that had been oiled, whether or not stone aggregate or gravel had been added. Road oiling originated in the California oil fields when crude oil, spilled around wells and on adjacent dirt roads, was found to dampen dust. Subsequent experimentation with gasoline, kerosene, and other distillates led ultimately to tars specifically formulated for road surfacing. Applied annually, road oil and gravel can build up as a hard surface, giving a road many of the characteristics of an asphalt road. However, such "tar roads" could not withstand heavy use. During the 1930s, planners generally considered it uneconomical to hard-surface a road if the traffic load was, on average, less than two hundred cars daily. Roads carrying between two hundred and fifteen hundred vehicles a day were appropriately oiled, while heavier loads required asphalt, brick, or concrete.[16]

Road planners recommended asphalt roads for various reasons. Such roads were smoother and generated less vibration and less noise than did gravel or brick highways. Not until the 1930s did shock absorbers become standard equipment on cars, so in earlier years, road vibration constituted a serious problem as concrete surfaces cracked and pitted with use. After 1920, asphalt was widely used to cap both aging brick and aging concrete pavements. Most roads eventually needed to be asphalted, according to the Asphalt Institute, the principal lobby group of the asphalt paving industry. Fully mechanized by the 1960s, asphalt paving was quick and inexpensive, certainly in comparison to concrete paving. Throughout much of the United States, especially in areas where cycles of winter freeze and thaw were less problematical, asphalt became the paving material of choice even for totally new highway construction.

Brick Paving

The first use of brick for street paving in the United States occurred in Charleston, West Virginia, in 1871. The idea followed logically from the then-widespread use of granite blocks (among other types of stone), asphalt blocks, and even wooden blocks (usually creosoted or otherwise treated) for paving, especially in towns and cities. True innovation lay in the perfection of very hard brick capable of withstanding not only ordinary weathering but the demands of wheeled traffic. The first vitrified pavers were laid in 1885 in a number of locations in Ohio, including Columbus, Zanesville, and Steubenville. The most durable paving bricks were made of crushed shale. Pulverized to develop full plasticity, the shale was then mixed with clay and water. At most brick plants, a raw paste was compacted and forced through a die to form a continuous ribbon, the cross-section of which equaled the length and width of the intended brick. Wire then sliced the ribbon into the proper size bricks. Damp bricks were stacked to dry and then placed in kilns and fired at temperatures that topped two thousand degrees Fahrenheit, a process of incipient vitrification. The fused brick was then allowed slowly to cool. Making bricks required from three days to two weeks, depending upon the exact chemical properties of the ingredients used.[17]

By 1932, the United States had about 3,500 miles of brick-paved state highway, including some 1,056 miles of federal-aid highway (or about 5 percent of the highways built with federal funds).[18] In 1940, fifty-one brick plants in fourteen states shipped approximately 66.7 million brick pavers, a sharp drop from the 277 million pavers shipped in 1929.[19] Very popular as paving material early on, especially in Ohio, Indiana, Illinois, and other states with well-established ceramic-pottery manufacturing, brick paving fell out of favor largely because of the fact that bricks had to be set into roadways by hand, making it an expensive way to construct roads. In addition, brick roads generally offered poorer traction than other surfaces, especially in wet weather: motor vehicles tended to slide when braking, especially on curves. Although the size of paving brick varied, the standard paver was 2½ by 4 by 8½ inches. Allowing for ⅛-inch joints between bricks, workers had to lay fifty-seven pavers per square yard if the bricks were laid on edge and thirty-six per square yard if the bricks were laid flat. A one-lane road nine feet wide and one mile long thus contained 192,000 bricks (if they were laid on edge) or 302,000 bricks (laid flat).[20]

Bricks were usually laid over a concrete base with a sand cap. Lugs—small projections one-eighth to one-quarter of an inch in size—on the sides of each brick facilitated positioning or spacing. In bricklaying, the "dropper" picked up and placed the brick into position, laying four to six rows at a time. A fast worker

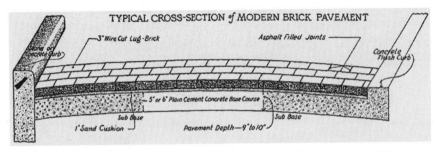

Figure 3.5. Typical Cross-Section of Modern Brick Pavement. *Highway Engineer and Contractor* 18 (May 1918): 65.

could lay thirty-eight hundred bricks per hour in four rows or forty-five hundred in six rows.[21] After the bricks were tapped firmly into place with hammers, rolled, and swept, the joints between the brick were filled with a grout of either cement or bitumen. Narrow single-lane roads—for example, the "farm-to-market" roads constructed in Vermilion County, Illinois—received gravel shoulders so that motorists approaching one another could pass. Two-lane pavements, however, usually had concrete curbs and, like other kinds of two-lane roads, elevated center crowns (figure 3.5).

Concrete Paving

Manufacture of portland cement began in the United States in 1872, and the Lehigh Valley of Pennsylvania became the nation's foremost producer. Lime, clay, and rock (especially rock strong in calcium silicate and calcium sulfate) were pulverized and thoroughly mixed, either wet or dry, and fired in kilns. The resulting clinkers, in turn, were ground into fine cement powder and bagged for shipment. At road construction sites, the cement was mixed with sand, gravel, and water and poured into forms, creating concrete pavement. Concrete was first used for road building in Bellefontaine, Ohio, in 1892. Streets around the city's courthouse were excavated to a depth of six inches; the ground was compacted with rollers; and a four-inch concrete base, one part cement to three parts gravel, was laid down. Over this was placed an additional concrete cap of one part cement to two parts sand, formed in wooden frames 5½ feet square. With the exception of the concrete base, the process used at Bellefontaine closely followed procedures already well established nationwide for the making of concrete sidewalks.[22]

The first concrete rural highway, approximately one mile long, was constructed in 1909 north of Detroit. It was seventeen feet, eight inches wide and thus could accommodate two-way traffic. It had compacted earth shoulders on either side,

Figure 3.6. Concrete Highway Construction. *Highway Engineer and Construction* 20 (April 1929): 42.

bringing the total width of the right-of-way to twenty-six feet.[23] By the end of 1912, the United States had more than three hundred miles of concrete highway. By 1931, the federal-aid highway system alone had more than twenty thousand miles of concrete pavement.[24]

As with asphalt paving, the laying of concrete was quickly mechanized. Portland cement was mixed in portable batching plants and transported to construction sites in trucks that used revolving cylindrical holders to keep the cement plastic in transit. More commonly, raw materials were trucked to a site or sometimes delivered on a narrow-gauge industrial railway temporarily set up for the purpose. The concrete was both mixed and laid down on the spot with a paving machine that had a large scoop for loading, a revolving mixer, and a boom-and-bucket arrangement to drop the concrete in place (figure 3.6). By 1930, most paving machines moved above the roadbed, riding, as with asphalt finishing machines, on secured steel side forms in a process known as slipform paving.

At first, concrete was laid ribbonlike, without expansion/contraction joints. But cracking pavement quickly demonstrated the need for jointing. By 1920, standard practice included molding each traffic lane separately, generally in slabs eight to ten feet wide and fifteen to twenty feet long. The slabs were separated by joints as much as three-quarters of an inch wide. Also by 1920, steel mesh and/or steel bars commonly reinforced the concrete. Individual slabs were stabilized by interlocking clips, and the joints between the slabs were usually filled with bitumen grout and then sealed with tar. One experiment that never reached wide use involved precast concrete slabs delivered from a manufacturing plant and then locked into place, grouted, and sealed.

Proponents claimed many advantages for concrete pavement. Concrete roads were thought to be resilient and thus longer-lasting. Concrete surfaces offered little resistance and were, like asphalt, much easier on car and truck tires than earth and gravel roads. When wet, concrete roads were less slippery than brick roads. The smooth surface meant relatively little tire noise, again quite unlike brick. Concrete was lightly colored, thus giving much better visibility at night than dark asphalt. Almost completely free of dust, concrete roads were even cleaner than asphalt surfaces, which were faulted for their slow flaking with use. Of course, concrete also had many disadvantages. The glare from concrete could blind in bright sun. With heavy use, even concrete roads deteriorated, and cracks and potholes remained all too obvious when patched with asphalt or tar. After construction, a concrete road required more than a month to cure even in the best of weather, lengthening the time that impatient motorists had to use detours. Early on, new concrete pavements were left with a rough finish with the intention of ultimately adding an asphalt cap. Later, however, concrete was fully smoothed for indefinite use without capping.

Highway Design

Most of America's new roads were upgraded old roads. The nation was rebuilding its rural highways, not creating a totally new system. Nevertheless, people speculated about what ideal highways built from scratch might look like. Some of this speculation took material form—for example, in the "ideal sections" built by the Lincoln Highway Association.[25] Planners really could not predict future highway needs, let alone how best to meet those needs through new highway designs. Prior to the early 1900s, most rural road improvements had occurred in areas peripheral to cities—for example, the placement of macadam on roads around Boston and New York City as prompted by the League of American Wheelmen. But as the nation began to look beyond the mere refurbishing of roads and to consider peripheral highways as axes for future urban growth, planners began to develop proposals for new approaches (figure 3.7). Traffic on the idealized 1906 road shown in figure 3.7 was fully divided, with the three lanes of traffic in each direction separated from each other by curbing. The two outer lanes were to be used by slow-moving horse-drawn traffic, since it was not yet clear that motor vehicles would completely displace horses. One inner lane in each direction would be reserved for autos and one for trucks. Footpaths would be provided along each edge of the highway, and lighting would be provided from poles arrayed down the center. The

Figure 3.7. Proposed Commercial Highway. *Good Roads* 7 (December 1906): 971.

road would be built as a commercial venture, with revenues generated both by tolls charged to users and through the sale and lease of adjacent real estate. Planners envisioned such boulevards connecting many of the nation's major cities—New York and Philadelphia, Baltimore and Washington, and Chicago and Milwaukee, for example.

Upgraded roads were intended to get motorists to their destinations not just speedily but also safely. Engineering for safe motoring necessitated knowing something about driver road response. How did motorists actually visualize and react to highway conditions? The specifics of grade, curvature (or turning radius), road width, and line of sight became design preoccupations. Good roads involved smooth, durable surfaces but also had to be structured so that motorists moving at high speeds could drive by instinct. Roads needed to fit the mental habits of the motorists who used them. Early study focused on how drivers positioned their cars relative to the road edge. Observers found that on two-lane pavements, cars were positioned an average of 2½ feet from the road shoulder and closer to the center when shoulders were low or rough or when a road surface was uneven. On curves, especially on narrow roads, motorists had a tendency to invade the oncoming lane.[26] New standards called for widened traffic lanes, especially on curves. In addition, the painting of lane strips became standard practice, first on curves and then on straightaways. Road designers also recognized the need for superelevation, the systematic banking of curves. Even the earliest motor cars traveled as much as five times as fast as horse-drawn carriages and wagons. New roads would require embankments that balanced centrifugal force (which inclined cars to slip off pavements) with centripetal force (which inclined them to move into oncoming traffic).[27]

Road gradients also were carefully considered. In the era of animal power, the most desirable maximum angle for a descending grade was the so-called angle of repose, the angle where tractive resistance balanced the force of gravity. Carriages and wagons could descend at this slope without a driver using a brake. Ideally, grades needed to be less than one in thirty-five, or less than 2.85 percent.[28] Equally low grades, of course, were desirable for ascending. In the horse-and-wagon era, roads were deliberately curved through hilly or mountainous terrain to maintain low grades. As early as 1916, however, five-ton trucks could ascend in low gear a brick-paved slope of 13 percent gradient. At this time most automobiles could easily climb a 6 percent grade in high gear if given a running start. High-speed driving, of course, required roads with but a minimum of curves—roads with long, sweeping tangents if there were any curves at all. As for descending, it was found that grades of less than 4 percent permitted motor vehicles to descend hills without use of either brakes or engine compression, although speed could be overly slow. Thus gradients of around 6 percent came to be considered ideal for auto roads, a clear compromise between automobile engine horsepower and braking ability.

When tight curves and steep grades were replaced by flat straightaways, extensive excavation and fill was usually necessary: debris removed from hill crests was used to raise embankments across valleys. However, not until after World War I, when large earth-moving machines were developed, were costs reduced sufficiently to encourage this and other forms of highway straightening on a large scale. Until then, most U.S. highway improvement was restricted largely to paving and bridge replacement. Motoring in hilly areas continued to be much like riding a roller coaster, with what highway engineers came to call humping or rolling grades.

As for sight lines, the American Association of State Highway Officials recommended that motorists be able to see at least 500 feet ahead at all times, sight distance being measured from an eye level of 4½ feet above the road surface.[29] To meet this goal, highway departments were encouraged, where necessary, to broaden curves, lower road grades, embank roads, cut down vegetation, remove billboards, and do whatever else was necessary to remove visual impediments. If highway rights-of-way could not be extensively rearranged, then they should at least be better signed. Association initiatives led to standardized traffic regulations and warning and guide signs along federal-aid highways (and consequently other highways as well). Signing of railroad crossings was especially important.

Through the mid-1930s, highway improvement remained primarily a matter of small-scale highway upgrades, each new project reflecting closely the specifics of physical site, economic context, and immediate need. America's good roads, in other words, evolved largely in an ad hoc fashion, rarely through the building of wholly new roadways over great distances. Important exceptions existed, of course, starting with William K. Vanderbilt's Long Island "motor parkway" opened in 1908, a totally new road intended to speed wealthy auto commuters toward Manhattan.

Determining the extent of a road improvement remained an unrefined art and mainly a matter of guesswork. Political reality rather than traffic need often drove particular road projects. It was obviously uneconomical to pave a road so that it would last thirty years but then to have to replace it by a new alignment in only ten years as a consequence of changed traffic demand. But who could be certain about what traffic demand, let alone road wear, would be? Highway planners, always constrained financially, tended to proceed cautiously, playing a game of problem response. Roads tended to be improved—or for that matter redesigned—only when situations became too problematic to further ignore. Such was the American way with most things.

Maintenance and Repair

Highways required constant attention. In the 1940s, West Virginia's State Road Commission set up a schedule for statewide highway maintenance. Snow removal and equipment overhaul were to dominate from December through March. Plans for summer construction were to be finalized and contracts concluded in February. March would be the month for bridge inspection, the cleaning of drainage pipes and ditches, and the removal of snow fences. Highway shoulders were to be dressed and guardrail cable tightened in April. May through August was a time for pavement patching, sign painting, and the removal of signs illegally posted on public rights-of-way. After May 15, new construction by contractors could begin. In June, mowing and trash pickup were to be emphasized. In September, pavement stripes were to be repainted. In October, snow removal equipment was to be prepared. In November, guardrails were to be loosened and snow fences set out. Finally, in December, the annual report was to be filed.[30]

The question of whether rural highways should be kept free of snow loomed large during World War I after truck convoys carrying war materiel became snowbound. In 1918, the Pennsylvania State Highway Department created a snowfighting force of two hundred men equipped with 105 horse-drawn road scrapers, seven motor trucks with snowplow attachments, and three gasoline-powered tractors. Pennsylvania officials thus kept clear the 225 miles of the Lincoln Highway between the Maryland and Ohio state lines. Drifts from three to six feet were common all along the road that winter. The work was begun by breaking a track through the drifts with teams and drags. This was followed by the road machines and trucks with plow attachments and by workmen with shovels. Turnouts were made at intervals and thereafter the entire road widened out to a width of between fourteen and sixteen feet, reported the *Buffalo Motorist.* "The snow at first was removed to within 3 inches of the road surface and what did not melt was afterward removed entirely."[31]

Roadside trash increasingly became a problem. But in California as late as 1953, the State Division of Highways allocated only five hundred thousand dollars for trash removal along fourteen thousand miles of road, an average expenditure of only thirty-five dollars per mile.[32] In many states, highway cleanup was left to the counties or not done at all. In some southern states, convicts did road cleanup, a practice that followed from traditional convict lease programs under which prison inmates were contracted out to brokers who in turn contracted the prisoners out to operators of mines, lumber camps, brickyards, and other places that needed unskilled labor.[33] Through the 1920s, the most important contribution to road building made by most state penal systems, even in the South, was supply of crushed rock, since many prisons were located at quarry sites so that inmates could be made to perform hard labor. But why, critics argued, deprive honest, law-abiding laborers of work and income? Road jobs should be reserved for those deserving. Highways affected economic well-being, they argued, not just through speed and convenience in transport but as a source of employment.

◆ ▼ ●

After World War I, when highway improvement moved rapidly forward, the construction detour became a persistent annoyance for motorists. The punctured tire, the broken spring, and the broken axle no longer disrupted travel as much as the red flag. "We would roll along a beautiful stretch of road, enjoying the breeze and the wonderful scenery," remembered one traveler, "when a red flag would appear in the middle of the road. 'Another detour, we can not make our distance today.'" "I would instinctively clutch the baby with one hand and the side of the car with the other," she continued, "and brace the steamer trunk with my feet, so it might not break loose from moorings and crush us, as we wallowed through the detour."[34] Such commotion suggested to at least one cartoonist that motorists who desired to see the country without the inconvenience of either bad roads or detours should stay home instead and rent a moving panorama (figure 3.8).

Perhaps the detour per se was less annoying than the way highway commissions allowed contractors to manage those detours: frequently without careful preparation, usually with a general lack of consideration for motorist sensibilities, and always with an arrogance of command. On the open road, motorists were supposed to be empowered, but on roads closed for improvement, highway engineers, contractors, and their minions dictated otherwise. Under the dictatorship of

Figure 3.8. Motoring without Detours. *Hoosier Motorist* 13 (May 1925): 13.

the highway engineers, roads were closed at will and for seemingly indeterminate amounts of time, the motoring public be damned. So popular, of course, was the cause of highway improvement that most Americans, including most motorists, were willing to suffer, though not necessarily silently.

During the 1920s, a mature highway industry evolved. It comprised governmental entities concerned with highway finance, planning, and maintenance as well as private entities concerned with supplying equipment, materials, and engineering and construction services. As a coalition of vested interests in league with the automakers, the gasoline refiners, the tire makers, and all the other auto-oriented businesses, the highway industry moved to dominate America's transport economy. In 1921, more than seventy-five thousand contracting companies engaged in highway construction.[35] If each firm employed 20 workers, the highway industry already involved 150,000 workers. Sixty years later, the industry accounted for 17 percent of the nation's gross national product, generating approximately 620,000 jobs.[36]

highways as public prerogative

"If the already improved roads of the Empire State were placed in the form of a loop," Robert Bruce noted in *American Motorist* magazine in 1918, "they would reach from Washington, D.C., to southern California over the National Old Trails, up to San Francisco, and thence again across the continent to New York City by the Lincoln highway, with considerable mileage to spare."[1] However, despite such a seemingly large number of improved roadways, American motorists remained mired in unimproved roads, which constituted roughly 89 percent of the nation's total three million miles.[2] And despite the existence of these improved roads, as in the parts of the state of New York, little coordination occurred between road improvements. Bruce's vision, shared by many commentators, called for network integration so that motorists would never be inconvenienced when speeding from place to place. What good was having automobiles if their potential for speed could not be realized on dependable pavement?

Automobiles and highways have worked in unison to kindle the excitement of motoring, with highways playing a special role in that synergy (figure 4.1).[3] The automobile's costs were far more apparent to motorists than the cost of highways. Motorists bought their vehicles, but beyond the first generation of motorists who witnessed transition from mud paths to an all-weather highway system with the universal adoption of the gasoline tax to pay for the new roads, highways have simply seemed to be there, waiting in obedient service. The open road, not just the motor car itself, supremely symbolized the automobile's freedom of release for both business and recreational motorists. Of all the forces stimulating the motoring phenomenon investigated in this book, highways have contributed most to the impelling and core belief in the blessed fantasy of flight. Roadside tourism could not deliver on pleasant expectations when painstaking travel preparations and possible annoyances cropped up along the way. Dealerships and garages dampened motorists' enthusiasm to various degrees, depending on the cost and complexity of the requisite cash outlays before motorists could start or resume

GREETINGS FROM THE ROAD

Scootin' down the valleys,
Climbing up the hills;
Eating up the distance,
Lots of fun and thrills.

Easy way of travel
In the good old bus,
Next time we go touring
Better come with us.

4844-29

Figure 4.1. Greetings from the Road, Postcard, 1929. Courtesy Lake County, Illinois, Museum, Curt Teich Postcard Archives.

their trips. Highways, however, seemed free and untroubled, not only embodying the actual path to the promised land but doing so without cost (the funds were hidden in the gas tax) or care (others constructed and maintained the roads). In addition to engendering feelings of liberation, highways emboldened motorists. The thrill of dominion over all that could be seen from the car, traversed over the road, and imagined ahead added to the rush. The extent and depth of those public longings were and remain reflected in federal and state governments' assumption of responsibility for a highway system.

Highway Construction

Before the 1920s, highway surfaces, quality, durability, and signs varied greatly among local jurisdictions. A magazine writer traveling in 1921, the same year the federal government legislated a national highway system, reported on the heterogeneous circumstances in the East and Midwest. (He did not even mention the West, where, except in a few states, automobile highways remained virtually nonexistent.) Roads adhered strictly to landforms, according to the writer. In the East, highways tracked "around swamps, hills, hillocks—the most trivial of obstacles, in fact." In the Midwest, it was "impossible to get seriously lost" because roads ran "straight east-west and north-south, with at most a little jog here and there to effect a more favorable crossing of a stream." Motorists counted turns to keep an accurate account of ordinal directions. "And one has but to watch the telephone wires to know whether one is approaching or receding from a town. If they thin out as you run past the widely spread houses[,] you are leaving a town behind you." Instincts could be no less effective than posted signs in helping motorists find their way: "'Straight Through' may be indicated by poles on diagonally opposite corners, and 'Turn' by poles set squarely opposite one another in such a fashion that one *must* turn to pass between them." However, "the strange driver approaching on the side road may be misled by the 'Straight Through' arrangement to suppose that he is on the highway." Tolerance for hazards differed so greatly from place to place that contempt for warning signs could result. Ohio and Indiana posted "sharp" and "dangerous" signs at curves that seemed very generous elsewhere. In New York, the terrain belied signs indicating "steep" and "dangerous" hills: they were not as bad as indicated.[4]

Other travelers imparted an appreciation of the varying quality of roads. Curiosity about the transcontinental Lincoln Highway, inaugurated in 1913, prompted *Collier's* magazine to invite socialite Emily Post to travel the road in the spring of 1915 and write a report for publication. She reproved the heretofore lauded highway as in fact a "meandering dirt road that becomes mud half a foot deep after a day or two of rain" and contrasted it with the state-maintained roads in the East.[5] In 1905, even Bruce's vaunted New York system had no improved road extending more than twenty-five miles.[6] In 1924, another magazine writer, amazed at how highway thicknesses had been increased to bear the weight of automobiles and motor trucks, insisted nonetheless that the "king of the highway" (the motorist as the supreme constituent of the new highway departments) commanded "not thickness of road so that it can be used to supplant the railroad, but . . . greater width and a greater paved mileage."[7]

Although Congress's legislative response to public demand innovated the practice of federal aid for a national highway policy and thereby transferred the highway project from exclusively local autonomy to a policy shared nationwide, the 1916 act frustrated many people by putting in place a framework but stalling execution. By the end of World War I, much of the existing road system lay in shambles as a consequence of accelerated wartime motor truck traffic, while less than $\frac{1}{75}$ of the funds appropriated in the 1916 act had been expended and a mere thirteen miles of road added.[8] In addition, more building might have worsened travel conditions because the 1916 act, which sought to end rural isolation and provide access from farms,[9] did not require the roads of contiguous states to connect and would soon have seemed incomprehensible in light of longer-distance motoring. The 1916 act did not account for later auto tourists and truckers. Nonetheless, Thomas MacDonald, in 1919 appointed chief of the Bureau of Public Roads to direct fulfillment of the 1916 legislation, felt confident that every state had taken steps of latent significance. He declared that "certainly the Federal Aid Road Act can be credited with having turned the attention of the public toward the expenditure of public funds for highway purposes."[10] The head of Wisconsin's highway department and president of the newly formed American Association of State Highway Officials concurred: "The American people, almost as one man, are demanding, and that instantly, a modern and comprehensive system of highways and are willing to pay the price" (figure 4.2).[11]

MacDonald began his tenure as head of the bureau by shepherding the Federal Highway Act of 1921 through Congress. Within a few months of taking his new job, MacDonald overturned his predecessor's commitment to a Washington-centered national highway commission in favor of truly federated cooperation among all groups interested in highways, especially the cadre of newly created state highway engineers. The 1921 legislation allocated as much funding for the following year as the 1916 act had provided for five years and required the building of an interconnected system of interstate highways that would link cities. Intracity and farm-to-market roads were excluded. The 1916 act had provided exclusively for roads that the postal service used. According to Bruce Seely, the 1921–36 period

Figure 4.2. Advertisement for Tarvia Asphalt. *Roads and Streets* 70 (December 1930): 73.

constituted the "golden age of highway building." During those fifteen years, states built 420,000 miles of roads and MacDonald created an aura of apolitical dedication and technical superiority for the federal venture that won public approval as the only way to realize the country's motoring needs.[12]

Out of the mounting pressure for a highway system emerged a strangely localized pattern. MacDonald's Bureau of Public Roads expanded the nation's total highway mileage but acceded to local interests less concerned with financing highways for travelers motoring through than with local use. Federally funded interstate networks were largely superimposed over intercity connections along existing railroad lines. Before automobiles inflated Americans' attitudes about spatial compression and interregional connectivity, local elites lobbied state highway departments regarding the location and building process for the first improved roads.[13]

Highway Finance

While MacDonald worked behind the scenes to guide and encourage the crafting of the American highway system, the issues resolved in public view, such as road location, engaged motorists. Funding was another principal calculation. John

Burnham, the first historian to fully explore the influence of funding on the automobile revolution in American transportation, pointed out that the voluminous purchase and registration of automobiles in the early twentieth century quickly outstripped the capacity of prevailing sources of highway funds (property taxes or poll taxes) or labor (the corvée) to satisfy the demand for improved roads.[14] The new class of highway engineers associated these sources with the obsolete "pay-as-you-go" policy, which limited highway construction, and preferred the issuance of construction bonds. Road builders viewed Virginia as one of the better practitioners of the "pay-as-you-go" policy when, in 1919, it started its automobile highway construction with a combination of a five-cent gasoline tax, vehicle registration tax, state convict labor, mill tax, and federal aid.[15] Many Virginians, however, regarded this system as a temporary expedient and hoped to spur completion of their projected thirty-five-hundred-mile system by amending the state constitution to permit issuance of bonds.[16] MacDonald argued that bonds were cheaper in the long run, reducing construction costs for all taxpayers by permitting the issuance of larger contracts; and enabling completion of highways as rapidly as the labor, equipment, and supplies became available; providing merchants and farmers alike with higher incomes; and allowing truckers to reduce the costs of operating on rough roads. In 1930, MacDonald pronounced, "There can be no question that the employment of motor vehicle revenues to pay for bonds is now the proper procedure."[17]

Bonds, of course, delayed payment, and money for their redemption eventually had to be found. The gasoline tax constituted the source. Its implementation indeed represented one of the most remarkable decisions in Americans' rapid adoption of the automobile, motor truck, and bus as *the* transportation of choice in the early twentieth century. No significant group of motorists mobilized in opposition to the gasoline tax. A few did question it, but in the legislatures, where it gained approval state by state, its proponents were motorists or automobile-oriented businesses. Between 1919, when Oregon became the first state to adopt a gasoline tax, and 1930, the gasoline tax supplanted all alternative sources as the means for funding the nation's highway system. In 1954, three tax policy analysts claimed that never had a major tax gained such wide approval in such a short time.[18]

This rapid and virtually universal acceptance was quite improbable in a nation that strongly resisted taxation. Theorists defended it as a user tax, a payment levied on those it most benefited, and the most equitable of that type. Highway advocates thus found it in agreement with the most accepted tax principles—in short, the fairest levy.[19] Competing alternatives for road development had required payment only from the owners of abutting property, from road users paying the maintenance cost, and from a general fund.[20] Advocates believed that gasoline consumption proved an accurate measure of road use as well as the damage that vehicles did to the roads traveled.[21] As one commentator observed, motorists "will pay a tax for the use of the road in the direct proportion to the weight and speed of the car and the wear and tear it causes to the highway."[22] Burnham showed that contemporary contingencies also entered into consideration. The gasoline tax, in several ways, proved too low to engender resistance. Social classes benefiting from the tax in the form of good roads were prosperous in the 1920s, when the tax began to be levied; thus, vehicle owners felt able to pay the new tax. Moreover, because motorists paid the tax every time they filled up at the pump, the loss came in small increments and the total amount did not seem onerous. But, most importantly, Burnham explains, gasoline prices declined simultaneously with the onset of the gasoline tax as the result of new gasoline-processing technologies.[23] Those who challenged the gasoline tax most vigorously, the petroleum companies and distributors, had lost their claims by the mid-1930s.[24]

Illinois illustrates how the financial factors worked to create one of the first trunk highway systems in a large state. Before federal aid, the Farmers' Good Roads League of Illinois lobbied for road improvement, the establishment of larger units of road administration, larger appropriations for the state highway commission, and bond issues for financing the roads. This effort showed that farmers, at least in Illinois, had abandoned their traditional resistance to road taxes. Along with the generally insistent urban dwellers, these newly affiliated agrarians demonstrated the existence of a true public groundswell for highway development. After surveying road conditions, a legislative committee reporting the numerous inadequacies in Illinois's roads—poor construction and maintenance, absence of uniformity between adjacent jurisdictions, and no through roads—endorsed a law to overcome those deficiencies and a bond issue to finance the work. Rising costs, however, precluded substantial building. Although the legislative committee's law passed in 1913 and the funds were ready by 1917, an 80 percent increase in the cost of cement after the passage of the bond issue resulted in a mere 550 miles of construction. Federal aid allotments matched by state funds from vehicle license fees enabled construction of twelve hundred miles by the start of 1921. The new governor inaugurated that year, Len Small, determined to build the network rapidly despite rising construction costs. At the height of this construction-induced frenzy, contractors laid sixty-three miles per week, or approximately one mile per hour, and employed twelve thousand workers and three thousand teams of horses.[25]

With such a pace rapidly exhausting the funds from the 1918 bond issue and faced with a rate drop to two hundred miles annually in a pay-as-you-go policy, Small recommended passage of a 1924 highway bond referendum yielding $100 million and a gasoline tax to add still more to the highway fund. The bond passed, but, on the oil companies' charge that the gasoline tax violated due process and equal protection of the laws, the Illinois Supreme Court declared the gasoline tax unconstitutional. Lawyers circumvented this block, and despite its leadership in rapidly building an extensive highway system through huge bonded indebtedness, Illinois became the last state to adopt the gasoline tax when it did so in 1929. Tax rates ranged from two to six cents per gallon nationwide, and Illinois supporters boasted that the three-cent-per-gallon charge placed the state among the eighteen states with the lowest rates. In 1930, two years into the term of the succeeding governor, who continued the construction program, Illinois had approximately seventy-five hundred miles of paved highway, completing about three-fourths of its primary system.[26]

Len Small's manipulation of the building program for his political advantage revealed how badly Illinois motorists had come to depend on highways, even before they were built. Small echoed those who extolled the highways' potential economic benefits and bragged of his accomplishments, earning the title Good Roads Governor, but punished his political adversaries by withholding highway construction in their areas. Areas pledged allegiance to him in hopes of receiving the blessings of good roads.[27]

Highway Signs

As politicians worked out schemes for highway financing, planners turned their attention to what signs would best serve motorists' requirements for directions and safety. The results, like the taxes motorists paid, became the most routine and enduring influences on every motorist's life. States had individually addressed questions about signage for some time before the emergence of the national interstate highway system in the 1920s. In 1918, Wisconsin became the first state to post official route signs for a highway network throughout its territory.[28] Even though the Federal Highway Act of 1921 stipulated no need for a common set of signs, the act's framework for an interstate system nudged state highway engineers toward cooperation. In January 1922, the five members of the Mississippi Valley Association of State Highway Departments appointed representatives to survey existing state practices. Representatives of Minnesota, Indiana, and Wisconsin conducted the survey in the fall of 1922 and at the group's annual meeting in January 1923 recommended the system that was adopted nationally two years later.[29]

On November 18, 1925, the U.S. secretary of agriculture adopted a final sign plan, acting on advice submitted by various professional highway groups and technocrats. Among the most important contributors was the American Association of State Highway Officials, the group of professional highway engineers born in

1914 out of the eastern states' dissatisfaction with the federal emphasis on rural highways. Association officials regarded the sign project as a natural consequence of members' overall commitment to fashioning an efficient highway system for their constituent motorists.[30]

In 1925, the head of Bureau of Public Roads Division of Design, E. W. James, explained to the National Safety Council some of the professionals' views about what motorists wanted and needed from road signs:

> It is estimated that about four percent of the population is color blind, in the general acceptance of that term. Fifteen per cent have defective color vision. Unfortunately, a large number of our public can not read English, or can not read at all. We, therefore, used the following four characteristics in each sign so far as possible:

"A distinctive shape"
"A distinctive color"
"A distinctive word"
"A distinctive symbol."[31]

According to planners' logic, a motorist who was both color-blind and illiterate could rely on the sign's shape and symbol to avoid trouble. At night, the glare of the car's headlight would show the sign clearly and alert the motorist to the proper action.[32] But planners did not ask motorists themselves to speak about what they required from highway signs; instead, professionals mediated for an assumed public interest, rejecting public hearings on the subject as unnecessary in the face of professionals' assumptions that they possessed superior knowledge. Permitting public testimony would have required planners to listen to both named highway and various civic groups, which, in the words of a later report, "would have prolonged the work of selection unreasonably, if, indeed, it would not have defeated the whole undertaking."[33] In addition, the Joint Board of Interstate Highways made the final decisions regarding signage, fearing that if it did not act unilaterally its members would have to arbitrate among the points of view of the named highway associations and local interests.[34] In the end, highway specialists simply reconfirmed their belief that they knew best.

What did motorists see in this uniform system? They saw, foremost, a system of numbers reinforcing the national highway grid (figure 4.3). All interstate highways were assigned numbers. Those running north-south received odd numbers, while those running east-west had even numbers. One- and two-digit numbers distinguished the main roads. Three-digit numbers distinguished alternate routes, crossroads, and branch roads. The numbers were displayed in black on a white background on a sign shaped like a shield to connote the federal union, one of

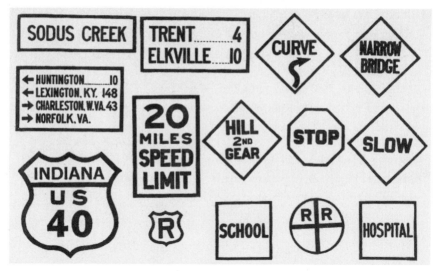

Figure 4.3. Examples of the Uniform Sign System. The sign on the lower left typifies the federal shields adopted for the interstate highways. *Hoosier Motorist* 14 (January 1926): 17.

whose unifying agents was soon to be these interstate highways. Because the signs sought to routinely assure and remind motorists of their path, the numbered highways absorbed motorists as a group into a homogenizing experience. Motorists achieved certainty of location but did so at the cost of adventure. Other signs reinforced this conditioning. Directions and speed limits, for example, also appeared on signs of white background with black lettering.[35]

Motorists reoriented themselves to the new system of uniform signs imposed from the top down. The system had a certain logic, if not necessarily every motorist's own; it seemed effectively to give directions and help elude traffic accidents. In the words of one motorist, "Stumbling through a two or three day journey, with the constant hope that when roads fail there will be a motoring Good Samaritan who can place the wayfarer on his proper route, will be at an end."[36] Most motorists accepted the new system, although a few holdouts grumbled. Wrote one,

> The scouts scouted, the presidents presided, and the pioneers pioneered. What of it! They are all long gathered to the shades and numbering the roads once named for them will push them still further down into the depth of oblivion. They were all very well in their day, but they have no claim on the "American" Association of State Highway Officials and the Federal Bureau of Public Roads. Our forts, parks, warships, libraries, etc., could all be numbered and catalogued, and all names of every kind relegated to the scrapheap.[37]

In the most celebrated case of adaptation to the new system, Route 66 from Chicago to Santa Monica, California, was personalized to an extent far beyond those that ever accorded to the named roads. The first lobbyists for the alignment that eventually became Route 66—the chief highway engineers for Illinois and Missouri and an early good roads spokesman from Oklahoma who wanted the alignment to pass through Tulsa—had sought to have the route numbered 60. But officials in Kentucky, led by the governor, and North Carolina also wanted the number 60. Both groups made their cases before the American Association of State Highway Officials, undertaking no campaign that would have attempted to persuade the association leaders about general motorists' interests. The struggle occurred behind the scenes, as one elite appealed to another. The Illinois-Missouri-Oklahoma faction lost the bid for the number 60 but soon came to appreciate the alliterative value of 66, led by Phillips Petroleum in Bartlesville, Oklahoma. The embrace of the number 66 thus constituted another commercial gambit rather than an outgrowth of motorists' feeling or their assent to the interests of the strategists who had wanted the number 60. A succession of writers and photographers as well as a television series eventually claimed motorists' commitment, as part of a wider popular interest, to the number 66. For most motorists, however, the highways' numbering remained unromantic.[38] Motorists as consumers were chiefly interested in *what* those numbers facilitated rather than *how* they facilitated it.

The public, including motorists, gently acceded to experts' decisions regarding safety signs. No significant dissent occurred against the government's invasion of personal rights when safety signs were designed and posted. Prior to 1950, Florida, for example, was plagued by collisions, sometimes fatal to humans, between motorized vehicles and cattle, but motorists did not lobby for warning signs and cattle owners did not tolerate control of unfenced stock. Despite the seeming lack of public demand, however, the state legislature enacted a fencing law that year. National sensitivity to highway dangers had first appeared during the 1920s, as many people were shocked by the mounting number of injuries and deaths. Between 1922 and 1927, approximately 3,446,370 people were injured and 114,879 were killed in auto accidents, numbers that safety advocates put in graphic terms, pointing out that someone was killed or injured in an auto accident every forty-one seconds. The most troublesome situations involved children between six and twelve years old and tired motorists: more than 7,000 schoolchildren died annually while crossing or playing in city streets or rural roads, and most accidents occurred between five and six in the afternoon, when traffic most congested thoroughfares and drivers tired after work were focused on getting home. In the case of uniform safety signs, people may have waived whatever distrust of big government they harbored in the face of the realization that this was one of those rare instances when government had to do what the people could not do for themselves. After 1925, therefore, octagonal, diamond, and square signs appeared to denote the varying levels of highway danger.[39]

Safety proponents laid special emphasis on "crossing crashes," collisions between cars and trains (figure 4.4).[40] As the most serious safety problem, level crossings required their own particular sign, a circular warning with yellow lettering on a black background. Even better than warning signs would have been separated grade crossings, but they were too expensive to build immediately, and the signs were accompanied by campaigns to heighten public awareness of the dangers of railroad crossings.[41] Railroads published a booklet to educate motorists about the problem and printed posters for the "Careful Crossing Campaign."[42] The National Safety Council extended its agenda of public education beyond the workplace to include highways in 1914 and subsequently sought to educate motorists and pedestrians alike.[43] Thus, motoring broadened into a general public concern rather than merely an issue for motorists alone.

Highway engineers preferred to think of motorists in the aggregate, gathering statistical data and referring to their "behavior." This paradigm became institutionalized in 1919 when MacDonald's Bureau of Public Roads and the National Research Council began the Highway Research Program, ultimately among the world's best scientific investigations of highway design.[44]

State- and federal-level research by the Bureau of Public Roads introduced more than highway signs and new highways into motorists' lives. By the late 1910s, for example, engineers had determined that motorists preferred clear sight for between two hundred and three hundred feet around an approaching curve; consequently, road designers lengthened existing curves, flattened inclines intersecting with curves, and cleared vegetation away from the shoulders. Research also fine-tuned highway width. "Lateral distribution," as engineering scientists referred to the subject of the distance between vehicles on a road, dictated enlargement of highway width beyond the narrow, sixteen-foot roads common in 1915. By 1920, eighteen-foot-wide highways and five-foot shoulders became standard for main highways throughout the nation. The Bureau of Public Roads studied lateral distribution in 1924, when the standard width of cars was sixty-eight inches and trucks was eighty-eight inches, and determined that extension beyond the twenty-foot standard added virtually nothing to two-lane highways' capacity to handle traffic. Through the late 1930s, studies of the "overtaking maneuver"—that is, how motorists passed those ahead of them on the highway—and bridge design, which influenced motorists' perception of a highway's width, came to affect highway design and the laws governing drivers. For example, the center line on highways, now taken for granted, became common in the late 1930s because engineers dem-

Figure 4.4. Safety Cartoon. *Hoosier Motorist* 16 (March 1925): 21.

onstrated statistically what they had suspected before: the presence of a center line regulated motorists' driving.[45]

Highway Accomplishments

Of the entire long period in American highway building, the 1920s are the most incredible years, setting the general template for all the years since.[46] Auto manufacturers, auto clubs, the trucking industry, and highway engineers came together to form in effect a single lobby for highway construction and maintenance, bearing on government at all levels. Most essential was the fact that the members of this coalition saw the "motoring public" as a strange and amorphous group despite its size. Motorists lacked formal organization in a legalistic society where the give-

Figure 4.5. Temporary Banking of a Sharp Curve on U.S. 19 in West Virginia as a Safety and Employment Measure. *Highway Magazine* 27 (April 1936): 87.

and-take of politics could not yield lasting results unless dedicated individuals influenced the formulation and passage of laws. The motoring public's numbers nevertheless could be measured, its agenda understood, and its undeniable clout felt in every public ballot about highways and every motorist's unhesitating payment of the gasoline tax, their "fair share," when they filled up at the gasoline pump. Between 1921 and 1930, highway expenditures more than doubled to $2.85 million annually, transforming the nation's collection of mostly dirt roads into the world's best system of paved or gravel-topped highways.[47] An academic historian soon dubbed the interwar period's building boom the "highway movement."[48] People at the time were fully aware that they were witnessing a historic watershed. Wrote one supporter of highway construction in 1930, "The automobile and the good roads have brought about the greatest and most sweeping changes in our transportation businesses that have yet come."[49] The adoption of a uniform sign system for motorists and the beginnings of the program to construct that sign system beside the new highways, although an adjunct, bonded the entire nation into one community sensitive to motoring.

Once established, the highway as public prerogative grew within the basic parameters set at the beginning (figure 4.5). Beginning in the early 1930s, Washington policymakers speculated about a coast-to-coast "superhighway," a state-of-the-art high-speed pavement across the nation's girth. The vision remained veiled, as highway planning customarily did, from public view through most of World War II. In 1944, Congress enacted another federal highway act that included plans for a limited-access interstate highway system. This measure extended the policy of state- and federally funded expenses, construction by state agencies through private contractors, and efficient and rapid traffic flow as the highest design goal. Planners tried to help motorists reach their destinations but did not grant them influence over choices regarding transportation or automobile-convenient urban development. Diversion of gasoline taxes from highways to other programs unleashed strong protests. Road building and motorists' appetite for more roads and higher speeds held sway. Claiming to speak for consumers, the chair of General Motors, Alfred P. Sloan, founded the National Highway Users Conference in 1932. Despite its broadly phrased name, the group lobbied solely for highway businesses—specifically, transporters, manufacturers, oil companies, and car and farm group executives.[50] Where were the motorists themselves? Did these corporate leaders misrepresent motorists' basic interests in highways? Hardly.

By the 1930s and 1940s, the highway system, previously a motorists' mirage to travel writers such as Robert Bruce, had become a reality. No longer was travel on the major routes a problematic event alternately kindling frustration and triumph, as Emily Post had experienced on the Lincoln Highway. In 1936, two Soviet travelers in America accorded their highest praise to the country's roads: "Our first impression remains ineradicable. We drove over a white iron and concrete plate, eleven inches thick. This ideally even surface, being slightly rough, had a large coefficient of traction. Rain did not make it slippery. We drove over it with the ease and noiselessness with which a drop of rain runs down glass." Americans passed in rapid flight along these sylvan pathways. "It is madness to think it possible to drive slowly down an American federal highway." Along these marvelously engineered speedways, Americans hurried unerringly to their destinations. "There is a great variety of signposts on the road, but—remarkable distinction!—not one among them is superfluous, not one might distract the attention of the driver."[51] Although a few Americans began at the time to reflect on some consequences of this highway system, motorists almost unanimously preferred to enjoy the experience as a dream come true.

◆ ▼ ●

Highways' design, construction, maintenance, and signage obviously transformed the motoring experience. Motorists could travel highways in almost any weather, with almost no chance of getting lost, potentially at speeds commensurate with their car's capacity, and safely, changes wrought by a succession of federal highway acts during the 1920s. The thirst for untroubled travel prompted motorists quietly to embrace the big taxes and big government required for those improvements, costs that seemed too dear to Americans with regard to other issues of profound social consequence.

5

dealerships and garages

Was anything more supportive of motoring than the commercial garage? There cars were stored, serviced, and repaired. Garages were closely related to new car sales and to the sale of tires, batteries, mufflers, and, early on, lubricating oil and gasoline. The garage mechanic quickly became America's quintessential problem solver, the nation's antidote to engines that would not start, axles that broke, and tires that went flat. By 1910, even the smallest hamlets and villages across the country had at least one garage, if only a converted blacksmith shop or livery stable. In the larger towns and cities, specially designed buildings with a layout and look quite distinctive from anything previously seen clustered around the edges of business districts and appeared along major streets as far out as the suburbs.

What few activities were more exciting than buying a new car? Was anything more tension filled than negotiating a purchase price? The elaborate sales floors that car manufacturers at first encouraged and then demanded that their dealers build brought architectural styling forcefully to the fore. A utilitarian garage might do out back, but only a grand emporium would suffice out front. Dealerships needed to attract on the basis of a quality product, but with so many different brands to choose from, at least through the 1920s, selling cars also required reinforcing customer aspirations by appearing modern, progressive, and financially sound. Importantly, premises needed to put customers at ease, inviting them to buy up, enhancing class and status aspirations. Next to houses, cars were the most expensive purchases most Americans would ever make. The automobile was not just a means of transport but also a symbol of family well-being. Motoring was rooted on the sales floor as firmly as in the repair shop. On the sales floor, dreams of mobility, both geographical and social, were enhanced. In the repair shop, dreams were physically sustained.

Joseph Corn astutely notes that consistent with the recent turn in automobile scholarship toward practical explanations for the auto's popularity, as opposed to the romance of the road or uncanny connection with the national psyche, the motorist's interface with the auto mechanic represents "one of the most psycho-logically charged relationships of modern consumer societies."[1] That relationship combines with the time and trouble of negotiating a purchase with a dealer to create a gauntlet that would-be motorists must run to convert their dreams of the open road into experience. The phrase "I wouldn't buy a used car from him" is the American vernacular for a dishonest person. And except for the comparative few who enjoy the sport of shrewd bargaining, haggling to buy a car ranks alongside motorists' fear of mechanics overcharging for repairs or for work that may not fix the problem. Motoring may be a fun consequence, but it is not without the mun-dane first tasks of shopping for, financing, buying, repairing, and refueling a car. "Sales and service," to borrow the auto industry argot, require examination lest one lapse into a mindless, one-sided rendition of motoring's felicities.

The interrelationship of dealers and garages has been very complicated. Some early garages, for example, specialized in service on certain makes and in the sales of used cars in that line.[2] Since the appearance of lube shops in the 1980s, auto owners can obtain oil changes in fifteen minutes or less plus tire and radiator ser-vice, but no engine work. Those areas have become a renewed stronghold of deal-erships. Even where sales and service have operated under separately owned busi-nesses, the relationship has been symbiotic. Obviously, new cars age and require maintenance; sales presupposes service, and service presupposes sales. Careful at-tention to the nature of both sales and service is required to adequately profile the motorists' relationship to each.

Dealerships

Matters of the manufacturer-dealer relationship may bear on the motorist's experi-ence, while salesmanship, negotiating a sale (whether of a new or used vehicle), and the architecture and layout of the dealership's showroom, business offices, service department, and outside lots always are a prelude to the motorist's time on the road. All of these phenomena, however, have a long, changing, and, there-fore, complex history best suited for treatment elsewhere.[3] This section will briefly outline the dealership's "front end" (as it is known in the trade) as a means of bet-ter understanding service anywhere—at independent garages or the dealership's garage, or "back end," as it is called in the trade. Only the aspects of the dealer-manufacturer relationship needed to understand the motorist-dealer relationship are detailed here.

By 1900, Americans were becoming accustomed to the mass-produced and highly complex machines with interchangeable parts that became a foundation of industrialization. This condition helped ready Americans to become a nation of motorists. From 1900 to 1920, manufacturers relied on numerous means to sell their vehicles, including factory stores, mail orders and consignment, retail department stores, traveling salesmen, wholesale distribution, and franchises. By the end of this trial period, dealers had sorted through the variations and operated through one of two formats, franchised or manufacturer-owned dealerships. Franchisees were required not only to purchase a predetermined number of the manufacturer's vehicles but generally to stock the parts necessary for servicing that brand and to make repairs at set prices. Parts and repair did not become standard in the agreements until after the 1920s, when the supply of vehicles began to exceed demand and necessitated thoughts about ways to enhance the deal for a new car purchase. Franchisees were "independent dealers," to use the industry's term, because they were not the manufacturer's legal representatives and could sell at any price. They constituted, in fact, geographic fiefdoms: their highway billboards and on-premises signs directing customers, the spatial arrangements at the lot and showroom, and their advertising's extension of the dealership beyond the lot and showroom were customarily stipulated in the manufacturer's terms. In return, an area was designated in which each franchised dealer would have no competition with other dealers in that manufacturer's line. Franchisees have been essential to the motorist's experience because they have been the most numerous dealers since the 1920s. Usually long-standing residents and often pillars of the community where they do business, these merchants have been highly sensitive to the local life and culture and to the local motorists on whom they depend for return patronage. Manufacturer-owned dealerships included salaried staffs working for the car company; in the early days, cars were also assembled on site. Because the manufacturers provided funding, such dealers have a competitive advantage over franchisees.[4]

Ford built the preeminent system of company dealers and in so doing helped usher in a general trend during the twentieth century away from merchant-dominated distribution and toward manufacturer-dominated distribution. Norval A. Hawkins, an auditor of Ford's books who became the company's general sales manager in 1907, reasoned that sales without middlemen would lower prices and thereby increase sales. Beginning in 1903 and motivated by officials' frustration with the original dealer network, Ford aggressively assembled a nationwide group of dealers, becoming the first company to do so. Few dealers had wanted to restrict their sales to one line of cars, and most dealers were poorly capitalized and unable to offer service or afford the expensive parts inventories required to establish a market of dedicated motorists. Ford had virtually been forced into the direct operation of its own dealerships in 1905 when department store titan John Wanamaker backed out of his agreements with Ford in New York and Philadelphia. Following the establishment of arms in Boston, Buffalo, Cleveland, Chicago, St. Louis, and Kansas City in 1906, nine company branches supervised 450 dealers.[5]

Franchising its dealers more than enabled Ford to decrease sales prices. Because production achieved legendary heights very rapidly, reaching almost 190,000 vehicles annually within a decade of the company's founding, the stipulated terms of franchising strengthened the corporate office's control of distribution and the terms under which motorists bought vehicles. Moreover, in giving terms that rendered the dealer legally independent, corporate executives could substantially lessen their responsibility for the franchisee's misdeeds with motorists.[6]

Hawkins's further persuasion produced the national network Ford coveted; by 1914, it included twenty-nine branches serving almost seven thousand dealers. Seventy-nine percent of Ford's sales by then derived from those company-owned stores, while the rest came from franchised dealers in small towns outside the service areas. Hawkins insisted on high-quality service, trained mechanics, and a large parts inventory. Branches telegramming for parts one day could count on receiving their shipments the next, and mechanics traveled from branches to local dealers to fix motorists' vehicles. This dealer network was at least as remarkable as the company's assembly-line system, its cheaply priced and efficient Model T, and the five-dollar-a-day wage for its workers, which earned worldwide praise. Ford service wedded many American motorists to the brand. Indeed, by the mid-1920s, half the world's cars were Model Ts (figure 5.1). Finally, Ford's highly integrated production-distribution system and high service requirements for even its smallest dealerships set standards that other American automotive manufacturers gradually mimicked.[7]

Ford, however, fell behind in sales techniques. In the early 1920s, with the market saturated, manufacturers shifted from production volume to marketing persuasion. Car companies now needed to convince people not that they wanted to be motorists but that they should buy vehicles they could not often easily afford. Henry Ford stubbornly resisted other manufacturers' solutions: new models, market research added to the distribution system, consumer credit, and acceptance of the dealer as an honored partner in distribution. In 1928, nine years after General Motors led the way, Ford grudgingly attempted the tactic of dealer financing, luring would-be motorists with the idea that they could drive a car away from the dealership for as little as one-third of the cost down.[8]

Motorists traditionally buy their vehicles from dealers on site, although e-commerce has lately entered the marketplace and there is as yet no way to know whether, to what extent, or how it will influence the traditional relationship.[9] The past, however, clearly demonstrates that considerable thought and wealth went into preparing the places where dealers meet customers in hopes of making a deal.

The showroom and lot were dealers' turf, the home place on which they inherently exercised the uppermost position in the relationship with the buyer. Motorists spoke the final word insofar as they did or did not buy a vehicle, but dealers had the advantage of contriving the stage on which products were shown, designing subliminal elements with the most persuasive powers to clinch a sale and maturing the relationship with the motorist to the point of convincing them they were getting a bargain when they chose to buy the dealer property while standing on dealer real estate. Buying a vehicle involved an adversarial relationship, even for those who enjoyed the event, because it required the customer to believe in the capacity to wrestle the salesperson and sales manager to the customer's most feasible terms.

The dealership sites into which motorists or would-be motorists stepped to inspect, test-drive, buy, and service their vehicles underwent several stages of evolution. Before the mass market gleamed, dealers adapted existing stores, carriage shops, and livery stables for their new automotive merchandise. William Metzger, who in 1896 became the first automotive dealer, ran a store in Detroit that sold bicycles, typewriters, and business machines before adding Waverly brand electric-powered cars. In 1907, Albert Kahn, subsequently one of the nation's foremost architects of automotive buildings, designed for Packard in New York City one of the first manufacturer-commissioned buildings for automotive display. Its neoclassical facade with terra cotta facing typified the foolish extravagance bankers generally associated with early automobile ownership. As late as 1929, bankers were on record against people of moderate means paying installments to buy a new car every two to three years. Chicago's "Motor Row" typified the grand assemblage of automobile dealers operating from palatial showrooms on the ground floor of multistory buildings that also included car and parts storage, assembly, and repair (figure 5.2).[10]

Following the downturn in economic fortunes through the 1930s, dealers turned to buildings of moderne fashion. Style but not intent changed. The purpose remained to sway motorists toward an experience detached from the mundane, an environment in which they dreamed about the open road behind the wheel of their new cars.[11]

The new automobile suburbs founded after World War II induced new dealership motifs. Most essential was the relocation to strips on the edge of suburbs as the older downtown dealership locations foundered along with most retailing there. Established consumer goods, automotive vehicles required less splendid displays. Dealers spread their merchandise in rows behind the street line and required small buildings centrally located for showrooms and business offices. Here was an architectural understatement relying foremost on an abundance of numbers, not

Figure 5.1. Bardstown, Kentucky, Ford Dealership, Typical of Small-Town Auto Showrooms. Courtesy of Dixie Hibbs, reprinted from her book *Images of America: Bardstown* (Charleston, S.C.: Arcadia, 1998).

Figure 5.2. Automobile Showroom for Harry Mapp, S. Western Avenue at 67th Street, Chicago, Illinois. Homer Grant Sailor Papers, Ryerson and Burnham Archives, the Art Institute of Chicago. Reproduction © The Art Institute of Chicago.

sumptuous show, as in the palatial settings of the prewar era. Showplaces nonetheless, the new dealerships positioned the service areas behind the facades in patient obedience. The new showrooms were brighter and cleaner; service managers now routinely greeted and discussed the impending work with approaching motorists; efficient clerks received the payments for the work; and servicemen returned vehicles to waiting motorists (unless they simply received the keys when they paid the clerks).[12] Yet in broad ways, service remained a secondary and unglamorous aspect of the dealership, although it was vital to selling new vehicles to returning motorists impressed with a competent and reasonably priced shop.

The mid-1950s marked the nadir between dealers and motorists. Problems started with manufacturers' arbitrary treatment of their dealers in the early 1950s. Never profiting from large sums on each car sold, dealers began complaining about distribution methods that allotted cars to dealers based on the number they had received in some past year. As a result, dealers complained, some dealers that could no longer sell the prescribed number received too many cars, while dealers in new areas capable of selling more cars did not receive enough. The situation resulted in the birth of bootleggers, unfranchised dealers who bought surplus vehicles from franchised dealers at factory prices, sold the cars at prices below those of other dealers, and included vehicles by various manufacturers. Bootleggers operated supermarkets on open lots with minimal if any showrooms along the highways at the outskirts of towns, where property values were lower than in the older inner-city locations of the franchised dealers. Bootleggers frequently offered neither parts nor repairs. In 1950, Dick Price, a De Soto dealer in Dallas, led a revolt among members of the National Automobile Dealers Association who sought to reform the terms of the centerpiece of the nation's dealerships, the franchise. Manufacturers, for their part, complained about lazy dealers who employed an aging corps of salesmen, aggressive as young men in the 1920s and 1930s but flagging in the 1950s. Manufacturers pressured dealers into "packing"—adding between two and five hundred dollars to the sales price of a new car in the comfortable knowledge that it could be traded away to a customer seeking some value for her or his secondhand car. One dealer told a Senate committee that he faced a choice of acceding to hucksterism or losing his franchise. Various other manipulative practices gave motorists a jaundiced view of dealers as hucksters. In 1958, Democratic Senator Mike Monroney of Oklahoma sponsored the Automotive Information Disclosure Act, which required a sticker posted on the driver's side rear window with the manufacturer's suggested retail price, the equipment included in the base price, and suggested prices for other equipment and dealer preparation. The "sticker price," as it is now known, went far toward alleviating the questionable practices but not motorists' lingering suspicion of dealer prices both on the lot and in the garage.[13]

Dealerships changed toward the end of the century. The big manufacturers granted dealership franchises to African Americans. Dealer service rebounded by the end of the century as the search for ways to attract customers continued. Although service contributed the smallest percentage of the dealers' three revenue sources (sales of new vehicles, sales of used vehicles, and service), it generated the highest profits. Motorist analysis proved that a dealership's good service boosted that dealership's repeat business for new vehicles. In a 1998 survey, 55 percent of motorists who said they would definitely return for service at a particular dealership said they would also buy another vehicle from that dealership. In contrast, of the motorists who said they would "probably" or "definitely" not go back to a particular dealership for service, only 3 to 4 percent said they intended to purchase again from that dealership. In the 1990s, a new effort to forge a brand-name store with a loyal national market spawned the superstore format wherein AutoNation sold new cars and ValuStop sold used cars. AutoNation's regional reconditioning centers made mechanical and superficial repairs for every car in the company's inventory. Thus, this new sales format did not include a new service format. Dealers in older formats, however, competed through improved sales and service, and motorist satisfaction with service rose by the end of the century.[14]

Garages

Garages have been polyglot operations since the dawn of the automobile industry.[15] Car owners could satisfy the various requirements for keeping their cars in optimum running condition—repair, storage, gas and oil, lubrication, painting, washing, and accessories—at various businesses. Some of these elements were housed in a single business, while others were diffused through several businesses. Few businesses supplied all the owners' repair and resupply needs.

Before competition between car brands became strong—when dealers simply demonstrated their cars and took orders and the demand for cars exceeded the supply—early car manufacturers and dealers could comfortably concentrate on their respective services while passing the responsibilities of repair and maintenance onto owners.[16] Salesman commonly gave flippant answers to first-time owners' naive inquiries about car care: "Oh, just keep her filled with oil, water, and gas, and be sure you use plenty of oil for a while."[17] Independent garages alone did not offer a serious alternative. First, until about 1905, few garages existed in big cities, where most motorists resided, and garages were even more scarce in rural areas and small towns, where bicycle and blacksmith shops adapted their services as best their willing operators could.[18] Second, early car owners were inclined to attempt to do repairs and service by themselves. The sporting element in early motoring assumed the challenge not only of driving over unmarked and often poor roads but also of keeping one's car running under those rough conditions. The advantage, of course, was avoiding poor or dishonest service: as one motorist stated, "If you actually oversee everything that is done—you *know* that your car is all right and you don't have to hope that nothing has been forgotten by a man who knows that he is not going to be the one to suffer if his work is not what it should be."[19] Performing repairs and maintenance required considerable knowledge, and as cars became more complicated, so did servicing them. As late as 1920, an experienced auto camper listed a long roster of requirements for readers on the eve of a motor tour. Those most important to "life and limb" included the steering gear (which needed lubrication and tightened bolts), brakes (both regular and emergency, which needed to be tested for relining), wheels (whose spokes had to be tightened and replaced), and tires (which had to be inspected for cuts, blisters, and wear). In addition, the cooling system had to be washed, hose and fasteners inspected, fan belt tightened, oil cleaned, motor cleaned of carbon, valves inspected for possible grinding, ignition system inspected, distributor cleaned, battery checked, gear case and differential housing cleaned, spark plugs removed and the oil drained from them, springs lubricated, clutch checked, and various accessories (spotlight and a light for working on the motor) supplied.[20] Men sought recommendations for building the ideal garage at home so that they could perform the mechanical work assumed to be part of a man's world, but many women too did not shrink from repairing their own cars as the era of the New Woman emerged.[21] Maxwell was among the early manufacturers that encouraged women motorists by assuring them that their models could be cared for without the auxiliary expertise of a male chauffeur.[22]

At the opposite pole from the painstaking motorist-mechanics, however, were those who willfully ignored simple instructions about use, such as the advice not to exceed certain speeds during a car's "break-in period." Toward the end of the second decade of the twentieth century, repairmen became more numerous and aggressive about advertising their services. Motorists who realized that they knew too little about their vehicles or believed that they lacked the time to keep their vehicles in the best repair gladly turned their work over to garages.[23]

Some motorists continued to do their own work, of course. Here and there across the nation through the 1970s, where the appeal of simplicity in a complicated world lured some motorists, they could rent shops and the use of equipment and tools and purchase parts. Motorists most commonly continued to change their own motor oil despite increasing garage competition for the task: in 1988, do-it-yourselfers installed an estimated 70 percent of all oil used. But after 1975, when automotive technology began to include electronic ignitions, emission controls,

fuel injection, and computerized engine controls, motorists patronized professional garages almost exclusively for more complicated work.[24]

Garage comes from the French, meaning "to protect," and the first garages often
combined repairs and refueling with storage. This combination was the most common grouping of services at first. Through the early 1920s, cars lacked the mechanical stamina for year-round use, and many had open rather than closed bodies,
making them unsuitable for winter driving. Motor clubs provided much of the first
shelter and service that the motoring elites required for their recreational toys, and
the Automobile Club of America, founded in New York City in 1899, was the first
to do so. As car ownership multiplied beyond the relative few, motor clubs across
the nation filled the need for garages. In 1916, for example, members of the American Automobile Association visiting Philadelphia were promised storage space
big enough for three hundred cars in a specialized three-story building as well as
numerous services, including washing, polishing, refueling, and air for tires; the
building also included quarters for chauffeurs. Increased auto ownership induced
nonclub motorists to seek the services of businesspeople eager for a new income
source through "dead storage." Motorists awaiting the return of mild weather, for
example, gladly paid a fee to be rid of the fall chore of draining the radiator and
gasoline tank and to store the vehicle until spring.[25]

Livery stables leased some of the first storage space in smaller towns, but within
a decade after the turn of the twentieth century, entrepreneurs, building contractors, and building suppliers began to appreciate the potentially big opportunities
specially fitted buildings offered.[26] In 1911, one author of a plan book referred to the
garage as the "present day livery stable."[27] The new facilities included interior provisions for turning radiuses, repair stalls, showrooms, and ramps to access upper
floors buttressed with reinforced concrete, earning such buildings the title *garage*
for their significant departure from facilities for horse-drawn transportation.[28]
Paramount was the motorist's rising expectation for fast service; overnight service
spelled doom for inefficient garages, one automotive journalist prophesized.[29]

Motorists' expectation of speedy service exacted a premium. While garages
began to add storage, they began to lose their popularity for refueling because
motorists grew disgruntled with the indifferent service (figure 5.3). Early garages
counted on gasoline sales for most of their income but frequently took motorists'
patronage for granted.[30] Texaco, one of the first independent petroleum companies to foresee a huge market through stations specializing in gasoline sales, outlined motorists' frustrations: "At the public garage it was necessary to pull into the
garage (usually the gasoline supply was located at the rear of the building) and
wait several minutes for someone to serve him, as it was not profitable to keep a
man especially for that purpose. Then it was necessary to back out the full length

Figure 5.3. Peotone, Illinois, Garage Offering Numerous Services, c. 1915. Authors' collection.

of the garage with a bunch of chauffeurs and garage men as a gallery; the driver often became rattled and a broken fender etc. was often the result." Nor were family members aboard comfortable entering the garage; they often waited outside.[31] Texaco tried to spur its gasoline sales in garages throughout New England by putting a company employee in charge of gasoline sales at the affiliated garages or making the garage owner the Texaco agent.[32] No single improvement, however, did more to lure motorists than the construction and operation of the filling station, a novel and specialized place seen easily, located on the streets motorists most used, accessed quickly but safely off the curb on the lot itself, and with attendants dedicated exclusively to filling customers' fuel tanks with gasoline and motors with oil. In 1916, Texaco's agent in Providence, Rhode Island, summarized, "The average person to-day, especially the motorist, desires and appreciates quick service."[33]

As motorists' demands satisfied enterprising garage owners' expectations for lucrative enterprise and as garage operators learned that reliable work, quick turnaround, reasonable prices, and ongoing attention to individual customers assured a steady or even rising income, garagemen turned their attention to pressing their services on motorists. "The bigger the volume of business handled by the large

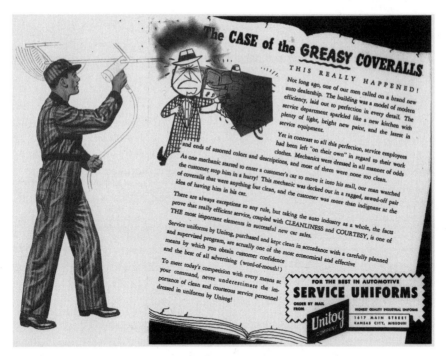

Figure 5.4. Advertisement for Unitog Coveralls, c. 1940. Authors' collection.

shops, experience seems to show, the better are they able to turn out good work promptly," the Buffalo, New York, motor club's magazine preached in 1925.[34] A 1928 book, *Garage Management and Control,* insisted that the owner of a growing garage trade "must, as quickly as possible, divorce himself from all details and spend his time in greeting his customers and developing his trade."[35] Managers should actively pursue methods of convincing motorists of a shop's virtues, the *American Garage and Auto Dealer* advised in 1927. In the case of the touring motorist, "*you must meet the customer and sell him* your tourist service. And the place is in your shop."[36] Garagemen should not rely on answering motorists' telephone inquiries but should lure them into shops or go to their homes, if necessary, to sell accessories.[37] Such bold moves could assure a financially robust garage. The service salesman became a recommended member of many large and profitable garages during the second decade of the twentieth century.[38] Image encapsulated the entirety of the business place, including clean uniforms to reinforce strategies of technical competence, cleanliness, and courtesy (figure 5.4).

A good salesman avoided selling motorists anything they did not need and did not prey on their insecurities about the highly complicated machines they drove. Fair-minded mechanics did not charge for work unless they did it and charged only for parts genuinely needed for repair. But many motorists believed such honesty to be all too uncommon. In the account of one traveler, "The garages which one passes at frequent intervals hover beside the trail like vultures waiting for their prey to drop."[39] Garagemen became so universally suspect that a popular literature developed about the dishonest mechanic, offering innumerable bad examples and rare speculation about the reasons for the fraud. Most writers gave no reasons, preferring to dwell on the bad cases and leaving the reader to infer that mechanics "were just that way." Even balanced accounts acknowledging that all mechanics could not be stereotyped as deceitful nevertheless insisted that evidence showed good reason for motorists to be wary.[40] In 1972, consumer counselor Ralph Nader charged that "many auto mechanics *will* cheat you, if you let them."[41] Such statements were tantamount to charges that fraud was the virtually the norm. Other observers attributed the tendency to a geographical contingency. Transients were subject to predatory mechanics who believed that they would never again have to deal with the hapless motorists who wandered by.[42] One cagey motorist out of state learned to tell mechanics casually, "Haven't bought my new plates yet," believing that such a statement would ward off any impulse to view her as an outsider who could be swindled.[43] Stephen McIntyre, a historian of honesty among mechanics, attributes motorists' belief in mechanics' dishonesty to class conflict between the blue-collar mechanics, who controlled the pace of work on the garage floor, and their managers and the motorists, who looked down on the mechanics. McIntyre locates the origins of this class conflict in the very early days of the automobile, when owners, expecting obedience from any servant, came almost entirely from the upper classes.[44] But why did motorists' distaste for mechanics not abate thereafter, when many blue-collar workers entered the ranks of the automobile owners? Mechanics' social rank appears to have risen by midcentury as young men were eagerly recruited for the trade to satisfy the increased need that accompanied growing ownership of vehicles.[45] The literature of the dishonest mechanic nevertheless continues into the present.

The persistent lore about the dishonest mechanic has made something of a folk hero of the honest mechanic (figure 5.5). Winifred Dixon titled a chapter "Saying Good-By to Bill" in her 1921 chronicle of a transcontinental trip. "Bill was Santa Fe's most remarkable institution," "surgeon general to all maimed cars in a radius of twenty miles," she wrote; to "Bill belongs the distinction of being the most honest, competent and intelligent mechanic we met in eleven thousand miles of garage-men."[46] The Alemite Division of Stewart Warner, a car parts manufacturer, arranged courses about car care especially for women in the early 1950s, when women comprised an estimated one-third of all motorists. Alemite eventually arranged for an estimated eight hundred courses throughout its dealer network, as company officials fully understood that simplifying the arcane knowledge of auto repair and maintenance was a clever strategy among women because the post-

Figure 5.5. Neighborhood Mechanic, Wabash, Indiana, 1999. Authors' collection.

World War II jump in suburban residences had put wives and mothers behind the wheel of the family car, ferrying husbands to the railroad station and children to school and various activities. Whether or not women enjoyed this automotive schooling—for theirs may have been mostly a matter of survival expedience—was unclear, Alemite officials understood. Whatever women's reasons, the high enrollments for courses nationwide gave the company reason to continue them.[47] Bill in the early 1920s and Alemite in the 1950s reflect the intermittently publicized attention to the honest mechanic. In addition, motorists who receive satisfactory service share information with motorists seeking advice about good repair shops, demonstrating that the appreciation for the sainted mechanic remains an obvious component of the motoring experience.

Suggestions for self-defense, meanwhile, stream through the garage advice literature. An article regarding New York state's 1974 law governing work at registered repair shops, for example, described the protections the law provided and outlined its loopholes. Because the law did not provide for restitution to the motorist in the event of a bad transaction, the motorist was advised to take the claim to court.[48] The former editor of an automobile magazine gathered the benefit of his long experience responding to letters to the editor about dishonest mechanics and recommended that each motorist patiently conduct a search for reliability by visiting garages and talking with their staffs: "In general hang around and soak up information."[49] The writer reminded his readers that the survival of local shops depends on satisfied local customers, so surveillance will disclose the quality of the neighborhood garage. Although the National Automobile Dealers Association established a program in 1970 to certify mechanics who obtained specific competence levels, the founders were aware that certification offered no guarantee against poor garagemen.[50] Observers ultimately have argued continually that each motorist was his or her own best guardian of a car's repair. The "chauffeur problem"—commissions and kickbacks extorted from garagemen and abuse of the owner's car—plagued the first decade of the twentieth century.[51] It thus followed that motorists should not rely on others. Repairs can be expensive and the transaction infuriating. Those ready to protect themselves occupied the best position.[52] The strained mechanic-motorist relationship therefore constituted a minor yet ever-present roadblock in Americans' faith in the open road.

Garagemen combined their skills in various ways as the twentieth century progressed. So diverse were the combinations that entrepreneurial advisers believed them a sign of poor business practices resulting in unrealized profits.[53] Garagemen could make better money, observers counseled, if they combined the right services and practiced the best salesmanship. Auto manufacturers and trade journals thus began to encourage scientific management, borrowing techniques from big factories.[54] These advisers prescribed flat rates, specialized mechanics and departments, progressive assembly methods, and piecemeal rates that presupposed heavy business flows.[55] The existence of many independent garages and many mechanics' resistance to imposed managerial standards, however, testified to the limited persuasiveness of such ideas. In fact, what appeared to industry reformers as wasteful and unsystematic or casual practices attested to the highly idiosyncratic preferences of garage owners, often master mechanics themselves, and the wide geographic differences in service opportunities that motorists induced. In 1924, for example, L. H. Brittingham operated a general repair service in rural Chadds Ford, Pennsylvania. A settlement of fewer than a hundred people, Chadds Ford was also on a well-traveled highway. Brittingham therefore operated a motor and repair service as well as a blacksmith shop and plumbing and heating business to satisfy local customers. The four service lines could be inseparable at times: on one occasion, Brittingham's call to a repair at an outlying farm so satisfied the customer that he had his auto's engine cleaned and repaired along with some farm machinery.[56] In rural East Lynn, Illinois, the garage was entirely community oriented. Built on the site of a livery stable in 1915 and without an appreciable highway business, its owners through the years first rented and serviced Willys-Overland cars, switched to Fords until 1936, and thereafter operated a service garage for school buses and a drainage tile business.[57] Modesto, California, despite its status as a midsize city, witnessed another variant in the bustling enterprise of William J. Silva Motor Cars,

Figure 5.6. Ink Blotter Advertising Beaver Brook Garage, Clinton, New Jersey, c. 1930. Authors' collection.

which rivaled the state's best garages outside of the big cities of Los Angeles and San Francisco. In 1925, this state-of-the-art garage offered battery service, lubrication, oil changes, car washes, four repair stalls, showers for motorists and mechanics, and a general manager's office permitting oversight of the entire main shop floor.[58] Profitable combinations eluded simple formulas.

Specialty shops proliferated, promising competent service of a complicated machine and thriving through reasonable prices. In 1929, Yarham's Brake Service in Des Moines, Iowa, specialized in the fairly complicated work of brake repair but added comparatively simple lubrications and car washes. In 1927 in Hollywood, California, Bill Ellenback predicated his comparatively expensive (a minimum of two dollars) brake work at Safety Corner on motorists' dawning appreciation that fifty-cent and one-dollar brake work was no longer reliable. Car washes, another specialty, long served as a secondary line for most garages. A few places had specialized in washing vehicles, but the coin-operated facilities that multiplied rapidly during the 1960s made it easy for motorists to wash their own cars.[59]

All work could not occur in garages, of course. Service on the road became critical to motorists stranded through breakdown or accident (figure 5.6). In 1926, the Hoosier Motor Club, located in Indianapolis and affiliated with the American Automobile Association, claimed an average of twenty calls every day and more than seven thousand every year for its road service cars, which either towed stranded cars to the club's garage or fixed the problem on site. Body shops, among the first specialty shops, added tow trucks or wreckers to increase their utility to motorists and thereby their income. Auto insurance helped defray costs. The Detroit affiliate of the American Automobile Association, for example, began offering auto insurance to its members in 1922 because other companies offered high rates and limited protection.[60]

Gasoline companies initiated some of the most important motorist services, chief among them free road maps. Governments, chambers of commerce, and various businesses eventually came to distribute maps free of charge, but the idea is believed to have originated with William B. Aiken, an advertising man tired of losing his way along poorly marked roads. In 1913, Aiken approached Pittsburgh's Gulf Oil with a proposal that the company distribute reliable maps with Gulf's advertising to motorists who bought gas at the company's filling stations, themselves a new marketing means. Early garage managers occasionally competed in giving travel advice by keeping current with the latest road conditions through local automobile clubs, but in the late 1920s, motorists grew accustomed to free gas company maps showing paved roads in red and "improved roads" with dotted lines. Such maps became a staple of the motoring experience and functioned as much to open roads to motoring as to tie the experience to the purchase of products by the distributing oil company. By the 1960s, Rand McNally, a mapmaker since the nineteenth century and the first producer of oil company maps; General Drafting, begun in 1909; and H. M. Gousha, begun in 1926, dominated the field, producing between 180 million and 250 million free road maps annually until 1972, when interstates diminished the maps' once-vital wayfinding function. In the 1980s, vehicle dashboards began to include built-in computerized navigation devices, giving a motorist a visual display of the vehicle's position and the streets required to reach the destination.[61] Oil companies ceased giving directional tips except when confused motorists stopped at gas stations as a last resort.

Motorists, however, came to rely on the gas station's malleability. By the late 1920s, increased gasoline and oil consumption plus increased competition among petroleum companies pushed them to build "service stations" in a constant effort to satisfy the motorists' demand for convenience. Motorists no longer drove up to "filling stations" selling only gas and oil but found "one-stops" that offered everything except mechanical repairs—oil changes, lubrication, tires, tire chains, antifreeze, car washes, and various small items such as lighter fluid and body polish. Petroleum retailers seized the opportunity to project a striking new image and to use subsidiary merchandizing techniques. Cities Service, for example, built attractive stations of white terra cotta tile with black-and-white metal tiles in a checkerboard pattern on the office roof. Green (the color on the company's gasoline containers) was used on the garage bay's roof and on display windows in octagonal towers at the office corners. The effect drew motorists to the products on display in the windows. Open to any new sales tactic, dealers discovered that cars raised on lift racks drew the attention not only of motorists but also of passers-by, who stopped to gawk.[62]

Along with the versatility of the gas station for motorist satisfaction, the petroleum companies enforced a strategy of uniform outward appearance known as place-product-packaging. Accordingly, the station's architecture and advertising, both on and off premises, corresponded to each petroleum brand's preferred image. Shell, for example, adopted a scallop shell logo derived from the original company's mother-of-pearl items. In 1930, Shell's jobber in Winston-Salem, North Carolina, Quality Oil, introduced its own shell-shaped stations. This bold gesture enabled Quality to gain recognition when it entered the local market, but later in the 1930s, corporate headquarters overrode this local eccentricity in favor of a moderne-style station uniformly imposed throughout Shell's market. Shell standardized its station colors, yellow and red. The ensemble of coordinated logos, colors, station architecture, attendant uniforms, and signs amounted to "total design" and resulted in locations that motorists easily recognized, even in unfamiliar settings. In this way, station design helped clinch motorists' loyalty to a brand after they had found their initial products and service satisfactory.[63]

In these settings, service stations became a means of marketing between the 1920s and the 1970s. Their diversified automotive services eventually gave way to the reduction of services to gas and oil, like the original filling stations, and expansion of opportunities for motorists to buy fast food and tobacco products. These latter-day convenience stores, which will be discussed more fully in chapter 11, further indicated the adaptability of the gas station format to motorists' changing demands.

Beginning in the late 1920s, tire stores began to broadening their inventories to include batteries and accessories—what was known as TBA. These three items comprised slightly more than one-fourth of motorists' annual expenditures, making TBA a lucrative market. Independent tire stores found TBA a means to regain profit when oil companies periodically cut the store's profit margins on gasoline. Tire giant Firestone joined the independents during the 1930s, opening a series of TBA stores capitalizing on "one-stop" convenience.[64]

Factors realigned in the 1960s and 1970s to put new service formats at motorists' disposal. Whereas price did not constitute motorists' overriding consideration through the 1950s and 1960s, it became paramount with the oil crisis of the early 1970s. The ritual of the motorist commanding, "Fill 'er up!" and the gas station attendant's free labor in washing the windshield gave way to self-service stations as a way to keep prices down. As oil companies reverted to their original "filling station" format, entrepreneurs took up the vacated garage work partly through the "fast lube" business, emphasizing quickly changed oil, lubrication, and minor services like replenishing windshield cleaner and rotating tires. The tune-up, a sales package of repairs created during the 1930s to give garagemen an opportunity to carefully inspect motorists' vehicles in hopes of increased work, required more sophisticated repair when engines became more complicated in the 1970s. Tune-up specialists then appeared to meet the rising demand for repairs because motorists kept their cars longer—an average of seven years. "Car care centers" became the new service stations, offering a variety of specialty shops under separate owners but clustered for convenience in groups, like neighborhood shopping malls.[65]

◆ ▼ ●

Dealerships and garages are ancillary to the motoring experience. Little of the exhilaration of flight along an untroubled path to some paradisiacal destination wells up from any amount of time or money spent fixing a problem at a garage. Of course, fantasy en route and on arrival are engendered by the vehicle bought and repaired. Except perhaps for shopping on the Web, vicariously enjoying the vehicles on television auto ads, test driving, and, for some, the gamesmanship of negotiating a final purchase price—all steps preparatory to buying a car and motoring—the experiences beckoning many motorists to the dealership turn just as mundane as that in the garage after arriving at the dealership.

This does not mean motorists do not appreciate the sales and service they receive. They seek, however, to have as little involvement as possible with the work of calculating the fairness of prices and to avoid any hindrance of roadside problems from bad repairs.

Dealership service, independent garage work, and sundry specialty shops stand in fairly plain view of any intrigued motorist. Indeed, of all the service people on whom motorists depend, those who perform automotive repair and service are the most prepared to make their craft public; theirs is at once the most central and complicated of the motorists' services. What motorist would assert the right to inspect a restaurant's kitchen before eating in the dining room? Who might require certification of safety of any amusement park's rides before getting on board? Yet cautious motorists seeking repairs or services are advised to ask questions of the service manager and possibly to inspect the garage premises before deciding where to have necessary work done.

Dealership service departments, independent garages, and specialty shops survive by providing quality work at what motorists consider reasonable prices. These are, after all, places of business, and their various permutations over the century of the automobile in American life illustrate the restless entrepreneurial search for optimum profits amid automotive technology's constant evolution and sophistication and motorists' demands for honesty and technical competence. Motorists willingly shed their anxieties about mechanical problems onto those who, for their livelihood, solved the most vital problems affecting happy motoring.

the tourist's roadside

With a plan in place for financing and constructing a nationwide highway system, plentiful auto salesrooms, strategically located gas stations for refueling and garages for auto repair, equipment for motorists and services beside the road became enabling complements of the motoring public. Motoring tourists knew that they could depend on the widely available goods and services of the roadside while making trips. The roadside both enabled and seemed to invite motor travel. From the first, motoring Americans set out in search of experiences that fell somewhere between challenging new circumstances and safe reassurances of familiarity; they anticipated a "trip." Roger William Riis's 1941 rhyme, "Song of the Open Road," captured the irony of a commercialized culture webbed in its limitations, dashing across the continent on branded fuel, looking for rest but finding noisy traffic:

> Ten million turning, churning wheels from Maine to Mexico—
> Socony, Purol, Shell, Good Gulf, Panam and Texaco—
>
> . . . .
>
> Ten million blatting, snarling horns from Mexico to Maine,
> It's been a lovely restful trip, and now we're home again.[1]

This dynamic of mass consumption for a limited range of psychic release, captured so well by Riis, has continued to determine the nature of the motoring tourist's roadside to this day.

Creating Confidence

The general public seems initially to have considered motoring an uneconomical activity. Early promoters of auto tourism often labored to persuade people that it was certainly cheaper than a railroad vacation and would even cost less than staying at home.[2] During his family's mid-1920s motoring trip, Myron Stearns, previously a skeptic, came to echo other experienced motorists' views of the benefits of car travel: "Everywhere we met 'tourists' of all descriptions who had discovered, as we had, this way to escape the complexities of modern existence."[3] The "minor conventions and necessities of a complex civilization," for example, included white collars and cuffs, tablecloths, and regular attendance at the theater. Motoring as the Stearns family did, tourists ate at lunch counters or picnicked on sandwiches. The options for overnight lodging ranged from hotels to sleeping out-of-doors in a consenting farmer's field.

Choices thus extended not only to material comforts but also to the awareness of choice itself. Motoring appeared to confer freedom. A process begun as testing frequently ended in cathartic conviction. "There's one of the first things you discover . . . to change your plans, all you have to do is turn the wheel."[4] Enthusiastic Bellamy Partridge, who turned his automania into a career writing books and articles on the subject, admitted to love at first sight in 1903, when he first saw a car. World War II–era gasoline rationing sparked in him an eagerness for "some bright future" when he could resume his wanderlust. Motoring became his hobby.[5] Others found different self-gratifications. In the early 1990s, Marilyn Murphy, a columnist for *Lesbian News*, wrote about how she and her partner, Irene, found RV-ing an extension of their lifestyle. In 1983, they escaped from their busy life in Los Angeles, full of lesbian and feminist political activities, and purchased a motor home. The RV enabled them to travel while surrounded by their possessions, creating a feeling of home: "We *were* home in our RV, with our things around us—our own bed, our favorite coffee cups and soup bowls—eating things we cooked ourselves and following our own schedule."[6] Marilyn and Irene eventually "no longer felt 'at home' in Los Angeles" and sold their house, bought a larger RV, and except for a small beach cottage in North Florida, lived exclusively on the road. They also joined a national organization, RVing Women, for both straights and gays interested in "becoming independent women, living their own lives, doing what pleases and nurtures them, and, for some, claiming for themselves the last decades of their lives."[7]

Although the motoring adventure could fulfill latent aspects of self, operational frustrations threatened to overwhelm the discoveries for those who failed to plan ahead. One popular columnist granted in 1920 that "motoritis" was an "agreeable malady" but also cautioned that "motoring has its essential hardships—what's the use of adding to them by wanton lack of forethought?"[8] Since that time, columnists have routinely filled magazines with motoring advice, some in lengthy prescriptions, some in short lists of tips, and others in the form of the writer's personal travel generalized for cautious readers. Yet these advocates also routinely interlarded tips with persuasions, seeking to spur the timid traveler. The mix reveals Americans' tentativeness in motoring. Elon Jessup, author of the 1921 *Motor Camping Book* and an exuberant proponent of motoring in the days before ubiquitous and reliable motorist services, offered recommendations about vehicle preparation, camping equipment, food, clothing, and temperament and averred, "I hereby elect motor camping the most democratic sport in America."[9] A proponent of the "rolling vacation" believed the best preparation was a positive attitude—just "start out for a ride," "don't let camping master you"—but also recommended certain equipment.[10] Most Americans were not the hearty breed just removed from the frontier who took naturally to camping beside the road. They had to learn how to consume motoring. Frank E. Brimmer, author of the 1923 volume *Motor Campcraft,* insisted from his "exhaustive survey of hundreds of motor camps" that "too much cannot be said about the spirit of good fellowship, democracy and friendliness encountered along every trail."[11] The implication: auto campers were solid middle-class citizens, no cause for fear. For those who missed the point, Brimmer spelled out his reassurance: "A few years ago it might have been a fact that the motor camper was only a stage higher than the hobo and the gypsy, but today auto-camping is a well-recognized American vacation institution."[12] The open road did not invite acquaintance with unfamiliar groups.

Selling the masses on motoring ultimately meant easing the activity itself. *The Delineator,* for example, hoping "you will want to join these happy millions after reading this article by a motor camper of many years' experience," offered two leaflets, "Cooking Equipment for the Motor Camper" and "Sleeping Equipment for the Motor Camper," at no charge except a two-cent stamp.[13] The specialized auto camping industry developed rapidly. Brimmer estimated that at least fifty varieties of camp beds had reached the market by 1923. Other available amenities included tents, camp bedding, camp stoves, kitchen cabinets designed for auto running boards, steel medicine kits, refrigerators, toilets, cupboards, washbasins, dressing tables, infant bathtubs, and lamps.[14] As motoring vacations became more common, authorities prescribed lighter travel and less commonly extolled the joy of the work ethic applied to motoring with the presumed rewards of sleeping outside under the stars. By 1931, one authority counseled tourists not to "make the mistake of cluttering up your outfit with too many elaborate accessories; rather select wisely a sufficient amount of equipment from the excellent suggestions, and load your car with only those which will be used and are essential for your comfort."[15] Physical comfort supplanted exertion as the consuming public expanded. In 1928, Brimmer judged that the "days of the tourist camp for tenters are apparently numbered."[16] The nascent motel industry helped explain the start of a different way of motoring, but as Brimmer wrote, another "reason is that tourists are a bit weary of pitching and breaking camp and generally playing Indian."[17] Buses and planes also eroded the auto motoring public: sights could be seen much more quickly and with less work from packaged bus and airline tours.[18]

Motoring lobbies targeted three specialized groups: women, motorists with small children, and motorists who wanted to travel with their pets. Virginia Scharff mines the sources of early information about women and the auto to conclude that by the end of World War I, women were gradually making their way from the passive role of passenger to the active role of driver. The sources, often indifferent, indicate that before 1920, the shift included only a small number of women, and cultural barriers to motoring's liberating potential remained numerous.[19] The existence of a fair number of women's published travel accounts documents the fact that some exceptional women participated in the motoring public.[20] More typical motoring articles in widely circulated popular magazines, however, routinely pictured women in supporting roles, frequently preparing meals. One magazine conjectured in 1925 that the common availability of labor-saving motor camping equipment such as gasoline, oil, and acetylene stoves resulted from the fact that women constituted a majority of the motoring public.[21] Jean Cunningham believed that too many women endured the privations of auto camping simply because their husbands liked it. Such a woman "will hang on grimly, with one thought uppermost in her mind—to get back home." If only she "can twist this new activity into something she can enjoy," the clever female motorist "will be as eager to get away as her man," Cunningham assured.[22]

Other women's accounts in popular magazines honored the ploy of the unempowered woman manipulating male vanity to achieve an end. Laura Breckenridge McClintock, after motoring alone and with a female companion, wrote that she had "become more and more convinced that the subtle art of masculine intercourse per the 'Oh, you-are-so-big-and-strong-and-I'm-so-dumb-and-weak' method has every other system beat a block."[23] Helen Mann, recounting a flat tire repair during the "pleasant adventures of two unchaperoned girls" motoring from San Francisco to Carmel-by-the-Sea in 1920, documented a case of chivalry.[24] A father and son in a passing car stopped, offered their help, and repaired the tire. Before leaving, the son declared, "I love to help ladies in distress." According to McClintock, for a woman, traveling alone was better than traveling with a man because police were more forgiving of mistakes. Gas station managers, innkeepers, and especially "mechanics seem to blossom forth into fits of unheard-of speed under a fire of ignorant questions and feminine flattery."[25] After midcentury, women more readily assumed motoring's responsibilities. Charlotte Montgomery's 1954 winter vacation tips for women did not hint at gendered considerations.[26] Still, authors of popular traveling guides singled out women; by implication, their participation in motoring required a certain amount of encouragement.

Child care represented an extension of the appeal to motoring women because this specialized concern customarily fell to women at home as well as on trips. Bertha Streeter stated forthrightly that motoring could be hard on children and their caregivers, but those difficulties could be diminished greatly with "proper preparations" and "if adults adapt their plans to meet the needs of the children." Adults should not expect to persist in their habit to "travel steadily and far into the night."[27] Instead, they should plan to stop by four or five in the afternoon so that children could exercise and should never pass a park with playground equipment without letting the children out to play. In 1951, Montgomery advised mothers to "keep the driving day short" and to include "side expeditions" such as model farms or ice cream factories.[28] Another good strategy was to collect shells or postcards en route so the children would have something to show their schoolmates after returning home. The child motorist's interests did not change substantially by the end of the century; in 1995, a father recommended the Story Land roadside amusement park in Glen, New Hampshire, as just the right scale for children aged three to twelve. "Outings to several attractions in Florida had ended in disaster. They were too big and overwhelming for a four-year-old."[29] One wife who had moved innumerable times with her children in the 1940s to join her husband on his various wartime assignments classified long trips as especially trying and decided that an entire day spent in a pleasant place en route was worth the therapeutic result despite the time lost.[30] Streeter insisted that maintaining the sleeping and eating routines of home would help children on the road. Small children's need to maintain a regular diet could be fairly easily accommodated with the prepared food that became available by the 1920s. Nevertheless, "meal time is the hardest part of the day for mother when there are children in the party."[31]

Infants presented even more specialized considerations. According to Dorothy Curd, writing in 1934, the paramount problem of food was "much easier if baby is breast-fed," but Curd believed that good foods for babies could be anticipated at roadside stores.[32] Another maternal counselor recommended adjusting the baby motorist to dry milk a few days before the trip so that it could be used on the road.[33] Special equipment for bedding and bathing was on the market; mothers were advised to bathe their babies just before they went to sleep for the night. One adviser alone cautioned that under no conditions should young babies go on long motor trips.[34] Most advice, however, echoed Jean Smith's 1940 words for anxious mothers on the eve of motoring trips.[35] As Montgomery summarized, "Remember this is *your* vacation, too! Having the children along can definitely add to family pleasure if you plan a little in advance and handle all situations with humor, flexibility, and good sense."[36] Behind the motoring experience with children loomed the tension between exertion and carefree release that familiar goods and comfortable services made acceptable.

Pets presented special considerations because they were often extensions of the family, especially among children. Pets not conforming to human expectations of obedience and cleanliness were thought best left at home. However, motoring authorities advised that well-behaved animals could be brought along. Some pets, especially young dogs, were prone to motion sickness. Advice-givers suggested treating pets much like children, with frequent stops for exercise, regularly scheduled feedings, and as much continuity between road and home life as possible.[37]

Sleeping and eating punctuated all motoring, and their demands soon eased travelers into commercialized services. Warren Belasco, foremost historian of motorists' lodging before 1945, explains that auto camping initially satisfied the robust with an opportunity to diverge from the drudgeries and bureaucratized constraints of work by providing opportunities for leisure, by expressing their individual personalities, and by offering families a shared experience of many days' duration.[38] Legions of outdoor zealots turned to auto camping as the first form of motoring, and many published their accounts—most of them unsurprising auto and camping industry paeans to outdoor living from which these businesspeople stood to profit. According to the May 1924 *Automobile Dealer and Repairer,* the "happiest of all is the motorist who, casting aside the trammels of high priced hotel and restaurant accommodations, plunges straight into the arms of nature with his own camp outfit."[39] Within five years, conditions changed, and the members of the mass motoring public turned largely to overnight accommodations suited to the desire for comfort with only a modicum of adventure. A veteran husband-and-wife motoring team concluded in 1928 that auto camps ultimately represented a "compromise between pocket and need of movement."[40] Motels became increasingly common in the 1930s, and while most were priced very inexpensively, the entrepreneurial response to motorists' demand for luxury on the cheap began with the industry's inception.[41] These establishments emerged as the new lodging mode, while hotels played an important but secondary role because of their comparative inconvenience for arriving automobiles and for parking.[42] African Americans experienced restricted opportunities in the same period. Not only did few own automobiles, but on the road, African Americans found few places willing to accommodate them.[43]

Roadside fare evolved similarly. For motorists enjoying auto camping, acquiring foodstuffs and preparing a meal provided welcome diversion. But as the motoring public grew, fewer converts saw meal making as a labor of love. One motorist swept up by the enthusiasm of buying her first car questioned the problem of food.

The indifferent food she and her companion prepared did not dismay her, but she certainly had been tempted to flee to a restaurant.[44] The late 1920s witnessed the creation of the first chain restaurants, designed to assure a menu of uniform quality and price.[45] In the 1950s, the most adventuresome motel habitués cooked breakfast in their rooms.[46] Franchised road food became the victim of a general backlash against the corporations' tyrannized consumer culture following the 1960s, and a literature grew about where to find wonderful but unknown one-of-a-kind restaurants.[47] Aficionados hunted restaurants in cities and in the countryside where the quality of the food was as important as its representation of regional cuisine and the personal eccentricities of the staff. Seemingly offbeat canonical guides for motorists in pursuit of "real" American fare simply produced standardized options of their own.[48] Others counseling on the ideal family motoring vacation regarded routine stops at fast food chains as acceptable as long as customers made healthy choices from menus once notorious as entirely unhealthy.[49]

While sleeping and eating on the road caused cautious motorists to think ahead about handling those elementary features of human existence, a host of unexpected predicaments could come into play after the adventure was under way. Such problems conditioned motorists' expectations when they came to rest at the roadside.

Handling Hardship

Through the twentieth century, the hell-bent driver represented the most consistently disagreeable feature of motoring. The subtitle of a 1921 article indicated the speed with which disdain for the maniacal driver arose: "If you like to tear along so fast that you can't open your mouth without having your teeth bent inward, why don't you go over to the electric light plant and ride on the flywheel?"[50] The author attributed the dysfunction to Americans' general habit of hurrying and believed that tarrying en route would not only stem the impatience but reward motorists with pleasant things to do and learn (figure 6.1).[51] A radio script published in a popular health magazine in 1936 dramatized the determination of a father, mother, and their two teenage children "to slow up and get a real rest instead of taking a vacation which calls for another vacation to recover from the first."[52] The alternative of racing through rural areas and small towns confronted unwary motorists with the proverbial speed traps where police waited to snare passers-by and thus raise revenue.[53] Vacation fatigue from the combination of navigating unfamiliar terrain, keeping schedules, and allowing for local customs bedeviled many motorists. Time away from home did not necessarily provide the freedom to relax.

Highways, whatever their condition, induced problems. Although two Soviets touring America in 1936 declared the nation's highways the best in the world, their

Figure 6.1. The Wrong Way to Spend a Vacation! *Buffalo Motorist* 50 (August 1957): 2; courtesy the Automobile Club of Western and Central New York.

high quality alone induced reckless driving. The Soviets found night motoring especially frightening because the headlights of oncoming cars came out of the darkness, flashed in the drivers' faces, and disappeared again into the all-encompassing darkness. Americans more often complained of bad roads, probably unappreciative of their good fortune relative to the rest of the world. Much long-distance driving was so uneventful because of the roads' high quality that motorists frequently complained about drowsiness and hypnosis. Glutted highways by the end of the twentieth century gave rise to "road rage," which occasionally resulted in angry motorists shooting or beating others believed to have disadvantaged them in some way. As late as the early 1930s, motorists complained about the frustrating local variations in traffic signs. Certain roads developed reputations as exceedingly dangerous. Authorities responded that safe driving would cure the problem, contending that no such thing as a dangerous highway existed. But officials' denials did not overcome the facts that many more accidents occurred on some highways than on most.[54] The public perception of the "dead man's highway" or the "hairpin turn" persisted.

Health, weather, and clothing called for expert advice. How to guard against contaminated food? How to determine the minimum necessary amount of clothing and provide clothing appropriate for the variety of places to which motorists were traveling? How to keep current with changing weather before confronted with inclement conditions?[55]

Some challenges and opportunities arose periodically. Other conditions of motoring remained constant. During World War II, for example, motorists no longer traveling for leisure still needed food and lodging. Nearly desperate owners of restaurants, cabin courts, and antique shops complained of a scarcity of customers while the few wartime travelers benefited from the surplus. In the early 1950s, hitchhiking seemed a big threat to safe motoring. The gasoline shortage in the early 1970s so sufficiently scarred motorists that travel writers encouraged people not to stay home but rather to substitute shorter trips. Aging baby boomers later raised the prospect that the start of the twenty-first century would see many unsafe drivers.[56]

Rather than addressing such innumerable considerations, the most certain advisers formulated broad prescriptions to revive the pleasure of motoring. According to a 1983 *Glamour* magazine article, the two problems that most often eroded motorists' anticipated fun were (1) different expectations among travelers in a party and (2) travelers' failure to talk with each other about their expectations. To avoid problems, all travelers should reach consensus about the trip before it began. Extreme opinions should be moderated through discussion but allowed some expression in determining how the trip unfolds. Another expert wrote about the pesky example of "Dogma Girl," who wanted no purchase along the road from any company that violated her beliefs about nutrition, the environment, or political issues. She consequently rejected franchised services that satisfied the other passengers. Motoring with a Dogma Girl would test *Glamour*'s recommendations that the interests of every traveler in the car should be accommodated. The magazine also reminded motorists that either something expected will not occur or something unexpected will occur; therefore, the article advised, travelers should think positively and plan without being rigid. Another expert touted the appeals of driving alone, providing a long list of the difficulties avoided by motoring solo. One could leave on time, if not ahead of schedule. One stopped to eat wherever one wanted. The driver was not disturbed by the passengers' exclamations about passing scenery. In a 1979 issue of *Car and Driver*, L. J. K. Setright dismissed consensus, instead expecting obedience from the other motorists because the driver was akin to the ship's captain. Each passenger's comfort was his or her personal concern. Nothing should be demanded of the driver: in fact, the passengers should serve the person at the wheel.[57] No simple remedy for motoring's various frustrations could be enunciated because motoring inherently combined in one vehicle several individuals with different interests and levels of authority. Which of them was to be pleased? Who was free in this apparently superficial frolic? Motoring, after all, resolved itself into a hierarchical relationship in which someone exercised power and someone else went along.

Finding Fun

The illusion of carefree adventure could be sustained partly because motorists' confinement to the automobile's small enclosure over long distances and under varying degrees of tension induced by fellow passengers made destinations, where other people took responsibility for activities, seem playful. Few people found driving itself liberating: destinations—both immediate and terminal—promised relief.

Intermediate destinations could offer some of the most playful settings, for they were not required to sustain long-term entertainment. Motorists happened onto them, stopped for at most a day, and accepted them as a playful diversion, as if they were not a staged reality. This "as if" frame of mind could even charm some critical travelers at places of advertised authenticity and high moral purpose such as historic sites or native villages along the routes to or within regional playgrounds. More often, this recreational tourism explained the massive numbers of delighted people seeking short-term and whimsical entertainment. Motorists enjoyed the enticements provided by these sites and moved on (figure 6.2).[58]

Santa Claus Land in Santa Claus, Indiana, and Silver Springs and Cypress Gardens in Florida exemplified the intermediate type of destination. Rural Indiana's late nineteenth-century economic descent pushed the town of Santa Claus to virtual extinction, but motoring infused new economic prospects. German settlers had named the town in 1849, and a retired toy manufacturer from nearby Evansville, Indiana, decided to build a children's park dedicated to the Santa Claus theme. The park was located approximately six miles from major highways and a national and state park dedicated to Abraham Lincoln, exemplifying the strategy of gaining support by clustering tourist lures. Santa Claus Land added attractions, including a Pioneer Village and a Wyandotte Indian Village. Publicity amplified. During the Christmas season, national attention focused on the community when letters addressed to Santa Claus flooded the local post office. Thus, from the first few years

Figure 6.2. Brochure for Gatorland Alligator Farm, on U.S. 1, Intended to Lure Motorists on Their Way to St. Augustine, Florida, c. 1950. Authors' collection.

following World War II, motorists to the nearby Lincoln sites or Louisville stopped and treated the children in the car to a combined fantasy and historic lesson.[59]

Silver Springs represented a variety of what Richard Starnes identifies as destination tourism in the South. Five miles from Ocala, Florida, and adjacent to the Orange Blossom Trail, Silver Springs offered motorists an adapted cave (sixty-five feet wide by twelve feet high) from which springwater gushed (550 million gallons daily) into a pool. Glass-bottom boats carried visitors, who looked onto the natural formations and wildlife at the bottom of the pool and adjoining White River. The surrounding semitropical jungle and handling of poisonous snakes enhanced the exoticism that was Florida's appeal to travelers, especially to the snowbirds from nearby East Coast and midwestern states who paused briefly at Silver Springs and similar places while on longer journeys to Florida.[60] Miniature villages, Native American teepees and villages, castles, petting zoos, model farms, Western frontier towns, and miniature golf courses (figure 6.3)—these roadside attractions for casual amusement along the way to primary attractions dotted the motoring landscape.[61]

Roadside farm stands were the intermediate destinations that most consistently scored high marks among motorists. These stands seemed to evolve naturally: "Our American habit of rambling over the highways on weekends has converted the borders of our concrete lanes into continuous shops," one writer concluded after the first half century of motoring.[62] Popular magazines paying homage to the faith in America as the land of small-business success periodically documented the histories of family-owned and -operated stands that popular demand inspired. In 1924, two motorists on their way home from northern California's beaches asked the Nelsons west of Sebastopol if they could buy tomatoes and so started Nelson's Gardens, fifty years later a legendary mom-and-pop roadside business.[63] Such places benefited from a combination of virtues. Selecting raw fruits and vegetables engendered a sensual delight and the competitive thrill of finding the most juicy or biggest item.[64] Motorists also felt a genuine sense of exploration and discovery: one farm stand owner testified that her business developed regular clientele when members of visiting school groups brought their families back on weekends.[65] Farm stands featured not lower prices but fresh produce, offering the aura of the fresh-picked even though some stands complemented their inventory with produce purchased from other dealers.[66] By 1965, the United States boasted at least eight thousand stands.[67] Some owners attempted to form an organization with certification powers, a code of ethics, and a logo, but it floundered, and the farm stand remained a darling holdout in the face of seemingly inexorable progress to ever-bigger businesses.[68] One dairy farm family recognized that motorists' pursuit of pleasure profited the family's ice cream stand. "Ice cream is a *happiness*

Figure 6.3. Children Playing on a Scranton, Pennsylvania, Miniature Golf Course, c. 1960. Courtesy Lomma Enterprises, Inc.

business," co-owner Dorothy MacKenzie announced. That statement also held true for many farm stands: in defying the perceived domination of big business, they offered novelty, satisfying the motoring formula of finding such novelties in unexpected places on a journey of discovery.[69] One example: the Nicolls sold date milkshakes at a stand beside the family's date farm outside Coachella in southern California's desert.[70]

Nothing so inexpensively fulfilled travelers' expectations of stepping into another realm and out of their routine as stopping, browsing, and perhaps purchasing items from souvenir stands. Although they ranged in size and extent of inventory, their architecture bespoke novelties that triggered memories long after one's trip, helping to stereotype the image of the place visited. These purchases could subsequently validate the visit to friends and associates back home and, depending on the perceived quality of the souvenirs, could establish high status for the owner. Souvenir stands also promised the joys of serendipity because they often loomed unexpectedly along the way to planned destinations.[71]

Terminal destinations tended to come with travel plans prepackaged for motorists. Popular magazines generated some of the most readily available discussions of the attractions as well as their cost and duration. If the motorist wanted an ocean voyage, *Better Homes and Gardens* in 1952 outlined a trip to Cape Cod. Another article demonstrated how a package could be opened: an uninformed young father and mother with two sleepy children drove to the entrance of the Skyline Drive at

Front Royal, Virginia, looking for advice. A beaming Shenandoah National Park ranger described a trip down the road and on south to the Blue Ridge Parkway as "one of the most remarkable trips in the world—about 550 miles of easy travel, most of it along the mountaintops, through the longest park in existence."[72] Melodic prose sold the couple, and the article, which appeared in *Better Homes and Gardens* in 1950, was intended to sell the reader. Travel guidebooks and travel agencies combined to undergird motorists' search for novelty without expending too much effort or wealth and certainly without life-threatening exploration.

No one has more fully unpacked the reasons for this delicately balanced quest among all tourists, motorists included, than Dean MacCannell. Building on Erving Goffman's thesis that the end of Western civilization's well-defined social customs has induced individuals' attention to appearance, MacCannell elaborates explanations of front and back regions. In front regions, customers meet hosts to view their performances. In back regions, hosts ready themselves for performances and close out customers from viewing.[73] Architecture was fundamental to relationships between people in front and back regions, acting as a screen, blocking the view behind the scenes and portraying a desired appearance for viewers in front. J. B. Jackson's characterization of "other-directed architecture" helps apply MacCannell's front and back regions to the motorist's roadside. Jackson understands that whether consumers liked or disliked what they saw in roadside architecture was the preeminent test of its virtue. It had to suggest "pleasure and good times," "the absence of any hint of the workaday world which presumably is being left behind," and "a dream environment for our leisure."[74] Strip architecture grew in places of long, linear display on suburban streets or outlying rural areas where the motorist's view from a passing vehicle was the first arbiter of commercial success. The roadside became another front region where architecture or the look of a place along the roadside became a performance staged for the touring audience by those seeking to make profit.

Motorists welcomed architecture contrived to cue them instantly and unerringly to what they wanted to consume. This programmatic architecture did not originate with motorists' eyes but reached bold forms especially among the diversionary motorist—pig-shaped barbecue stands, cone-shaped ice cream stands, and motels that looked like haciendas, to name a few (figure 6.4).[75] Motoring through programmed landscapes reinforced and multiplied travelers' sense of autonomy. Stopping, starting, going where one desired, and perhaps most of all, being certain of where one was—motoring helped satisfy all of these needs in an American culture that exalted individualism.[76]

The hunt was also on for "authentic" experiences, engagements with people and places uncontrived for the motorists' consumption. Motorists plunged into natural

Figure 6.4. Postcard Advertising the Zuni Motor Lodge in Albuquerque, New Mexico, c. 1935. Authors' collection.

areas and historic sites, seeking settings that rewarded the search for the enduring back areas. Marguerite Shaffer convincingly demonstrates that motoring tourists pursued the "real" America through the period 1880–1940 in terms prepared for them by local boosters and the consumption industries' advertising and that those motoring consumers emerged approving what they were told they visited.[77] In 1916, the *Ford Times* beckoned its readers to "reach the beauty spots deep in the mountains, where Nature has held sway for countless ages." The culturally thirsty could follow "miles of excellent roads, logged and well marked by signs, which will lead the wanderer to the haunts of the big game and the tumbling, foaming streams where live the wily trout."[78] The government built highways that not only enabled tourists to reach isolated spots but also, like the Redwood Highway begun in California in 1923, conveniently joined natural sites in long alignments beside which arose motorists' services (figure 6.5).[79] In 1916, the National Park Service opened its vast assemblage of reserves to auto tourism, in accordance with Assistant Secretary of the Interior Stephen T. Mather's strategy of preserving wilderness by informing the public about it.[80] Within thirty years, travel columnists like one for *Highway Magazine* asserted confidently that there existed "tourist accommodations to fit every taste and every budget so that every citizen can enjoy the scenic wonders of Grand Canyon."[81] Behind the front regions, motorists had arrived in droves into the back regions while advocates of wilderness stood firm in their determination to spare it from automobile invasions.[82]

Figure 6.5. Castle Rock, a Profitable Roadside Attraction in Michigan's Upper Peninsula since 1927, c. 1935. Authors' collection.

Historic sites underwent the same process. The fate of historic Weaverville, California, alarmed preservationists who challenged the necessity of a highway down the town's main street in 1934. More often, however, highway planners and local boosters alike welcomed motorists through historic areas by the 1930s.[83] Motorists were often satisfied in such front areas perceived as back areas. As David Lowenthal points out, many tourists went uncritically into historic back areas convinced of their authenticity before arriving.[84]

Authenticity tended to be an elusive goal, however: the more motorists entered the back regions, the more they came to be like the front scenes. Advertisers followed motorists onto their favorite pathways, bill posters especially seeking the coveted "circulation" that passing consumers represented. Increased highway construction throughout the nation during the 1920s produced a concomitant reaction against billboards as blight. Kenneth Roberts, one of the period's most outspoken supporters of the visual management of the roadside, for example, chronicled how the state of Maine's Arnold Trail, named for Colonel Benedict Arnold's military expedition against Canada during the American Revolution, was only half completed in 1929 when the road grew thick with billboards that blocked views of historic markers and scenery. In addition, motorists jettisoned their litter along the route, forcing residents to clean up the mess (figure 6.6).

Elizabeth Boyd Lawton's National Committee for the Restriction of Outdoor Advertising took on the task of national control and publicized the cause between

Figure 6.6. Antilittering Cartoon. *Western New York Motorist* 67 (August 1970): 2; courtesy the Automobile Club of Western and Central New York.

the 1920s and the 1950s. Ramshackle stands and, more often, stands covered with garish advertising aroused the committee's ire, and resistance to such eyesores has continued through the present. Motorists' expectations regarding clean and reliable services pushed roadside architecture above the minimum threshold of appearance, but billboard advertising has remained embattled because motorists rely on information from billboards for the nature of and direction to roadside services.[85]

Motoring spawned an insatiable appetite for novelty among those who could pay for its luxury. While the roadside responded to motorists' ceaseless demands for personalized services, their modes of lodging simultaneously took similar forms of self-indulgence. Tourist courts, motels, and later motor hotels—each form outstripping the previous one in the process away from the Spartan necessities of travel and toward the manifold amenities of the reproduced home on the road—housed most motorists overnight, and those who could do so reproduced their homes in mobilized form. Reflecting their eventual foundation in the consumer culture, the various forms of mobile lodging were collectively grouped as "recreational vehicles" toward the end of the twentieth century. Five forms have been distinguished: travel trailers, motor homes, truck campers, folding camping trailers, and van conversions.[86] The most numerous of those, travel trailers, originated in the 1930s with the practical needs of numerous members of the working class who pursued employment wherever they could find it on the road (figure 6.7). War production in the early 1940s further increased the number of transient workers housed in trailers and, despite their contributions to winning the war, did nothing to erase the stigma attached to "trailer trash" that had arisen during the 1930s.[87] The glamorous variation of trailer living for pleasure won far more attention in the printed media. Manufacturers spun a mystique of motorists' self-satisfaction, cleanliness, convenience, economy, outdoor living, and above all freedom.[88] For every unheard itinerant worker, many more writers, including famous post–World War II novelist James Jones, rhapsodized about the advantages of "Living in a Trailer," the title of his article for *Holiday* magazine that appeared in 1952, when many people had come to covet trailers as a remedy for the housing shortage. A quarter of the trailers sold during the postwar period were bought by soldiers who found other housing unsanitary and incredibly expensive—when they could find it at all.[89]

Retirees, however, added further luster to the trailers' postwar appeal, and life in a trailer park became idealized (figure 6.8). One of the largest parks in the early 1950s, located in Bradenton, Florida, featured landscaped grounds, shuffleboard contests, card games, hobby clubs, dances, and weekly stage shows.[90] By the end of the century, mobile home parks defining the upper end of the scale had full-

Figure 6.7. A Trailer Tourist Camp in Dixieland, Postcard, 1937. Courtesy Lake County, Illinois, Museum, Curt Teich Postcard Archives.

Figure 6.8. The Retiree's Roadside Idyll, Postcard, c. 1960. Dorsey Trailer Company, Elba Systems Corporation.

time security with gatehouses to gain access, fully equipped exercise rooms, and organized participation in the latest forms of recreation.[91] Those highly publicized places enjoyed positive media attention, confirming occupants' well-earned success. Itinerant trailerites moved north to permanent homes in the summer and south to their trailer park communities in the winter. Small, utilitarian mobile home parks were more common but remained invisible in the communities on whose physical fringes they were located. The inhabitants of these parks were permanent residents who were seeking an alternative to more costly housing and who no more contributed to the recreational roadside than the idealized suburbs. Ironically, these steadfast residents were not welcomed as integral to the "normal" communities beside which they grew.[92]

Motor homes comprised the most opulent form of mobile roadside lodging. These self-sufficient vehicles necessitated incredible size, weight, and accessories to transport all their motorists' demands of home. Family-christened names like "Gypsy Van" and "Autobungaloafer" for these hand-crafted, one-of-a-kind vehicles verified the playfulness of their owners and the vehicles' indulgent uses. Roger White ably chronicles the history of the motor home.[93] Accounts of happy vacations and circumspect spouses converted to ardent devotees are common. Like auto camping in the 1920s, the arduous demands of their repair, resupply, and reluctant passengers are brushed aside in exultant declarations of their benefits.[94] In 1993, two people who preferred living exclusively in a motor home to living in a conventional home echoed the century's past motoring enthusiasts: "This is what fulltiming is all about: Being able to go where you want, when you want, see new places, revisit old ones, and make friends wherever your fulltiming takes you."[95] Although believers in the advantages of the open road, these authors acknowledged that although "fulltiming" offered freedom from the confines of a routine work schedule, real estate tax payment, and home care, it also required considerable introspection about one's life expectations before selling one's house and buying a recreational vehicle. "Fulltiming" was not for everyone.[96]

Most Americans believed that motoring's challenges were far outweighed by its advantages. In many ways, the most fully self-dependent motorists, the campers, speak for the entire motoring enterprise. Ethnographers Margaret Cerullo and Phyllis Ewen found that family camping in the mid-1980s was fraught with limitations similar to home: adult men with organizational experience (often business ownership) dominating the power structure, whites far exceeding racial and ethnic minorities, and hard work. The perceived rewards, however, more than compensated. Camping, especially at the national parks, avoided the excessive acquisition of goods that characterized home life and implied a simpler life. Camping invoked nostalgic faith in a better time that could be relived, if only occasionally.

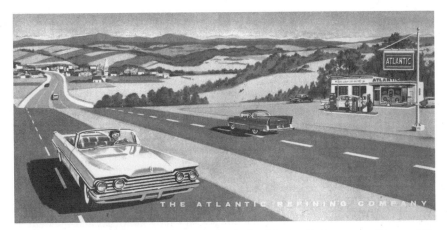

Figure 6.9. The Atlantic Refining Company's Standardized Station Design, c. 1955. Courtesy BP America.

Neighborhoods of adjacent like-minded camping families materialized the comforts of self-defined communities: everyone was an insider. Campers often shrank from the crime and chaos they associated with urban scenes. They sensed none of the density, lack of privacy, poor commodities, and food additives that urban critics found replicated in campers' temporary homes. Camping represented freedom from round-the-clock wage labor and the rigors of house and grounds maintenance. Campers instead enjoyed "getting away," intimate life with their family members, living a timeless existence, and relaxing, although they worked. Women especially welcomed their reprieve from the chores of homemaking because men shared the work more equally on camp outings and women overcame their housework-imposed isolation because they could enjoy the casual friendship of other women in the camp.[97] Self-renewal may have been more important to these campers from the 1980s than to the century's earlier motorist pursuers of history and the "real America." Camping echoed the use of vacationing to refortify oneself for a return to the workplace, as Cindy Aron proves of Americans' vacations in general.[98] These seekers were as enmeshed in the culture of consumption and production as were the motorists between branded gasoline stations that Roger William Riis's poem noted ironically (figure 6.9).

◆ ▼ ●

Americans have frolicked along the automobile roadside for a century, having fun in various attractions designed especially for their style of travel. Amusement parks, zoos, natural features, and roadside farm stands joined the required gas stations, motels, and restaurants to create the roadside as a place of legendary recreation.

All the privations of impatient passengers, provisioning for the trip, and racing to keep preset schedules were discounted. Motoring Americans pushed from their preoccupations all the hazards and petty irritations of traversing long distances over unfamiliar terrain and dealing with strangers along the way. The auto—or whatever more specialized mode of motoring was used—enabled this feeling of carefree rambling and seemed to put the land at the motorists' disposal. The consumer culture mediated between motoring's plusses and minuses and refocused attention on the obvious pleasantries while introducing considerable outlays of cash for the specialized equipment—the means of transportation included—and its costly and relatively scarce repair. At century's end, campers expressed their disdain for the superabundant material goods and plush services of most motorists, preferring instead closer acquaintance with fellow motorists and the natural outdoors itself. They sought entertainment in decreased levels of sophisticated technology. Yet the cycle endured. While many looked for frivolous diversion in roadside entertainment, others, even the atavistic campers, negotiated the delicate balance between uncharted adventure and enveloping luxury. Motoring was as much several states of mind as a group of activities.

rejecting the roadside as landscaped landscape

"Roadsides constitute the front yard of every community," wrote city planner J. M. Bennett in 1936, "and because of this, if for no other reason, they should be developed and maintained in a manner befitting such distinction."[1] But most American roadsides, especially well-traveled routes peripheral to cities and towns, were rather helter-skelter. In 1930, Elizabeth Lawton and W. L. Lawton wrote of North Carolina that when a new highway was completed, "hot dog stands, filling stations and billboards spring up like magic with no regard for the appearance of the roadside or its immediate vicinity. Raw cuts have been left in the construction of the road. Trees have been sacrificed by road builders and public utility companies. The new highway, designed to open up the beauty of the state, has become itself a thing of ugliness."[2]

Highway planners had been preoccupied with meeting the nation's demand for functional roads. In the financial climate of the time and with Americans clamoring for more and better roads, visual attractiveness fell by the wayside. Editorialized *Good Roads,* "There are thousands of miles of highway to be built and their building will require millions of dollars and much time. Because of the urgency of the road betterment program, comparatively little can be spent for beautification."[3] Argued a Wisconsin highway engineer, "The highways are too badly needed, in the opinion of most people, to permit the spending of large funds in beautifying them. A good many feel that they cannot admire landscapes and artistic effects so long as the roads are impassable, and prefer to spend money in building roads first and develop the beautiful later."[4]

The valuing of individual prerogative, especially in regard to protecting property rights, was also at work. A new or improved highway created new opportunities not only for road users but for owners of adjacent real estate. The nation's highway margins—what James Agee, writing in *Fortune,* called the "Great American Roadside"—was a new kind of frontier that fully invited commercial pioneering. Americans were building, Agee exclaimed, the "greatest market the human race has ever set up to tease and tempt and take money from the human race." Roadside America was, he noted in 1934, already a $3 billion enterprise.[5] Who could deny, especially on aesthetic grounds, a property owner's right to profit as he or she saw fit from highway proximity? By what right could government curtail, contain, or control what happened along a highway's margins?

Commerce and the Roadside

Motoring generated roadside selling through garages, gas stations, drive-in restaurants, motels, and other venues convenient for if not oriented to automobiles. Because many early twentieth-century motorists drove mostly for pleasure, the roadside tourist attraction came to figure prominently, especially in resort areas. The structuring of the early roadside was flimsy and ad hoc. Highly speculative investments in buildings, signs, driveways, and parking lots, the principal architectural signatures of roadside commerce, tended to produce structural impermanence, as roadside businesses constantly changed. "We are building a cheap, disposable environment," argued Edmund Faltermayer as late as 1968, "containing hardly any man-made *places* that people can love and feel and identify with." This situation represented a function, he said, of America's "rootless, nomadic nature."[6] Moreover, during times of economic boom, American optimism produced too much of nearly everything—gas stations, for example. America's commercial strips evolved largely without plan, and critics described them as visually chaotic.[7] But it was not clear that Americans disapproved of this chaos.

The roadside was not just a place to sell things to motorists. It was also a place to advertise. Motorists represented a kind of captive audience: signs and other prominent displays along a highway margin were difficult to ignore in passing. Billboards and other kinds of advertisements thus proliferated along the nation's main roads (figure 7.1).[8] Two journalists, motoring to write a travel book, found the highways of southern New England lined by pictures of "soft drinks, cigarettes, motor cars and pink cheeked ladies preserving their 'schoolgirl complexion'" and described New York state as a "playground . . . clamorous with advertisements."[9] In Louisiana, another writer derided the "nighttime luridness": billboards that flashed "invitations to buy cigarettes or gasoline or a pleasant lot in a distinguished cemetery."[10] No other country so commercialized the landscape, critics claimed. The director of the Bureau of Public Roads, Thomas H. MacDonald, termed the situation a "national disgrace."[11]

Critics also decried the utility poles between which unsightly wires were strung. Not only were utility lines themselves unattractive, but numerous roadside trees had been removed to accommodate the poles, resulting in the outright destruction

"TO HIM WHO IN THE LOVE OF NATURE HOLDS COMMUNION WITH HER VISIBLE FORMS, SHE SPEAKS A VARIOUS LANGUAGE."—WILLIAM CULLEN BRYANT

Figure 7.1. Advertising Signs as Roadside Epidemic. Courtesy *Evansville Courier and Press;* reproduced in *American City* 41 (October 1929): 131.

of beauty. Critics also complained of the trash that littered highway margins. In the words of one writer, the "windrows of luncheon boxes, sardine tins, paper bags, wrapping paper, and discarded newspapers—the miscellaneous filth of countless thoughtless tourists of doggeries and crab-meateries and doughnuteries." Litter was an important dimension of the roadside's "tawdriness, cheapness and bad taste."[12] In addition, road cuts and other landscape scars often were left unattended after highway construction, and new roads frequently did not fit well into the topography, further violating landscape unity in a visual sense. Highways, critics asserted, should add positively to what motorists saw. Did it really cost more, one writer asked, to build a road "with pleasing curves and with well-trimmed shoulders and slopes" than to construct a route "with monotonously long tangents and with rough, untidy slopes and shoulders"?[13]

Highways that were visually displeasing for whatever reason depreciated the motoring experience, thus denying motorists the full benefit of a landscape's scenic value. And scenery was important, especially to motorists who traveled for recreation and pleasure. Roadside ugliness was a form of deprivation, of abuse, not only of the environment but of person. Most Americans remained oblivious to any sense of problem, however. Highways were new and thus symbolized a progressive modern America. And people generally prized change, almost always seeing progress and benefit in all new things. Most Americans prized speed, especially as it brought places closer together temporally—the main purpose of the new highways.

Roadside Landscaping

Except in areas of outstanding natural scenery, like the national parks, or in unusually scenic hilly or mountainous areas, most motorists were content with the utilitarian. A trained eye might discern the picturesque everywhere, but relatively few Americans had such ability. Landscaping as an aesthetic enterprise was only slowly entering American consciousness early in the twentieth century. Of course, the wealthy prized domestic lawns and gardens in status-conscious display, but most Americans still kept their front yards and especially their backyards rather indifferently. Why should streets and roads be any different? Why should they be ornamented with trees, shrubs, flowers, and grass? An important exception, of course, involved the village beautification movement, confined largely to New England, where cow commons were converted into village greens and streets were lined with elms and other trees.

"A completely landscaped highway is perhaps a desirable ideal," wrote J. M. Bennett, "but the cost of proceeding . . . is prohibitive and it savors of the impractical because motorists in reality see a very small part of the detailed landscape as they pass. Furthermore, the intensive maintenance necessary . . . is practically impossible." Beauty, in other words, was a luxury. If Americans wanted beauty, Bennett added, they should plant flowers in their home gardens.[14] Even some prominent landscape architects agreed. Why should countryside imitate a city park, asked Wilhelm Miller? "The country is a big, open place that is beautiful in itself, and people flash through it in automobiles, seeing only the big things." Let the public right-of-way be merely "laid down in grass, so that it can be cheaply mowed."[15]

A few highway officials attempted to advance the cause of highway landscaping. "It is not enough to build good roads," wrote the chair of the Wisconsin Highway Commission. "We should beautify them." "Any progressive and self-respecting community ought . . . to give attention to beautifying the highway," he asserted. Concrete roads in particular were "cold" and needed a "softening influence."[16] For most highway planners, however, unadorned highways constituted improvement enough. Follow an unimproved road in any farm area, the argument went, and you usually found countryside in deplorable condition: "homes dilapidated, front yards scarcely recognizable among the tangle of broken machinery, old wire and various other objects placed 'out of the way.'" But improved roads led to ready evidence of better farm management and of domestic life.[17] Improved accessibility and highway utility had the power to translate efficiency, orderliness, and cleanliness into beautiful practicality. The result was "honest" rather than pretentious beauty.

Of course, responsibility for property improvement adjacent to roads lay mainly with private landowners, who could turn road and other public improvements to personal advantage. But might not private interests also sustain road improvements? Road upgrading inflated property values. Might not that added value be taxed, if not in dollars and cents then perhaps in some other obligation? Might not citizens be expected to take at least some responsibility for maintaining roads adjacent to their properties? Wrote one observer, "I am in hearty sympathy with the man who brings a fine level field of wheat right to the roadway, but there are ugly spots on every road that are of no value, seemingly not for any purpose. I refer to the cuts, fills and gullies along the roadside . . . usually barren and scarred and generally unattractive."[18] Indeed, in New York as well as in some other states, adjacent property owners' bore legal responsibility for healing such wounds. "Besides the legal duty every dweller by a highway is under, to use it with due regard to the rights of the public, he is under a moral and Christian obligation to maintain order and neatness within and without his roadside," asserted the author of *The Road and the Roadside.*[19]

Trees, Shrubs, and Grass

Early advocates of roadside landscaping emphasized tree planting. In the pioneering phase of farm development on the American frontier, land clearing had fostered almost complete forest destruction, and commercial lumbering had stripped extensive areas clean. "Through a wasteful and unfortunate system of lumbering a large part of the timber has been cut off and the aftermath of repeated burnings has reduced large areas to unproductive barrens," wrote one Michigan highway engineer in 1920. But highway construction, he observed, only compounded the problem by necessitating the felling of additional trees. Michigan advertised itself as the "Play Ground of the Middle West," but tourists could not be expected to believe that slogan when so much of the state looked so awful. Existing trees along new highways needed to be conserved; even more important, new trees needed to be planted.[20]

However, truly practical rationales for doing so had to be developed: beauty alone would not suffice. In hot weather, proponents of landscaping argued, shade retarded evaporation, keeping road surfaces moist, an especially important consideration with macadam roads, which could flake into dust as a consequence of dry conditions and the pounding of high-speed auto traffic. In addition, during the era of open automobiles, road dust necessitated the wearing of goggles, dusters, and other paraphernalia. Trees served as windbreaks, preventing road surface materials from blowing around in the summer and preventing snow from drifting in the winter. Shaded roads were of course more pleasant than sun-baked routes for hot-weather driving, and shade retarded weed growth, thus reducing mowing costs.[21] Trees also protected against erosion, especially along slopes, and could screen objectionable land uses such as junkyards (including auto salvage yards), dumps, and borrow pits. Fruit and nut trees could produce valuable crops, while maples could provide maple sugar. Roadside tree planting might be considered a form of reforestation, a means of increasing the nation's dwindling supply of timber. The editors of *Good Roads* calculated in 1921 that the United States had approximately 2.5 million miles of rural road. If trees were planted every fifty feet along these roads, the country would gain more than 264 million new trees—the equivalent of a fifteen-million-acre forest, or about one-thirteenth the size of the existing national forests.[22]

The chief opposition to tree planting, admitted Maryland's chief state forester, came from farmers who objected to trees shading fields and extracting moisture and soil fertility from the ground.[23] Other opponents argued that trees interfered with electric wires and could start fires. Falling branches broke power lines. Trees obscured signs. Falling leaves clogged drainage tiles. Trees could cut off motorists' view, especially on curves and at intersections. Close to the road, trees posed a danger to erratic drivers.

> I think that I shall never see
> Along the road, an unscraped tree
> With bark intact and painted white
> That no car ever hit at night.
> For every tree that near to road
> Has caused some auto to be towed.
> Side swiping trees is done a lot
> By drivers who are not so hot.[24]

Nonetheless, various states encouraged roadside tree planting. In 1903, Connecticut, building on the work of the state's village improvement societies, empowered individuals to plant trees along public highways and at schools and other public places in lieu of paying property taxes. Wrote James H. MacDonald, at the time Connecticut's state highway commissioner, "Nothing makes a journey more pleasant [than] to have the road upon which we travel skirted with some beautiful touch of nature to enliven the occasion and enhance or add to the pleasure of the traveler on the road."[25] In Michigan, property owners had the right to prevent tree cutting along state roads. This provision implied the "right of adjacency," the legal principle that an owner of land adjoining a public road was entitled, by virtue of that ownership, to prevent the "doing of any act" in the public right-of-way that would render land occupancy "less enjoyable and beneficial."[26] Many states empowered local governments to raise and use tax monies for tree-planting purposes. By 1920, Illinois, Massachusetts, New Jersey, New York, and Pennsylvania had established roadside tree-planting programs under the auspices of the highway department, the department of forestry, or both.[27] In 1921, California established a tree nursery and systematically undertook to line its highways with trees, making planting an integral part of highway planning. More than a million trees were planted along some seven hundred miles of highway during the program's first ten years.[28] California's population boom was prompted in no small measure by the state's dramatic scenery in addition to its mild climate. Most Californians strongly supported roadside beautification as a means of protecting the state's attractiveness.

Tree-planting projects were undertaken as memorials to servicemen killed in World War I. At the forefront were women's clubs, encouraged by the General Federation of Women's Clubs, and garden clubs, encouraged by the Garden Club of America. Other organizations prominently involved included the Daughters of the American Revolution, the American Legion, and men's service clubs such as Rotary International. The Lincoln Highway Association led the way, integrating tree planting into its "demonstration miles." The formal allées created in France beginning in the eighteenth century presented a model for many advocates of twentieth-century highway landscaping. Most landscape architects, however, recommended that trees be planted informally to achieve "natural effect." Trees should be spaced unevenly to avoid "soldierly rows."[29] Trees were best clustered according to species and these clusters arranged irregularly. Tree planting, supporters asserted, completed highways as visual display, predicting a new era of highway building where the road would become a work of art. "The appeal of the countryside is no longer to be that of nature alone and unaided," one landscape architect wrote. "Landscape art, here and there very simple, here and there very elaborate, will add a human touch, a new appeal . . . on varied fascinating roadsides which extend to the horizon for hundreds of miles across the landscape. And thus the traveler will find that everywhere . . . the human spirit expresses itself."[30]

Only after World War II did advocates of roadside landscaping vigorously promote the use of shrubs and ground cover, including wildflowers. Shrubs along highway median strips could help screen oncoming headlights at night and could help combat drifting snow. Both shrubs and ground cover, like trees, were useful in erosion control. More important, if the goal of landscaping was to make public rights-of-way look "natural," then attention had to be given to understory vegetation, not just to tree canopies.[31] Across the Great Plains, grass was the most common vegetative cover. Wildflowers greatly enhanced the motoring experience there when massed by color and texture. California again led the way in diversifying plant material used in highway landscaping, eventually employing on urban freeways exotic succulents requiring irrigation. Nonetheless, even in California, grass became the predominant expedient. Grass dominated highway margins not so much for its look, ecological value, or any other reason except that it was relatively cheap and easy to maintain. Closely trimmed, lawnlike roadside margins became the ideal, perhaps in imitation of the urban park. More likely, roadside lawns simply reflected most farm communities' traditional penchant for neatness: the cleanliness of the farmer's field had long symbolized his or her worth both as farmer and as citizen.[32]

Boulevards

Landscaping was far from the whole story when it came to highway beautification. A highway (and its adjacent landscape) looked better when careful attention was paid to issues of grade, curvature, and alignment. Motoring became easier and thus safer when multiple lanes were provided in each direction, when oncoming traffic was fully segregated, and when intersections were configured as roundabouts or as cloverleafs. And such highways also could be designed to provide motorists with scenic vistas. These considerations were especially important in areas of natural beauty, where highway travel clearly underpinned tourism. Through the 1920s, these ideas came together in the design and building of urban boulevards and of so-called scenic highways, especially in mountainous terrain.

U.S. urban boulevards reflected Baron Georges-Eugène Von Haussmann's nineteenth-century Parisian thoroughfares. The roads in New York City's Central Park as well as Brooklyn's Ocean and Eastern Parkways, all designed by Frederick Law Olmsted and Calvert Vaux, set clear American precedent. In the decades after the Civil War, a city's well-to-do paraded in their fashionable carriages along boulevards that linked city parks. In Boston, Chicago, and Kansas City, as elsewhere, many boulevards were lined by the mansions of society's elite. But with the coming of the automobile and especially mass automobile ownership, those thoroughfares were seen as attracting mainly the hoi polloi driving for pleasure. The scenic Sunday drive became popular as motorists sought pleasure both in town and out (figures 7.2 and 7.3). Rural roads offered motorists the opportunity to press down on the accelerator pedal, with the result that new boulevards, especially those located just outside cities, became known as "speedways."

Figure 7.2. Forest Park, St. Louis, Missouri, Postcard, c. 1915. The caption reads, "The view shows the popularity of this park for a Sunday drive." Authors' collection.

Figure 7.3. Lampooning the Sunday Driver. *Concrete Highway* 8 (December 1924): 279.

Auto-oriented boulevards not only served the weekend motorist but represented a means by which cities could physically expand. Like earlier streetcar thoroughfares, along which electric power, water, and sewer lines were run, subdivision developers oriented construction toward peripheral boulevards that either encircled or radiated outward from cities. The first section of Philadelphia's Northeast Boulevard (later renamed Roosevelt Boulevard) was completed in 1914 with a total right-of-way of three hundred feet, including a center drive sixty feet wide; two lawn areas, each fifty-six feet wide; two side drives, each thirty-four feet wide; and two sidewalk spaces, each thirty feet wide.[33] By 1930, the boulevard was fully lined by houses and businesses.

Scenic Highways

As a visual experience, motoring was much improved when long stretches of straight road were made serpentine—broken up, in other words, by gradual curves. Long curves were thought more pleasing to the eye than combinations of short curves separated by short tangents. Road designers had previously sought to prolong tangents as much as possible, but in the early 1940s, U.S. public roads administrator Laurence Hewes advised the use of long sweeping arcs more sympathetic to topography. Roads needed to orient motorists through the serial vision of sequenced vistas, to "flow with the country," Hewes emphasized. Anything that "broke the beauty of the line" needed to be avoided—for example, a summit or hump in the profile of an otherwise smooth concave curve. Nor should a curve be allowed to begin at a summit. Motorists should always see curves looming ahead. Bridges, guardrails, and other highway structures needed to be carefully designed, not just in terms of driving safety but in terms of how well they visually fit the landscape.[34]

The Columbia River Highway in Oregon was the outstanding early example of what highway planners could accomplish when scenery remained foremost in their thinking. Samuel Christopher Lancaster, the principal engineer on the project, envisioned a road that would "lay lightly on the land," which constituted some of the most scenic but also most difficult terrain in North America. As a young surveyor on the road later wrote, "The ideas sought were not the usual economic features and considerations given the location of a trunk highway. Grades, curvature and even expense were sacrificed to reach some scenic vista or to develop a particularly interesting point. All the natural beauty spots were fixed as control points and the location adjusted to include them."[35]

The first section of the road, some 42 miles long, opened just west of The Dalles in 1915. It paralleled closely the Columbia River, accessing scenic spots such as

Figure 7.4. Mitchell Point Tunnel, Columbia River Highway, Oregon, Postcard, 1930. Courtesy Lake County, Illinois, Museum, Curt Teich Postcard Archives.

Multnomah Falls, down which water rushed 850 feet. By 1921, work was complete along the highway's entire 365 miles from Astoria in the west via Portland and The Dalles to Pendleton in the east. But the section along the Columbia River gorge offered the most excitement. Not only did the river remain almost constantly in view (figure 7.4), but the road itself was a scenic attraction, an engineering marvel with numerous tunnels and bridges as well as a work of art. The steel-reinforced concrete bridges were ornamented by Italian craftsmen brought to Oregon specifically for that purpose. "Rest houses" were constructed at intervals, most in association with scenic overlooks, waterfalls, or other natural attractions. The road was paved with concrete in some sections and with Warrenite in other sections. Pavement was eighteen feet wide, with two-foot shoulders on either side. The maximum gradient was held to 5 percent and the minimum radius of curvature set at one hundred feet. The highway could be comfortably motored at speeds above forty-five miles per hour. Mile after mile, the road was supported by masonry retaining walls and protected by guardrails configured to look like low fences.[36]

California's Carmel to San Simeon Highway, part of today's scenic Route 1, was begun near Big Sur in 1919 but was not completed until 1937. Scenic highways in other states, designated as such mainly to stimulate tourism, included the Apache Trail in Arizona, the Mohawk Trail in Massachusetts, and the Storm King Highway in New York. In 1963, California established a scenic highway system "as a vital part of the all encompassing effort which the State must make to protect and enhance

California's beauty, amenity, and quality of life."[37] Some five thousand miles of road were proposed for designation, with the first official section a seventy-two-mile stretch of Route 1 in Monterey County designated in 1964.

Parkways

Parkways evolved as scenic roads that went beyond mere tree planting and, for that matter, tasteful road design. Parkways also embraced land-use zoning, use of real estate easements, and sign control. Not only was access limited, but accessibility was restricted to users motoring for pleasure. Parkway development was justified on a variety of grounds, including economic development through growth of tourism, land reclamation through the elimination of toxic wastes, historical commemoration, and urban renewal. Plainly stated, a parkway was an attenuated park with a road running through it.[38] The American Civic Association defined parkways as highways that mainly connected parks but also extended "some definite recreational facility in addition to its connectional value."[39] The American Association of State Highway Officials defined parkways as arteries for noncommercial traffic "with full or partial control of access, and usually located within a park or a ribbon of park-like development."[40] As recreation, parkway motoring celebrated the open road but did so sanctified through ambience of scenic beauty.

The first parkway built for motor cars was William K. Vanderbilt's "motor parkway" opened in 1908 to speed travel from Long Island's estate country toward New York City. "And now the day of the automobile has come," *Good Roads* quoted Vanderbilt as predicting. "A highway is about to be constructed for its use, free from all grade crossings, dust and police surveillance, and country opened up whose variegated charms are hard to equal in any part of the world."[41] The road, surfaced with bituminous asphalt, was twenty-two feet wide, but Vanderbilt and his associates had purchased a right-of-way from one hundred to two hundred feet wide. Motoring into the city would be not only fast but scenic.

The fifteen-mile-long Bronx River Parkway, completed in 1923, was located just north of New York City in Westchester County. "In the layout of the drive," historian Gilmore Clarke summarized a quarter of a century later, "careful attention was given to preserving the existing amenities of the valley, to the control of floods, to the elimination of dumps, billboards, and other existing unsightly features, and to planting with native materials. Engineers were no less concerned with the careful grading of slopes and the appropriate design of all the related elements, such as bridges, guardrails, light standards, direction signs, and gasoline stations."[42] The road was patterned after the drives in New York City parks and was thus antiquated from its inception. Traffic lanes were only ten feet wide, and there were no

Figure 7.5. Hutchinson River Parkway, New York. *Motor Travel* 20 (February 1929): 8.

shoulders. Bridges were low, and curves were not properly banked. The parkway's main purpose had actually been to clean up the polluted Bronx River. "Rubbish and garbage all went into the river," one member of the Bronx Parkway Commission remembered. "Disorder, dirt, filth and unsightliness reigned supreme."[43] Yet motoring for pleasure had been very much in the commission members' thinking, with one stating that the "whole automobile fraternity" would "rise up and bless" the parkway.[44]

The Bronx River Parkway was eventually rebuilt as part of a very ambitious 140-mile parkway system serving the whole of Westchester County. During the 1920s, Westchester, like sections of Long Island, was rapidly developing as one of metropolitan New York City's most affluent suburban areas. Through its park commission, the county bought rights-of-way varying in width from two hundred feet to more than a mile as well as land for parks, including nine miles of shoreline.[45] The first section of the Hutchinson River Parkway opened to traffic in 1928, its two-lane concrete pavement darkened to a gray-black to blend better into its parklike surroundings. Access was limited, with all other roads carried above or below the parkway on bridges or in viaducts (figure 7.5). There were no traffic lights.[46]

The parkway scheme included several gasoline stations carefully designed, like the road itself, to blend into nature. This approach represented an "improvement of the roadside by replacement of the ugly, garish type of gasoline dispensing emporium by one carefully planned, possessing artistic merit, and providing a less blatant and ugly aspect," wrote Clarke, who served as the project's consulting landscape architect. "Competition in the gasoline business is the breeder of ugliness," he continued. "Each dealer in gas and food along the roadside tries to have more pumps, more signs of brighter colors, than his competitor; the result is what we see along most of our highways."[47] At Hutchinson Parkway stations, gas pumps were hidden in what appeared to be old-fashioned well houses or built into the columns that supported overhead canopies. Each station bore only one sign. It was a way of preventing the type of roadside sprawl that had beset one Westchester town when land use was not controlled along a bypass highway: "Within a few months this delightful stretch of new road was lined with billboards, hot dog stands, and gas stations, which blotted out views of the farm land, and decreased the efficiency of the road. Each new enterprise introduced a point of danger because it had direct access to the road. It was not long before a bypass of the bypass was needed."[48]

Other parkways in the New York metropolitan area were developed under the auspices of the New York State Council of Parks, dominated by Robert Moses, including both the Long Island Park Commission, which Moses fully controlled as chair, and the Taconic State Park Commission, initially chaired by Franklin Roosevelt.[49] The Taconic State Parkway gave access north as an extension of the Westchester County parkway system. But most of the state's parkway building took place on Long Island. Brooklyn's Belt Parkway was built and then extended eastward as the Southern State Parkway. The Grand Central Parkway in Queens was built and extended as the Northern State Parkway. Shorter roads (including the Montauk State Parkway, the Jones Beach Causeway, the Ocean Parkway, the Babylon Spur Parkway, the Wantagh Spur Parkway, and the Meadowbrook Causeway) gave access to various state parks and beaches built under Moses's direction. By 1940, 325 miles of parkway either had been completed or were under construction.[50]

Moses deliberately set parkway bridges low to prevent trucks and especially buses from using the routes. His roads were not intended for New York City's less affluent or its racial minorities—that is, the people who would ride buses to get to Long Island's parks and beaches. He intended his roads for the car-owning middle classes, those deserving people who wanted to escape the heat and crowds of city streets through weekend and holiday motoring.[51] Moses also headed the Triborough Bridge Authority, which oversaw the bridge that connected his Long Island parkways with midtown Manhattan by way of the East River Drive. He developed the Henry Hudson Parkway along the Hudson River to connect Manhattan with the Westchester County parkway system. From the 1930s through the 1950s, Moses's influence on highway development nationwide was most profound: numerous state highway departments and city planning agencies sent representatives to consult with or train at his office on Randall Island under the Triborough Bridge.

In the 1930s, parkways were also completed in the Washington, D.C., area. Within the District of Columbia was the Rock Creek Memorial Parkway in Rock Creek Park. Across the Potomac River in Virginia was the Mount Vernon Memorial Highway, built to commemorate the two hundredth anniversary of George Washington's birth. The highway linked the Arlington Memorial Bridge near the

Lincoln Memorial with Washington's Mount Vernon, although the road was broken into two sections separated by a surface street in downtown Alexandria.

National Park Roads and Parkways

In 1927, Congress authorized $51 million to improve roads in the national parks. At certain parks, such as Glacier National Park and Rocky Mountain National Park, the roads themselves (the Going-to-the-Sun Highway and the Trail Ridge Road, respectively) were to be the major tourist attractions. But most park roads were merely intended to provide access to park facilities. The National Park Service managed more than twelve hundred miles of road plus some four thousand miles of trail. Planners had sought to contain the amount of road built within the parks, imposing a limit of an average of no more than one mile of road for every three miles of trail. The "cheapening effect" of easy auto accessibility, park officials argued, needed to be avoided.[52] In the 1930s, the Roosevelt administration moved to create parkways and to manage them as auto-convenient parks that were little more than motorways, a strategy that caught park service officials by surprise. But parkway popularity grew quickly with completion of the first section of Shenandoah National Park's Skyline Drive. Running down the spine of the park, the road gave access to some of the highest elevations in the Blue Ridge Mountains. "Oftentimes the roadway runs along the mountain," wrote E. S. Matheson in the *Motor News,* and "is so narrow the motorist sees the world seemingly falling away on either side."[53] Approximately fifty thousand motorists visited during the first five weeks after the road opened.[54]

In 1935, Congress authorized extension of the Skyline Drive 460 miles southwest to the newly created Great Smoky Mountains National Park, dubbing the new route the Blue Ridge Parkway. The states of Virginia, North Carolina, and Tennessee were to acquire land and scenic easements using federal funds and then to cede the land to the park service, which would construct and manage the parkway. One hundred or more acres per mile would be purchased, land adequate for a right-of-way some eight hundred feet wide. The new parkway would be a two-lane recreational road from which commercial vehicles would be excluded. The parkway's principal designer, landscape architect Stanley W. Abbott, worked diligently to fit the road to the Blue Ridge crest. Construction started almost immediately, but only two short sections were complete when World War II halted construction. Nonetheless, early travelers submitted glowing reports: "At times the road is up in the blue or smoky haze so prevalent in this region. Then for short distances, it passes down a valley, racing parallel to a tumbling mountain stream.

Many 'saddles' or gaps are crossed, with mountainside dropping precipitously to patterned farmland and mountain cabins far below."[55] Motorists could now venture where few tourists had gone before.

The National Park Service also began the Natchez Trace Parkway during the Great Depression, and as with the other parkways, this timing reflected the Roosevelt administration's desire to stimulate employment through public works projects. Following the course of the Old Natchez Trace between Nashville, Tennessee, and Natchez, Mississippi, the route was anticipated to stretch 450 miles, with 245 of those miles either completed or under construction by 1959.[56] A 1970 park brochure described a "drive along the gently rolling, sometimes precipitous hills" during which "lush vegetation, stately trees, vines, shrubs and other flowery plants provide a variegated background of beauty . . . a segment of the American landscape that is rapidly regaining its frontier characteristics."[57] Along much of the parkway, reforestation was very much apparent.

Congress and Highway Beautification

In 1932, the White House convened the Conference on Natural Beauty, which concluded that roadside development needed to conserve and effectively display natural beauty in landscape.[58] The conference, which drew members from both the American Association of State Highway Officials and the Highway Research Board, called for the "complete highway": a road engineered to provide utility, safety, economy, and beauty. Highways needed to be functional—that is, able to accommodate all kinds of traffic. Highways had to be safe. Construction and maintenance costs needed to be kept low. But highways also needed to be attractive—in particular, they needed to be harmoniously integrated into the surrounding landscape.[59] The chief of the Bureau of Public Roads, James McDonald, sought "to beautify and enhance the usefulness of highways" in four ways: "First, the complete elimination of commercial advertising signs, not only those within the rights-of-way, but those on private property along the rights-of-way. Second, the removal of oil filling stations, 'hot-dog' and lunch stands, and roadside markets that encroach upon the rights-of-way, a regulation of distance from rights-of-way at which such establishments may be located on private property; Third, the planting of trees and shrubs along the roadsides; Fourth, the location, design and construction of the highway in such manner as to preserve the natural beauty of the countryside."[60]

The Federal Highway Act of 1938 was the first measure to authorize landscaping and roadside development as part of the normal costs of highway construction. In 1940, the act was amended to allow land acquisition for purposes of preserving natural beauty within highway corridors.[61] Nonetheless, until the mid-1950s, federal-aid highway funds tended to stress issues of utility, safety, and economy and to neglect highway beautification. Not until the Federal Highway Act of 1955, which amended legislation creating the nation's interstate freeway system, did Congress move highway aesthetics to the forefront. The measure focused on billboard blight, empowering the secretary of commerce to acquire "exclusive advertising rights on lands adjoining certain rights-of-way of the Interstate System for a distance not exceeding 500 feet from the highway right-of-way."[62] Three years later, the Federal Highway Act of 1958 extended a carrot to the states: a 1 percent bonus in federal-aid highway money should billboards be restricted and a 3 percent bonus to states that engaged in certain kinds of roadside landscaping.[63] The Highway Act of 1959, however, marked a substantial step back, excluding from billboard control land along interstate highways zoned as either commercial or industrial.

During the Lyndon Johnson administration, the issue of billboard control again took center stage, pushed there in no small part by the president's wife, Lady Bird Johnson.[64] Much to the chagrin of the outdoor advertising industry, the Highway Beautification Act of 1965 threatened states with the loss of federal highway funding if they failed to control signs for up to one thousand feet alongside both interstate freeways and federal-aid primary roads. All off-premise signs were to be prohibited after January 1, 1968. Sign owners were to be compensated, however, with sign removal funded through annual congressional allocations. Oversight for the program fell to the Bureau of Public Roads, acting under the Federal Highway Administration. In 1967, both organizations were moved from the Department of Commerce to the new Department of Transportation. Although these measures seemed to indicate significant accomplishments in the arena of highway beautification, in fact they did not. Congress subsequently proved reticent to fund the program, and many of the act's more controversial provisions were simply allowed to lapse. Today, only Hawaii, Maine, and Vermont ban billboards from highway margins.

Roadside Rest Parks

For the most part, America's highways remained fully utilitarian. With the exception of the nation's toll roads and freeways, roadsides largely remained open to commercialization. Thus, along most highways, landscaping was restricted mainly to wayside rest parks, facilities justified as means of reducing driver fatigue by giving motorists opportunity to break the tedium of long-distance high-speed driving without straying far from the road. Texas launched its wayside park program in 1933, asking property owners to donate land for the purpose. By July of that year, 125 "pocket-sized" parks had been completed thanks to twenty-seven-year-old Congressman Lyndon Johnson. As Texas director of the National Youth Administration, Johnson found federal financing for the parks, rationalizing their construction as a way to put unemployed youth to work. Ohio's roadside park system was started in 1936 and, by 1958, 300 units had been established, averaging 2½ acres in size and with accommodations for roughly fifteen cars each.[65]

Parkway Motoring

The nation's roadside rest parks, its few parkways, and its still fewer scenic highways represented scant reward for the decades of effort expended by advocates of roadside beautification. Some of their ideas were incorporated into the nation's new interstate freeway system: restricted access from adjacent private property, alignment of roadways with topography, and even roadside landscaping, although it was highly standardized and formulaic in most states. Along the new freeways, retailing would be limited largely to interchanges, but billboard advertising, despite modest restrictions, would flourish largely unhindered. Were these changes too little or too much? Should the nation have done more or less? Did the landscaped roadside really receive its due, or was it a failed experiment?

In the mid–twentieth century, most American roadsides remained fully utilitarian, and most Americans were content with that approach. In *The Last Landscape*, William Whyte champions the traditional highway and the traditional American roadside, "at once rustic, sometimes ugly, but seemingly always entertaining."[66] Traditional roads kept motorists fully in the landscape close at hand. But the freeways, the roads of the future, kept motorists at a distance, substantially disconnecting the road from its surroundings. "Landscape," he reminds readers, "is built up by people, accumulatively, over a long period of time, and it is around roads that they build it."[67]

The nation's parkways of the 1930s had promised a kind of motoring alternative. Parkways reflected the ideals of highway beautification. But was it all for the good? In 1940, Jonathan Daniels, a southerner exploring New England, drove on Connecticut's Merritt Parkway, an eastern extension of Westchester County's parkway system, where he "escaped the . . . seeing of hamburger and the clam stands, the dime-dances, the tourist homes and the automobile graveyard," he wrote. "Maybe this was pure gain. I am not sure. For the man whose only interest in travel was the end of his journey here is perfection. But I ride as one who wanted not only to go but to see, and as one to whom a hot-dog stand was as much an item of civilization as a transplanted spruce."[68]

In 1950, Volney Hurd motored on the Skyline Drive. "The natural state of the roadside is clutter," he noted, "but the eloquent testimony of the parkways is that the customers don't like it. Wherever their comfort has been planned for, clutter disappears." The Skyline Drive was lovely, he thought, at least for the first ten miles, but after that his appetite for manicured nature (which he believed ought to have gone out of style with topiary gardens) rapidly began to flag. He once had motored on the Merritt Parkway and had found it "deadly dull." "So befuddled have we been by the love of 'scenery,'" he concluded, "that the tensed nervous systems of drivers struggling against sleep have been our first indications that the parkways are not as reasonable as we thought." Motorists were being "artificially protected from commercial taint," perhaps out of deference "to the unspeakable thought that actually, the rest of the country looks like hell." In choosing between "the park and the dump," Americans had succeeded in "producing only a few parks at the price of allowing everything else to become a dump."[69]

In 1986, Nigel Nicolson, custodian of one of Britain's outstanding landscape gardens, which his parents had created, motored on the Blue Ridge Parkway. "No other nation could have built such a road purely for the motorist's enjoyment," he wrote to his son. For nearly five hundred miles, the road had no traffic lights and very few intersections. The parkway resembled a country road that by twists and turns climbed up mountainsides and ran along mountain ridges. It was beautifully made and quite "geographically sensational." "You overlook on both sides a tossing mass of forest-covered hills, and every few miles a scoop or driveway leads you aside to a vantage point where the designers hoped you would be amazed by the view. You are, for the first three or four times, but the views are inevitably very similar," he concluded, and very soon there was little "scenic surprise" left to be had.[70]

◆ ▼ ●

Advocates of highway landscaping hoped that landscaped roadsides would prove the wave of the future, believing that Americans certainly would opt for roadside beauty over the chaos of uncontrolled commercialism. The parkway would surely become America's highway norm. But parkways were built for pleasure. Around cities, they fostered the leisurely drive out into open countryside. But the countryside around cities rapidly became urbanized after World War II. Other kinds of traffic demand, especially commuting to work and long-distance driving between cities, quickly overwhelmed the parkways—for example, those of New York's Westchester County and Long Island. They became high-speed expressways fully integrated into the region's interstate freeway system. Today, only the parkways of the National Park Service serve their original purpose. Only they remain essentially as built, examples not so much of what is to come but of what might have been.

limited-access highways as dream fulfillment

Highway promoters through the 1940s principally achieved government commitment to construction and maintenance and public sanction of the various means of financing. The way seemed unbarred to limitless highway expansion and the fruits of a robust motoring agenda. Government prerogative and public endorsement affirmed the tacit and sometimes articulated assumption that highways represented an essential ingredient of the motoring life to which Americans eagerly bound themselves in the early twentieth century. The apparent triumphs over space and time introduced unintended and unexpected consequences that required innumerable adjustments, some of which gradually revealed the costs of those triumphs. Soon obvious among the adjustments were new varieties of highway that were required to sustain the blessed fantasy of flight through increased speed, greater carrying capacity, and surer safety. Automobility's assets could not be fully achieved unless the debits of congested traffic, diminished traffic volume, and higher incidence of accidents were checked. Those debits first became obvious in the high-density traffic of urban centers, where motorists faced the conflicts between their vehicular-induced expectations of untroubled passage and the realities flowing from more highways carrying more vehicles. Limited access, the highest construction standards, aesthetic amenities, and carefully planned trajectories between destinations set the subjects of this chapter apart from the highways treated in chapter 4, where the joy arose simply from gaining them.

The Limited-Access Highway

The idea of highways is ancient, but the limited-access highway is new, dating back no more than a century and purely a response to motoring. English law recognized the concept of the "land service" road, which served society when roads were needed almost entirely to provide access to homes, farms, businesses, and places of recreation. With motoring came a new type of road, the "through" road, which served travelers passing through, on their way beyond the immediate residential or business neighborhood. Traffic numbers ballooned first in high-density cities during the 1910s and first on certain interstate roads during the 1920s with the effects of slowed passage, increased accidents, and eventually costs calculated not only in lives but, in a capitalist society, by money lost. Traffic engineers soon defined the through road as one that would "facilitate the safe movement of large numbers of vehicles with a minimum of obstructions and a maximum of speed."[1]

Limited-access highways did not come simply because their greater speed and safety for motorists easily trumped the illogic of traffic flow stalled by intermittent stoplights and intersection accidents in addition to the human and financial costs of such accidents. Bruce Seely conveniently summarizes the legal hurdles traffic engineers had to overcome beginning in the 1930s to build the limited-access highways they prescribed as the best solution to the apparently worsening traffic problem.

First, engineering efficiencies contradicted history in the form of the long-ingrained precept of common law that property owners adjacent to a public highway had the right of access from their property. That tradition had to be overturned before any limited-access highway could be built. In 1935, Colorado enacted a weak law permitting the construction of limited-access highways; starting two years later, Rhode Island and New York passed stronger laws establishing the right to limit highway access. By 1950, thirty states had enacted similar legislation. Limited-access highways gained acceptance only gradually, with some states at first allowing restrictions that limited the enabling legislation. Model legislation prepared by the Bureau of Public Roads helped facilitate the transformation from common-law precedent to contemporary expedience. The high price of funding added a practical impediment through the 1940s.[2]

The fact that both motorists and roadside businesspeople endorsed the change to limited access reemphasizes the revolutionary nature of travel by motoring. Roadside strips, known initially as "ribbon developments," mushroomed across the nation, proving that motorists enjoyed the freedom to turn off the highway wherever they saw something they wanted and that opportunistic entrepreneurs were equally glad to please passers-by.[3] Alarmed traffic engineers saw chaos resulting rather than choice exercised. A 1943 study of thirty-six miles of New Jersey's state routes 41S and 43, for example, reported that a "traffic hindrance appeared every 300 feet on the average, plus 538 signs and billboards."[4] Other studies found similar conditions elsewhere. Traffic planners might have been expected to argue against the excesses of such roadside laissez-faire, but more surprising was motorists' willingness to forgo the convenience of roadside shopping, which limited-access highways restricted to off-ramp interchanges.[5] Whatever welcome benefits the limited-access highway offered motorists, it ran counter to Americans' prevailing libertarianism. The limited-access highway also ran counter to what opponents of unplanned roadside development found to be a powerful determinant in motoring. "For a dispersed pattern of travel desires, and intermediate travel distances, the relative flexibility of the automobile seems essential. . . . Psychologically, the automobile seems to satisfy a human urge to control one's destiny in movement."[6] Limited-access highways, as their name indicates, limited choice. They channeled travel, rendering impossible hastily chosen excursions off the main road.

Parkways Revisited

The parkway represented the first form of limited-access highway. Parkway design in practice evolved in intervals of intense activity separated by periods of inattention—until the coming of the automobile.

The term *parkway* was first used in Williamsburg, Virginia, in 1699 to refer to roads of wide and grassy central medians. In 1857, landscape architects Calvert Vaux and Frederick Law Olmsted created the first widely remembered formulation of the parkway concept from the era of horse-drawn transportation with their design for New York City's Central Park. Carriage drives, bridle paths, and pedestrian walks introduced pathways separated by function. Bridges and grade separations were designed to frame scenery, making passage through the park an experience of visual edification. Four transverse roads were built eight feet below grade to screen pleasure seekers from the commercial traffic carried above on bridges. Bold European antecedents such as Baron Georges-Eugène Von Hausmann's redesigned Paris perhaps inspired the grandiose extent of the landscape architects collaborating on Central Park, but lesser-known colonial American street patterns, which separated foot and carriage traffic and installed central medians to divide two-way traffic, also played a role. Vaux and Olmsted proposed Brooklyn's Ocean and Eastern Parkways a decade after their Central Park collaboration.[7]

William K. Vanderbilt's Long Island "motor parkway" and then the Bronx River Parkway, after it was improved for car use, brought the American parkway more into the auto age (figure 8.1). However, the parkway's potential not merely for pleasure driving but for very fast pleasure driving was fully demonstrated when the Merritt Parkway was completed. Problems aside, the Merritt Parkway's 37½-mile span across Connecticut's Fairfield County, a bucolic suburban reserve for residents who commuted to work by car, has remained the most popular of parkways with its motorists. The Merritt Parkway opened in 1939 as an alternative paralleling the Boston Post Road between New Haven and the New York state line. The inordinate volume of truck traffic on the post road during World War I surprised many, sounding one of the first serious alarms not only that motor trucks were serious conveyances but that mobility not properly handled threatened congestion. The road's respect for the area's natural beauty earned it acclaim as one of the most

Figure 8.1. Bronx River Parkway, New York, Postcard, c. 1920s. Authors' collection.

aesthetically sensitive parkways in the automotive era. It was originally designed as a relatively straight forty-foot-wide path with no center median—a purely utilitarian conception for motoring convenience. The parkway as built, however, included two twenty-six-foot-wide paths with a landscaped median measuring just over twenty-two feet wide. The parkway's narrow overall width dictated narrow tolerances on its bridges, and even at its inception, its tight entrance and exit ramps and lack of acceleration and deceleration lanes seemed insufficient for speed limits of thirty-five or forty miles per hour.[8]

From among the parkways in the Washington, D.C., area, leaders of the Bureau of Public Roads selected the Mount Vernon Memorial Highway as a model for the federal-state relationship on parkways. The highway, which opened in 1932 as a link between George Washington's home at Mount Vernon to Washington, D.C., at the Arlington Memorial Bridge, blended the older aesthetics of the parkway with the most recent engineering elements of the high-speed highway but was not named a parkway, perhaps because the Bureau of Public Roads leadership felt that the word smacked of elitism and would condemn the idea among the state highway engineers the federal officials were trying to win over to the parkway concept. The bureau's attempt failed, however. Parkway finances were seen as exorbitant, and no one was prepared at the time to sponsor legislation authorizing substantial numbers of limited-access highways. Just as important, highway engineers, who held great sway over what was built, resolutely rejected the aesthetics of the landscape architects who promoted parkways.[9]

Parkways doubtless reached the height of their acceptance among highway planners and designers during the interwar years. On the West Coast, traffic between Los Angeles and Pasadena seemed justification for the six-mile-long Arroyo Seco Freeway. It opened in 1940 with six lanes, a median, and narrow strips of vegetation adjacent to both shoulders, adding an attractive amenity to the narrow land segment adjoining the Arroyo Seco Drainage Channel and the Union Pacific Railroad. Its designers added the nationally significant innovation of extralong on- and off-ramps to accommodate acceleration and deceleration, a feature subsequently adopted by the designers of the Pennsylvania Turnpike.[10]

At the twentieth anniversary of the Arroyo Seco parkway's opening, the governor of California characterized its original design as "bold" yet "rather simple," "obviously necessary," and "wholly practical," demonstrating that advances in motoring on limited-access highways induced an amnesia.[11] Reducing the challenges of motoring elided the distinction between the past and present so much that the rush forward induced a keen awareness of the present, leaving the past virtually forgotten.

The highly publicized Bronx River Parkway, on the verge of opening when Robert Moses conceived the highway to Jones Beach, helped him conceptualize his first work, a five-mile section of the Meadowbrook Parkway. Its opening in 1929 not only made six miles of beach available but added parking for twenty-three thousand cars. Although Moses was fond of the parkway conception's arboreal and scenic splendors and exploited them in the parkways under his supervision, his appetite was whetted by the idea of motoring uninhibited by traffic lights and intersections. Commuters on the Saw Mill River and Hutchinson River Parkways (begun in 1925–26) were the first to travel on automobile parkways in Moses's network. His prevailing utilitarian bias likely explains why some have criticized some of his early work as hardly deserving the term *parkway* because their rights-of-way permitted merely accompanying narrow strips of park. In contrast, the 105.3-mile-long Taconic Parkway (built 1927–63), originally an extension of the Bronx River Parkway to which Moses contributed, has won praise as the culmination of the parkway concept because it combined the earlier landscape traditions of the parkway with the safer, broader curves of later highways.[12]

Whatever critics have charged about Moses's hubris and political maneuverings to achieve his ends, his grandiose conception of highway transportation, including parkways, to facilitate travel throughout metropolitan New York and his efforts to undertake such redevelopment on the scale of regional planning placed him among the best planning minds of his era.[13] He helped make easy motoring an imperative of twentieth-century America. Modernist philosopher Sigfried Gideon writes lyrically of Moses's handiwork, giving rare voice perhaps to the thrill motorists experienced on Moses's parkways: "As with many of the creations born of this age, the meaning and beauty of the parkway cannot be grasped from a single point of observation. . . . It can be revealed only by movement, by going along in a steady flow as the rules of traffic prescribe. The space-time feeling of our period can seldom be felt so keenly as when driving, the wheel under one's hand, up and down hills, beneath over-passes, up ramps, and over giant bridges."[14]

Toll Roads

Toll roads were a form of limited-access highway with a pedigree stretching back to the colonial period. Americans adapted the idea to motoring with a parkway built on Long Island in 1908. A few other short toll roads functioned by the late 1920s. The financial rationale that a road's chief beneficiaries should pay for it had won strong endorsement in the wave of gasoline taxes adopted by the states during the 1920s, before motoring interests similarly justified toll roads. Special authorities created to administer the tollways both grounded them legally and circumvented the debt limits imposed on most governmental entities as well as various state constitutions that required referenda or constitutional amendments before funds could be borrowed. The timing of the tollway construction boom from the late 1940s to the mid-1950s resulted from certain state leaders' conviction that toll roads were the quickest option for financing urgently needed limited-access highways in the wake of the federal government's failure to undertake a national network of such roads.[15]

No sooner had the network of federal-aid highways begun to take shape in the late 1920s than some motor industry officials began lobbying for what they projected as the motorists' new rights to speedy and accident-free travel over long distances. One lamented that automobiles "have been vastly improved in the past decade, they are dependable, powerful and capable of speeds sixty, seventy and even eighty miles an hour and yet these speeds can only be used at very infrequent periods and short distances because the development of our highways has not kept pace with the developments in motor transport."[16] In 1928, Lester Barlow, a Detroit engineer, propounded a plan for a nationwide system of toll roads that would be overseen by a federal commission and would include grade separations for intersecting traffic and a uniform signal system as well as provisions for proper drainage, frost resistance, and long life. Neither of the existing alternatives—federal aid to states or private enterprise—could create such a toll system, Barlow contended.[17] Barlow's prime motivation was facilitating intercity travel, especially in the Northeast.[18] In 1929, Congress established a commission to study a toll-funded "National System of Express Motorways," but so vast a project produced no quick results.

Advocates of the Federal Aid Highway Act of 1944 foresaw a postwar need to plan and construct an express interstate system because of the pent-up consumer demand for motoring. President Franklin D. Roosevelt had begun to consider the need for such roads in 1939, when he hosted a White House dinner for a select group discussing the prospective authorization of a federal road-building body. Norman Bel Geddes showed those in attendance his sensational Futurama exhibit of an ideal limited-access interstate highway system, which he had created for the New York World's Fair. Roosevelt also had two New Deal agencies provide Pennsylvania with the initial funds to build that state's turnpike but soon seemed less interested in the system itself than in its ancillary benefits of job creation. He later began to focus on funding highways via property condemnation, but World War II ultimately submerged the idea.[19] The Federal Aid Highway Act of 1944 created a third category of highways, the interstates, in addition to the existing primary and secondary roads, but legislators could not agree on funding details, so the new interstates existed in name only.

Tolls seemed the most prevalent funding source discussed in conversations about the creation of a limited-access highway, but federal officials could reach no consensus. Some planners contended that tolls were the fairest way for motor transportation to compete with other transportation modes in any federally sponsored system. Chief of the Bureau of Public Roads Thomas MacDonald consistently favored a interstate road system of express toll roads but opposed congressional plans for toll-based financing in a 1937 report, "Toll Roads and Free Ways," concluding that such financing was simply impractical. A year later, state and federal road engineers, biased perhaps by a vested interest in maintaining the federated system of highway construction, persuaded the Senate to defeat a plan for federal toll roads.[20] Toll roads may not have been suitable as national remedies, but they worked regionally. Individual states threatened by traffic congestion, highway accidents, and the consequent costs took the initiative for toll roads.

October 1, 1940, saw the opening of the Pennsylvania Turnpike, the nation's first long-distance limited-access highway. Motorists found the initial 160-mile stretch between Carlisle and Irwin a genuinely remarkable accomplishment. Driving along the parallel Route 30 (the Lincoln Highway), truckers encountered hazards caused by its steep inclines—as much as nine feet up for every one hundred feet forward. The turnpike through the same area avoided those problems because it employed the abandoned South Penn Railroad alignment, with its far more level grades; the turnpike also had four lanes and a center median at least ten feet wide, and there was no speed limit. Ten turnpike stations spaced approximately fifteen miles apart on alternating sides supplied food, gas, lubrication services, and lodging for truckers—all intended to make limited-access motoring as speedy and effortless as possible. Despite the skepticism of the Bureau of Public Roads and its estimate of a meager 715 vehicles per day on the turnpike, average daily use reached nearly 6,000 by the end of 1940. On the first Sunday of the turnpike's operation, cars queued up for a mile at the entrance tollbooths. The turnpike's full 327 miles opened in 1954, slicing in half travel time between Philadelphia and Pittsburgh.[21] During the first nine years and eight months during which the turnpike operated, an average of 6,211 vehicles per day traveled the road, yielding revenues of $1.65 per vehicle. Such palpable demand permitted retirement of the original debt in 1965, twenty-three years ahead of schedule.[22]

The Pennsylvania Turnpike's funding and engineering set a precedent for the succession of state toll roads in the offing.[23] Moreover, as one enthusiast correctly noted in 1951, "A dozen other states are moving ahead so that the great Pennsylvania Turnpike will become the nucleus of a super-highway system of 1000 miles that will extend from Maine to the nation's capital and across Pennsylvania and Ohio, including the links already constructed, without a single traffic light or crossroad."[24] Some states had begun to collaborate on what the federal government was not yet ready to do.

Maine's Turnpike Authority, enacted in 1941, opened an express, limited-access, toll-financed road as an alternative to Route 1 in 1947. New Jersey, Ohio, and Indiana authorized turnpike authorities in 1948, 1949, and 1951, respectively. Between 1955 and 1957, New York, where the toll road authority antedated the post–World War II stampede, built the 427-mile New York Thruway from New York City to Buffalo and south toward Erie, Pennsylvania. Ohio's public plans demonstrated the zeal and purpose that accompanied these plans for a "new and possibly revolutionary development in transportation. [Ohio's tollway would be] part of an 812-mile turnpike system which will carry automotive travel across four states from New York to Chicago without a single light or intersecting railroad or highway or a single traffic jam to impede traffic" (figure 8.2). By 1956, a total of fourteen states in addition to those in the northeast corridor prodded the boom in toll road construction, thereby affirming the eagerness with which motorists harnessed public budgets.[25] And then a new alternative loomed in the ongoing program to satisfy Americans' seemingly insatiable appetite for motoring.

The Interstate

Highway engineers, motoring lobbyists, and politicians had used the term *interstate* as a noun off and on for half a century before 1956, when the nation committed its wealth to a federal scheme to build an enormous national network of limited-access highways and to build it quickly—forty-one thousand miles by 1970 (figure 8.3). This product, not its antecedents, is what the term *interstate* now refers to. The terms of the Interstate Highway Act of 1956 resolved a quarter century of

Figure 8.2. The Ohio Turnpike, Postcard, 1955. Courtesy the Ohio Turnpike Commission.

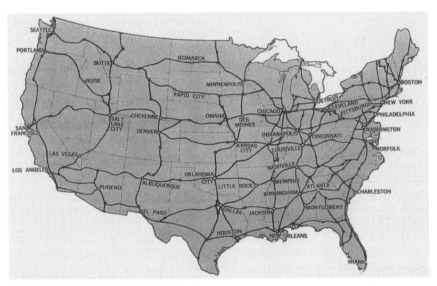

Figure 8.3. The New Interstate System as Proposed in the Interstate Highway Act of 1956. *Highway Magazine* 57 (March 1957): 44.

rising demand not only among motorists but among commercially and professionally vested interests—highway engineers, government bureaucrats, truckers, automobile manufacturers—for a highway system that would eliminate the traffic glut caused by increased dependence on automotive vehicles for travel and business. The system would link forty-two state capitals, 90 percent of all urban centers with more than fifty thousand inhabitants, and 65 percent of the country's urban and 50 percent of its rural inhabitants. The result satisfied the demands of the time and the locally oriented interests that had guided federal road construction since its earliest days. Americans were well on their way, although they were virtually unanimous in their innocence of it, to an imbalanced dependence on cars, trucks, and the interstate. By 1984, 84 percent of all intercity passenger traffic and 23 percent of all freight tonnage would be hauled by automotive vehicles, and 20 percent of all traffic would be carried on the interstate, which represented 1 percent of all highways. This entire limited-access network included at least four twelve-foot-wide lanes, a median separating the opposing traffic streams, wide paved shoulders, and curves and slopes sufficient to enable motorists to drive without slowing (figures 8.4, 8.5).[26]

Mark Rose authoritatively chronicles the fifteen years of industrious exchanges that culminated in the 1956 act. His study reveals a compromise between government officials and the American Automobile Association, which preferred to shove the financial burden for the interstate onto truckers, and the trucking industry, which eventually agreed to some higher taxes. Thus, in more than the ways treated in chapter 9, motorists and truckers uncomfortably cohabited in the highway space each group coveted for itself. Truckers accepted higher taxes only if they were not prey to public funding raids for "diversion," the catchword for funds applied to projects other than that for which the monies were collected.[27]

Agreement finally occurred because the feeling that a crisis threatened the open road. Congressman George A. Dondero, a Michigan Republican who chaired the U.S. House committee in charge of road legislation, for example, pointed out to fellow legislators the geometric expansion in vehicle registration after World War II and concluded that highway programs no more than kept pace. Instead, he argued, planning for future growth needed to occur. In a 1955 article, *Life* magazine claimed that the nation's highways were twenty years out of date and that one-third of the mileage had been constructed for speeds half as fast as the prevailing forty-seven-mile-per-hour average.[28] Motorists may have sensed those deficiencies, but such clarion calls probably readied motoring and nonmotoring readers alike for new financial measures to remedy the "traffic problem."

The terrifying Cold War further shoved parsimonious legislators toward the interstate system. President Dwight D. Eisenhower, from the vantage point of his

Figure 8.4. Interstate 5 in California, c. 1960. *California Highways and Public Works* 40 (March–April 1961): front cover.

experience in two world wars, extolled the interstate as a route of flight should any city be bombed and foresaw the pavements as emergency runways for military aircraft.[29] No one has studied the influence of military preparedness on motorists' support for the interstate, but it seems a likely factor at a time when the fear of global communism gripped much of the nation.

The winning financial compromises in the 1956 Boggs-Fallon Bill and the Highway Revenue Act stipulated a tax on gasoline and diesel fuels, lubricating oils, tires, and new trucks that yielded a Highway Trust Fund rather than "pay-as-you-go" financing. The financing plan also set aside the fifty-fifty split between state and federal funding that had prevailed since the Federal Aid Highway Act of 1921 and substituted a formula under which the federal government paid 90 percent of construction costs. This satisfied the Eisenhower administration's heretofore frustrated desire to build roads without adding to the federal debt.[30] The president's exaspera-

Figure 8.5. Interstate 5 Interchanges in California, c. 1965. Authors' collection.

tion likely mirrored that of the average motorist—most people just wanted to get on with the building and using of roads. Motorists wanted "better roads now," a spokesman for the American Automobile Association declared in January 1956.[31] In April, two months before signing the final legislation, Eisenhower declared, "We need highways badly, very badly, and I am in favor of any forward, constructive steps in this field."[32] Previously antagonistic interest groups, such as the tire industry, also had stopped lobbying against taxes on their commodities, thus clearing the way for the bill's passage and the president's signature.[33] Numerous observers, beginning with the interstate engineers themselves, have stood in awe of the physical result—the world's largest public works program and engineering's largest structure—tending to overshadow the fact that its magnitude corresponded to the huge public demand that made it possible.[34] Highway interest groups tried to wriggle out of financial responsibility for the interstate undertaking while pushing the inordinate weight onto others, but beneath this instability was an unmistakable unity—motoring was a national urge.

Not only did the interstate deliver the rewards motorists had anticipated, but the interchanges along it offered opportunities of often unforeseen significance. Half of the first funds allocated went toward construction of five thousand miles of bypasses around 90 percent of the cities with populations above fifty thousand; these bypasses reduced motorists' travel time by an average of sixty-six hours a year and created a suburban growth spurt as commuting from interchange-accessed suburban homes to downtown workplaces became easier and faster. In addition, although individual businesses had been attracted to interchange locations off toll roads before their incorporation into the interstate, the development of "interchange villages" around 10 percent of the interchanges has had a far more dramatic effect on land use. These interchanges became centers of service not only to passing motorists but also to local populations, offering commerce, manufacturing, distribution, and administration. Churches and governments, for example, have constructed new buildings at those interchanges to provide motoring members and constituents easy access and comfortable commutes from far away.[35]

In rural settings, the interstate tested the assumption that motorists' craving for efficiently spent time dictated that short-term roadside services such as gas stations and fast food restaurants be located close to the interchange, while longer-term or overnight services such as motels were located farther away. In fact, a study in the 1980s showed motorists on I-75 were served by gas stations near the interstate, but motel spacing varied according to the clientele. Motorists prepared to pay higher hotel/motel chain rates found lodging near accesses, while more frugal travelers drove farther from interchanges to save money at individually owned lodgings. Independently owned restaurants often were closer to I-75 interchanges than were those of the large chains. Real estate departments for those chains counted on clustering with others in a fast food agglomeration where motorists could exercise their choice in outlets side by side rather than searching for outlets made distinctive in their isolation from competitors. In addition, the fast food chains purchased or leased land later than other services and consequently had to settle for locations relatively far from interstate interchanges. No evidence indicated that such locations cost those chains any profits.[36]

Surveys of Denver's expansion around the I-470 Beltway determined that it had less revolutionary effects than opponents of "urban sprawl" customarily charge. In 1979, residents began moving to suburban homes in a planned community, Highlands Ranch, but more than a decade passed before a big shopping mall, the Park Meadows Town Center, followed in 1996.[37] This finding seems to counter the common belief that motorists are motivated exclusively by convenience—travelers on the I-470 Beltway seemed prepared to commute home and shop elsewhere before both aspects of urban development were gathered into a single center. The issue of urban sprawl along interstate corridors as well as along primary roads merits more study.

While the interstate's influence on land use may not yet be fully understood, its importance to the act of motoring itself was soon clear. The interstate's midcentury turnpike antecedents produced a rash of popular articles about a new driving hazard, the "false sense of security" induced by long, straight roads and reduced traffic volume.[38] Highway engineers referred to mastering a "feel" for the novel motoring experience, rather like the sensation Gideon had enjoyed on Moses's parkways, and referred to a fluidity of movement defying the friction that kept motorists alert on ordinary highways.[39] "Highway hypnosis" became a dreaded symptom under such conditions.[40] One article invoked the motorist who "maintains a constant speed mile after mile. The engine—and on some roads the whump-whump of the wheels over paving joints—purrs him into drowsiness. He relaxes. His reflexes dissolve. He drowses. Then *wham*—he drives full tilt into a bridge abutment or the side of a mountain."[41]

Popular magazines offered antidotes to their wary readers. Editors urged readers to learn about the potential dangers of the "loss of sensitivity" induced by interstate motoring and to break the numbing flow by stopping at rest areas and reducing the number of hours behind the wheel. Motorists were also advised to drive at the prevailing speed of the surrounding motorists but to drop out of the packs that tended to come together. Of course, motorists were also advised to continue practicing old principles of car care. Tires and engines suffered special failures on the interstate, warned magazine writers, with motors burning out because of the high speeds and threadbare or improperly inflated tires blowing out more quickly. Motorists should plan ahead and should not fumble with maps while at the wheel to avoid a rapid decrease in speed that could result in an accident; traffic flow needed to remain steady. Advice givers told motorists to learn to rely on the interstate route shields: two digits numbered the main routes, and, as had been the case since 1926, odd numbers marked north-south routes and even numbers east-west routes. Three-digit numbers with even first digits denoted routes through or bypassing cities, while three-digit numbers beginning with odd digits indicated spur routes that might not necessarily connect motorists to adjacent interstates. Red, white, and blue shields connoted long-distance routes, and white and green shields directed motorists between business areas and interchanges.[42]

The interstate conferred the benefits motorists had sought. Traffic was three times safer on interstates than on previous highways carrying the same traffic. By 1970, motorists averaged twenty-four hundred miles per ten-day trip, eleven hundred miles more than the preinterstate average.[43]

After the initial demand for the interstate and its bypass appendages faded, they came in for some disapproval, but more recent years have brought at least some renewed appreciation. As a type of freeway, the interstate has been derided as separating motorists from the surrounding regional environment at the gain of efficiency, yet people absorb some of its features into their routine experiences.[44] Even critics can support the interstate through their own motoring—disapproval from the perspective of outside the system turns to tacit approval when looking at the system from within, from behind the steering wheel. Theirs is not less an objective criticism than a perspective arbitrarily taken or overlooked depending on personal advantage. These observers fail to give substantial credit to what uncritical interstate motorists find advantageous or distinctive about the road.

◆ ▼ ●

From the first, motoring kindled a zeal for vaulting time and space to distant destinations, as Robert Bruce's admiration for New York state's highways illustrated at the start of chapter 4. And degrees of accomplishment only made motorists zealous for more. Motoring generated a self-perpetuating dynamic, as if drivers and passengers alike became extensions of the machines they had formerly controlled. Successful motoring required not only ever-more-reliable cars but also ever-better highways in terms of greater safety and greater speed. The apparent contradictions between those twin goals disappeared from consciousness as highways improved. The influx of tax monies and engineering expertise bred impatience with any obstruction to the free flow of traffic. Paradoxically, Americans even relinquished their time-honored goal of freedom in favor of the benefits of limited-access highways. They followed their dreams of an open road headlong to whatever new land uses nurtured those dreams. Were there no limits?

motoring by truck

In the motoring experience, truckers and trucking represent a significant deviation from the pleasantries that define the norm. A type of labor that can be grueling, trucking is nonetheless also enshrouded in one of the most romantic variations on the open road theme. Truckers are not ordinary motorists, although they too drive automotive vehicles, but motorists view truckers through either a rose-colored lens—shared by some truckers—or a dark lens. Because trucking is widely misunderstood as another fanciful behavior that driving automotive vehicles stimulates—one whose mystique most people are satisfied not to go beyond—this chapter will deal first with the business facts of trucking history before exploring its evocatively ahistoric folklore constructed substantially by motorists. The magnitude of the open road theme cannot be appreciated without a baseline comparison of the trucking mystique against the utilitarian circumstances transformed by motorists' imaginations.[1]

A Historical Sketch of the Trucking Industry

Truck at first gained currency slowly in the English language. The word, meaning a vehicle for hauling, dates only since the seventeenth century; in the nineteenth century, usage expanded to apply to the carts used for moving goods around railroad depots. In the early twentieth century, however, *truck* acquired a new and spectacular meaning with the invention of the internal combustion engine. In 1898, two commercial manufacturers, Alexander Winton and Duryea Motor Wagons, and a dry goods store, B. Altman, produced small automotive delivery wagons, the first recorded. By 1900, the Stanley brothers of passenger car construction fame and White Sewing Machines entered the new truck field with lightweight steam models. Motor trucks, like many new technologies in the consumer culture, benefited from their entrepreneurs' staging of sensational public displays to attract attention and demonstrate the merits of their products. A Swiss-designed Saurer

Figure 9.1. Packard proudly advertised to diverse customers, including farmers and urban truckers, hoping to persuade them to purchase its motor trucks. *The Farmer and Facts about His Motor Truck* ([Detroit]: Packard Motor Car, n.d.), 29.

Freighter set out in 1911 to prove the capacity for long-distance truck service by hauling a 3½-ton load from San Francisco to New York City by way of Denver. Although the load traveled by railroad from San Francisco to Pueblo, Colorado, it completed the first transcontinental truck crossing. The next year, a Packard carrying three tons broke the record when it traveled cross country in forty-six days, and Philadelphia hosted a parade of five hundred trucks (figure 9.1). Numerous manufacturers arranged perhaps less exciting but nonetheless eventually persuasive intercity and interstate sprints.[2]

Although the romance of the road multiplied the charm of these stunts, as pioneering routinely does, motor trucks in fact developed greater popular appeal than actual utilization early in the century. By 1910, the United States had 10,123 registered motor trucks, just 2 percent of the vehicle total.[3] Trucking was limited to some intercity deliveries and a few short farm-to-market hauls, but growing numbers of people understood the greater potential. In 1912, a widely read general news magazine, the *Literary Digest,* assessed the field: at most one hundred trucks per year had been manufactured a decade earlier, but "there still remains 'a big field for the commercial car.'" According to the *Literary Digest,* truck prices would soon level off, leading to a bright future for the vehicle.[4] Horses, which provided most of the nation's short hauling at the time, were less economical than trucks, the *Literary Digest* argued a year later. Horses required food, and in a nation with an accelerating population and a high cost of living, feeding the animals was financially unsound: 125,000 people could be fed from the land committed to feeding the nation's horses.[5] The partisan *American Motorist* reasoned that one truck could serve an area between two and three hundred square miles, whereas three or more horses would be required to cover the same area. Horses had a radius of eight to twelve miles from a central destination; trucks had a radius of between twenty and forty miles. In urban areas, said the *American Motorist,* "street filth, the dust nuisance, the fly pest" clearly doomed the horse, while in the countryside, farmers would come to realize that trucks were cheaper and speedier and would bring into production acreage now considered too remote.[6] Confronting paralyzing traffic congestion, early city traffic experts soon reasoned that trucks not only gave swifter service but resulted in fewer accidents than did horse-drawn wagons.[7] New York's farmers were not readily convinced of trucking's virtues, as reflected in the state legislature's 1907 debate about the need for "radial highways" reaching from cities and towns into the countryside. *Good Roads* attempted to persuade the state's reluctant farming community by outlining financial reasons that came to be common tactics used by the automotive lobby nationwide.[8]

Whether or not motor trucks were to realize their potential ultimately rested not with debaters and their discriminating audiences but with the structure of the nascent trucking industry and its accessories. Several preconditions were necessary for growth. James Flink convincingly demonstrates that trucking's radically cheaper economies of scale could not be obtained in practice without widespread adoption, which awaited creation of a sufficient pool of capable drivers and mechanics. Other preconditions had already been satisfied. Automotive technology in general advanced remarkably. Gasoline-powered vehicles benefited when the Burton cracking process yielded less expensive and more efficient fuel and invention of the electric starter replaced the time-consuming and often injury-inducing hand crank. Motor trucks especially improved with the abandonment of the inefficient chain drive for a power shaft to the driving wheels and adaptation of the steering knuckle, which permitted wheels to turn free of their axle, thereby enabling trucks to negotiate the tight quarters they often faced in narrow city streets not designed for automobiles. Manufacturers and transporters began capably organizing their markets. For example, after 1909, White trucks came to the forefront when the company shifted from the production of steam-powered vehicles to gasoline-powered models, and in 1912, Norwalk Produce, one of the nation's first trucking companies, started as an intercity line headquartered in Cleveland.[9] But nothing spurred advances like the exigencies of World War I.

War heightened the existing emphasis on efficiency, speed, labor saving, and productivity. Even before the United States officially entered the war, foreign orders and their subsidiary effects on the domestic economy loosened money heretofore loaned cautiously to truck builders and drivers. Truck sales rose 100 percent between 1914 and 1915, and the number of truck registrations leaped from 99,015 to 158,506 during the same time. The term *motor express* found its way into the transportation trade's new vernacular for speed, which was the most obvious advantage the light (defined as two tons or less) motor truck offered over the railroads, which had been unchallenged in heavy hauling for three-quarters of a century. Trains took a day or more to make deliveries between Detroit and Toledo, a distance that motor trucks could travel in a few hours. In addition to saving time, the use of trucks eliminated labor and packing costs, and goods suffered less damage because they were handled only twice, at loading and unloading, rather than between destinations, as railroading required. Detroit's Sullivan Packing developed innovative refrigerator trucks that delivered meat to Toledo in six hours, a substantial improvement over the 2½ days the same shipment took by train, and with far less shrinkage. Such cases dramatized for the general public the trucking industries' claims of transportation superiority, while more subtle evidence persuaded the accountants and merchants responsible for shipping merchandise. The use of motor trucks enabled marketers to respond more quickly to changing conditions than did trains. Not only were motor trucks free to travel almost anywhere, with no limits imposed by stations and fixed rails, but trucks permitted merchants to reduce expensive inventories to levels of minimum sufficiency. If something was needed, it could be delivered quickly.[10]

Historian William Childs describes a trucking revolution during World War I. A combination of farmers' reasoning and the insistence of commercial and governmental authorities on maximum productivity drew agriculture, previously the economic sector most resistant to trucking, more closely into the nation's economy. Farmers realized that either their own vehicles or trucking companies could enable the shipment of products to market faster than railroads could; moreover, by using trucking companies, manpower could be reserved for farm production. Because truckers charged flat rates without fees for loading and unloading, as the railroads did, total shipping costs dropped. So eager for business were many in the infant trucking industry that they also welcomed shipments of less than carload lots (LCL), unlike the hesitant railroads.[11] National and local councils of defense advocated those smart tactics as well as "back loads," having trucks carry goods on their return trips to their points of origin rather than traveling empty. The Indianapolis Chamber of Commerce declared it "unproductive to wear the road without the load," operating a stockyard information exchange at which truckers

Figure 9.2. Use of Trucks for Local Deliveries during World War I. *Motor Truck Club Bulletin* 5 (February 1918): 7.

could learn where in the city to obtain return loads within a sixty-mile radius. Everyone came out ahead, noted the chair of the Indiana State Council of Defense: "The Rural Motor Express means more food for the consumer, a bigger market for the producer, lowered costs of transportation and the taking of the big burden off the congested means of transportation."[12] The federal Railway War Board reinforced the shift to trucks for short hauls, urging railroads to give as much short-distance business as possible to the trucks (figure 9.2).[13] The postal service added momentum. Rural free delivery, begun in 1896 and buttressed by the Federal Highway Act of 1916 dedicated to post roads, remained in the hands of mail carriers on bicycles, on horseback, or in horse-drawn wagons until World War I, when the Post Office Department began serious consideration of trucks.[14] Like its commercial predecessors, the department began with a publicly acclaimed demonstration, putting a 1½-ton Autocar on a route between Lancaster, Pennsylvania;

Philadelphia; and New York in early 1918.[15] By midyear, several parcel post routes had begun to operate.[16]

Motor trucking emerged stronger as a result of the war. Motor truck production alone multiplied twentyfold between 1910 and 1918.[17] Railroads forsook contentious rivalry for grudging if temporary embrace as they conceded trucks a role in short hauls, thereby freeing up an estimated fifteen thousand rail cars and easing terminal congestion.[18] Pneumatic tires, long mounted on bicycles and previously adapted for passenger automobiles, became practical for trucks beginning in 1916 when P. W. Litchfield of Goodyear Tire and Rubber developed a durable product. The new tires outperformed the old hard rubber tires in many respects, doing less damage to roads, providing better traction in mud, and enabling trucks to travel faster, since fear of overheated tires had previously limited trucks to speeds of fifteen miles per hour or less. Three days after America entered the war, Goodyear started the Wingfoot Express demonstration truck line between Akron and Boston, proving the pneumatic tire's practicality for trucks.[19] Motor trucks became an accepted part of American life, and by 1919, the United States had 897,755 registered motor trucks. That number would never again drop below a million.[20]

Still, problems arose during the 1920s. Motor trucking's wartime success and its legitimate claim to patriotic service led to a flood of new trucking companies, some of which survived and some of which failed. In the reversion to a peacetime economy, surplus motor trucks ill fitted for general cartage enabled almost anyone to enter the field, and many hardworking men attempted to enter the business without full awareness of the pitfalls. "Gypsy truckers" drawn between sites wherever opportunity seemed to present itself, for example, hauled coal from the mines in the eastern states directly to city consumers, in the process weakening retail coal dealers. Comparatively few operators realized, as did the independent truckers who solicited work from Norwalk Produce and took back loads from around Norwalk and Cleveland, that a lucrative long-term future lay in regular work with a shipper rather than in continued wildcatting. Firms consolidated throughout the 1920s, but as late as 1932, nearly two-thirds of all trucking firms (2.2 million truckers) were one-man firms. States regulated rates but enforced those regulations only sporadically, and truckers accordingly adjusted their rates to achieve competitive advantage against one another and the railroads. Many rates were cutthroat, barely above the breakeven point. Fluidity and intense competition—in short, an overall atomism—characterized trucking through the 1920s.[21] The American ethos of self-taught competence being rewarded in improved incomes if not status undercut calls for educated transportation specialists.[22] Novice truckers seldom knew how to calculate the cost of fuel, oil, and food or how to think ahead to the costs of depreciation, the wisdom of insurance, or the arranging of back loads.[23] Customers routinely offered and bought the transported goods at bargain prices, unsure of what they were getting from unfamiliar truckers. A man's truck could produce his livelihood while functioning as both his office and home.[24]

Trucking in the West suffered from the peculiarities of its sparse settlement pattern and topography. Unlike eastern truckers, who picked from an abundance of shippers, westerners took what business they could and consequently developed general rather than specialized services. Often hauling with only half loads, western truckers routinely handled agricultural as well as manufactured goods and navigated icy mountain passages on crudely engineered roads. For example, when Federal Auto Freight of Yakima, Washington, started business in 1920, only six miles of paved roads south of town existed. Given the fact that railroads outperformed motor trucks over long distances with heavy loads, railroads remained the primary means of shipping into the 1930s.[25]

Manufacturers began to develop and produce the various specialized chassis and bodies that trucks needed to function most effectively. Through the mid-1920s, most motor trucks were standardized, little more than modified passenger cars weighing one ton or less. Companies—most notably Mack and Kenworth—entered the field with custom-made models and workmen who called themselves "truck tailors." Trailers became the single most influential adaptation in the industry's wartime and postwar growth spurt. Trailers dated from the first decade of the twentieth century, but demand for them did not accelerate until the end of the war, when their ability to at least double motor trucks' tractive power became desirable. Trailers could be operated and maintained cheaply, reducing shipping costs and helping clinch their rapid appearance. Initially the lumber and building supply companies' conveyance of choice, trailer trucks gained wider usage with the invention of the fifth wheel and satisfactory coupling steer, which prevented loads from weaving, enabled adjustment to change axle loads, and facilitated uncoupling.[26]

Among the conditions affecting the rise of trucking through the 1920s, none was more expensive and drew more resistance to the young industry than the construction of highways adequate for trucks. Private associations undertook much of the responsibility for the developing highway system, but soon after the war, it became evident that the federal government would have to design, fund, and build that network to satisfy the expectations of automobile and truck motorists alike. Trucking added compelling reason to the good roads lobbyists who influenced passage of the Federal Aid Highway Act of 1921.[27] Proponents of enhanced transportation throughout the nation ranked trucking's capacity for better service as a strong reason for more and better-designed highways. In 1917, for example, *Good Roads* magazine found cause for its advocacy of smooth, rigid, and durable highways in a Wayne County, Michigan, road commissioner's assurance that trucking's expansion in his area indicated that the "freight highway" would constitute a fact of the immediate future.[28] Both short-distance motor express and long-distance hauling had registered proof of the truck's potential. At the same time that highway engineers began the practice of designing roads for the heaviest trucks,[29] the motor trucking industry labored to prove that various innovations such as trailers minimized damage to highways. Assuming that the public remembered how trucks had outshone the railroads, especially during World War I, the head of the Trailer Manufacturers Association of America aggressively advocated better highways: "So, in the final analysis, it is for the public to decide whether it prefers to pay for suitable motor truck roads that will reduce the cost of haulage or continue to pay the high cost of living."[30] Government answered in the affirmative, but the matter remained a continual source of debate as automobile motorists especially have chafed at sharing highway space with trucking motorists.

The Great Depression of the early 1930s worsened old problems that truckers found less disturbing in the economically flush 1920s.[31] Gypsy truckers, who comprised just 5.4 percent of all trucking firms by the late 1920s, jeopardized the virtually equal number of common carriers (5.5 percent), who were legally obligated to serve shippers regardless of load size or remoteness of the destination.[32] Declining business volumes in the 1930s did not discourage enterprising men who took advantage of the easy purchase terms on the oversupplied used truck market.[33] The unsuspecting often overloaded their rigs beyond safe capacities, resulting in costly broken axles and mechanical failures, and the dishonest bootlegged loads below established rates and without cartage permits.[34] Under the cover of night, some truckers not only avoided the heavy traffic of daylight hours but also evaded law enforcement.[35] Truckers' reputation for night driving thus spawned their stereotype as reckless.[36] The rough-and-tumble competitiveness among early truckers also produced a novel cartage category, the contract carrier, who, unlike the common carrier, offered services suited to specialized trucks. Refrigerated trucks might remain dedicated to shippers of certain foods, but flatbed trucks could transport various loads if none of the heavy equipment for which such vehicles were best suited was available. However, unlike common carriers, contract carriers remained unregulated and consequently had an operational advantage over common carriers.[37] Railroads called anew for truck taxation amid the decline in demand for shipping services. Truckers persistently countered that they paid their fair share of highway construction and maintenance costs and did not disadvantage the railroads, which were unable to avoid paying for their right-of-way.[38]

For an industry of hard-earned profits, the depression of the 1930s only increased the pain caused by the eccentric government regulations inherited from the 1920s. Complicated U.S. Supreme Court decisions during the 1920s had said that state trucking laws to promote safety and protect pavements from overloaded trucks did not interfere with federal authority but that the licensure of companies to block excessive numbers interfered with interstate commerce. Much of the new motor trucking industry consequently remained largely unregulated. And those regulations in force often varied so much between states that truckers not uncommonly had to unload quantities at one state line and take on loads at another. "Border wars" erupted intermittently when states fined entering truckers for failing to comply with regulations; temporary reciprocity agreements put an end to these conflicts. Michigan, with some of the nation's best-defined early truck statutes, faced the problems of erratic enforcement within its borders and truckers' ability to elude enforcement. Truckers developed the habit, still in existence, of blinking their lights at oncoming truckers to alert them to law-enforcement personnel—originally, the locations of the portable scales Michigan authorities used to weigh trucks for compliance with load limits. Although proud of his state's practices, Michigan's assistant maintenance engineer could not provide assurances that the state's highways were free of dangerously overloaded trucks. Overweight motor trucks combined with driver fatigue to threaten highway safety. Truckers with helpers commonly traveled eighteen, twenty, and twenty-four hours without stopping.[39]

A 1935 Senate report described transportation in general as in a "chaotic" state and recommended legislation to remedy the situation.[40] Small truckers generally disliked "government interference," although larger firms welcomed the government's role in putting an end to what they perceived as unfair competition through rate cutting and the welter of confusing state laws.[41] With a minimum of involvement from the New Dealers in power, who were concerned principally with social policy reform, the bigger truckers and allied technocrats and highway lobbies formulated the nation's first significant trucking law, the Motor Carrier Act of 1935. Its guiding principle was a concept of public interest aimed at preventing excessive competition. The measure empowered the Interstate Commerce Commission to require published rates, established schedules, and financial responsibility for loss and damage.[42] Motor truck rates were to be kept equal to or lower than railroad rates, new trucking firms had to prove that they merited admission to the industry, and minimum rather than maximum rates were set for contract carriers.[43]

Motor trucking grew through the 1930s despite the depressed economy, with several general trends becoming apparent. In 1933, the President's Research Committee on Social Trends, in keeping with the rising general awareness, took trucking into its field of vision and made important discoveries. Committee members attributed the assembly of the nation's "modern economic regionalism" to motor trucks linking rural hinterlands within a forty-mile radius of adjacent urban cen-

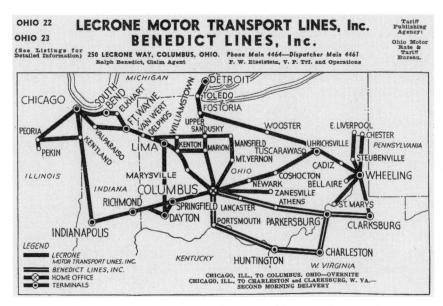

Figure 9.3. Advertisement Showing Motor Trucking Network between Chicago and Eastern Ohio. *Official Motor Freight Guide* (Chicago: n.p., 1941), 130.

ters (figure 9.3). Department stores in those cities marginalized small-town rivals not only through more diverse inventories but also because trucking fleets made door-to-door deliveries possible.[44] Chicago's dominion over the midcontinent urban hierarchy grew even greater as a consequence of motor trucking links to national production and consumption centers.[45] Farming became more tightly woven into the economy as trucks transported produce into urban markets on a daily basis.[46] Intercity motor trucking remained in use primarily for short hauls, although the railroads remained alarmed because they had lost about 10 percent of their business to their new, motorized competitors.[47] Clarence Aspinwall, a pioneer in the moving and storage industry, recalled the truckers' characteristic optimism of the late 1920s: "Household removals to another city were no longer accomplished by crating and shipping by rail, but by loading into a long-distance moving van. Hence, the interchange of shipments between members and problems of packing and shipping were transferred to questions of motor haulage and return loads."[48] Paralleling the maturation of such business practices was the increased registration of trucks throughout the 1930s and 1940s. Although the number of registered motor trucks declined for four years after its 1930 zenith of 3,518,747 vehicles, the total then grew every year thereafter except for 1938.[49] Federal regulation under the 1935 act prompted consolidations among firms, resulting in an increase in big firms and a decrease in small companies. In 1938, public and Teamsters

Union concern resulted in the first Interstate Commerce Commission limits on driving time—no more than ten hours per day before an eight-hour rest, with a sixty-hour maximum per week for any driver. And the infamous logbook became the means of checking on compliance. All truckers were supposed to record all their activities, an honor system that became prone to cheating.[50]

Cartelization, or the establishment and enforcement of operational terms including permission and rates, gradually grew dysfunctional. While the 1935 act satisfied the depression-era assumption that unbridled competition had run amok and required government regulation, by the 1960s the Interstate Commerce Commission's supervision had slipped into a protectionist mind-set benefiting existing truckers and disadvantaging consumers, whose guardians found evidence that trucking costs were higher than they would have been in a free-market competition. Presidents John F. Kennedy, Lyndon B. Johnson, and Richard M. Nixon considered deregulation but dropped the idea because the political gains seemed insufficient. Not until the oil crisis of the early 1970s combined with the inflation of the late 1970s did the second great reform of the trucking industry under federal auspices occur, the Motor Carrier Act of 1980.[51]

Dorothy Robyn explains that post-1945 highway construction, galvanized especially by the creation of the interstate system in 1956, gave great impetus to the volume of goods shipped by truck. Standard truck size grew from twenty-seven feet to forty-five feet. Between 1950 and 1970, the number of registered motor trucks more than doubled from 8,233,146 to 17,800,000. More highways, more trucks, and longer trucks produced a boom at the same time that federal regulation kept shipping rates above a competitive level because the number of firms was limited and they were allowed to collude in price setting. Robyn identifies the four underlying problems as monopoly profits, excessive costs, insufficient price service, and discriminatory rates. Participating carriers created and staffed "rate bureaus" that set rates within various regions throughout the nation, and the overworked Interstate Commerce Commission seldom overturned those rates, instead routinely approving them. Because the Reed-Bulwinkle Act of 1948 exempted motor trucking from antitrust prohibitions, the rate bureaus were free to fix prices. Cutthroat pricing no longer jeopardized the truckers, as had been the case before 1935, but analysts concluded that rates above market level disadvantaged the public interest. Existing companies sold portions of their rights to new companies wishing to enter the field, but fixed rates blocked the lower rates that uncontrolled competition would have offered. A combination of factors produced excessive costs of operation. For example, the Interstate Commerce Commission's practice of approving rates set based on average industry costs tended to protect the less efficient firms. Route and commodity restrictions resulted in smaller loads and excessive interlining (the transfer of cargo between shippers) and gasoline and labor consumption, to name only a few problems. In the category of inefficient price service, prices above competitive levels left shippers with less choice about their inventory size, production schedules, and plant location. Discriminatory prices resulted when the regulated rates overcharged some shippers yet in effect subsidized others.[52]

The Motor Carrier Act of 1980 loosened the forty-five-year-old policy of regulation but did not completely deregulate the industry, as some observers had sought. The foremost change involved a reorientation that created a "presumption in favor of entry and competition" for new firms.[53] New firms also gained expanded access to routes, commodities carried, service points, and directions. The 1980 measure ended the sharp distinction between common and contract carriers: common carriers were no longer limited to operations for a particular industry or within a particular region, and the Interstate Commerce Commission was no longer required to consider the number of shippers an applicant would serve. Owner-operators also no longer had to demonstrate the commission's formerly coveted "public convenience and necessity."[54]

Deregulation resulted in a substantial jump in the number of carriers, which rose from 18,212 in 1979 to 27,517 in 1983. Most of the new entrants were small carriers. More common carriers entered contract work. Few owner-operators took advantage of the expanded privileges to carry food products, agricultural soil conditioners, and fertilizers. Consistent with the trend toward deregulation, the Surface Transportation Assistance Act of 1982 legalized the use of twin trailers, forty-eight-foot trailers, and 102-inch-wide trucks, which some states had previously prohibited.[55]

More and bigger motor trucks on the open road that passenger car drivers preferred to think of as their own periodically refocused public attention on the truckers' responsibility for highway safety and highway upkeep. The threat of overbearing and recklessly driven behemoths on the highways never disappeared completely from public consciousness. Few were bold enough to admit, as did one highway engineer, "If I had my 'druthers,' I'd rather have *no* bus or truck traffic on the particular roads and streets over which I travel."[56] Trucking's sharp increase from 9.1 to 21.3 percent of the total intercity cartage between 1949 and 1969 and the adoption of piggybacking on railroads in the 1950s made trucks ever more apparent.[57] Their bulk, their volume, and their noise threatened.[58] The early 1970s fuel crisis reopened the issue as people saw televised incidents of truckers blocking highways and confronting National Guardsmen, read newspaper editorials attacking the oil companies and truckers, and wondered when or if a truckers' strike would jeopardize the shipment of food from the countryside.[59] These fears threatened a highly integrated economy and unnerved a nation that would have preferred to forget the potential for civil unrest that had so recently flared. Taking responsibility for some conditions on the new interstate system, the federal government had enacted its first limits on vehicle weight, dimensions, and configuration in 1956,[60] but states continued to set and enforce their own limits. States might undertake safety studies prior to legislating remedies.[61] Illinois began using truck weighing stations in 1936 but in 1949 started constructing additional weighing stations on highway shoulders to avoid blocking the increased postwar traffic flow.[62] In the mid-1960s, Pennsylvania was the only state that required all motor vehicles licensed under its authority to undergo periodic inspections at authorized stations, a practice it had begun in 1929.[63] Engineers designed improved highway technology to handle increasing loads under the nation's widely varying climatological and traffic conditions. Eased load restrictions during World War II had resulted in pulverized pavement, and engineers—for example, at Purdue University during the early 1950s—began developing ways to stabilize grades below the pavement.[64]

The 1982 federal legislation's liberalization of truck dimensions gave renewed stimulus to public alarms about trucking. Severe and spectacular large-truck accidents and massive traffic congestion garnered extensive press and television coverage and helped engender a study of how twin trailers in fact influenced traffic. Although the study was conducted too soon after the passage of the 1982 act to obtain definitive results, twins were thought to be more prone to rolling over as a result of erratic steering, less likely to warn drivers about stability, more likely to encroach on outside lanes on curves, and more prone to rear-end sway. These traits made twins slightly more likely to be involved in accidents, but their greater cartage capacity actually lowered the number of accidents per truck mile. Deregulation's critics, however, blamed rising violations on old equipment and delayed repair. Twins seemed to have no effect on traffic congestion, taking up more space but also lowering the number of smaller trucks in use. Furthermore, the study acknowledged that although twins likely increased pavement wear and highway costs, these expenses probably were offset by reductions in shipping costs brought about by increased capacity.[65]

The study affords an opportunity to pause and reflect on nearly a century of highway interactions between truckers and autoists. While the study took neither the truckers' nor the public's side, it lends credence to the fact that the public was not entirely comfortable with the motoring experience, notwithstanding people's fabled love affair with the open road. Perhaps the public—especially the autoists, who comprise the preponderance of all motorists—resents having to pay for highways even if those costs are hidden in the price of fuel, and this resentment is displaced onto truckers and trucks. Passenger car, RV, and travel trailer devotees have overtly declared their distaste for sharing the highway with motor trucks. Fear of collisions seems largely to be rooted in the dread of the possibility of a collision with an overpowering machine more than in the likelihood of such an occurrence. But, since worry, unlike actuarial statistics, cannot be quantified, there is no unarguable way to test the proposition that passenger car motorists are unduly upset by big trucks. The problem's insolubility thus goes to the heart of the benefits in the motoring experience, suggesting that it will perpetually be plagued by the rivalry between truckers and autoists over who owns and who deserves the open road.

Truck Terminals and Truck Stops

Two very different types of places framed the trucker's motoring experience—the truck terminal and the truck stop. The former stood behind the scenes, out of public view except perhaps in rare distant glimpses from interstate overpasses above railroad lines or even more uncommonly when motorists got lost in industrial and warehouse areas. Truck terminals were working scenes. Truck stops stood in plainer view along highways, where motor car travelers might occasionally pull in to refuel and eat, if they wished, and share the setting with truckers who required rest, room, and board. Truck stops were places of exchange, if only visual, between people at rest and people at play.

Considerable heterogeneity applied in the arrangement of early trucking terminals. By midcentury, parking lots and converted warehouses served as the most crudely improvised of this potentially sophisticated category of truck place type. Charles Taff groups truck terminals into four classes according to ownership: (1) space rented by one motor carrier to others; (2) a cooperative association of carriers paying shared expenses; (3) a terminal company with leases to carrier-tenants; and (4) space operated on a system of rates depending on the amount of business hauled in and out. All types of these facilities were commonly built according to a T plan in which the offices filled the crossbar and loading and unloading docks occupied the vertical bar. Long-haul trucks loaded or unloaded on one side of the dock, and delivery trucks picked up or unloaded on the opposite side of the dock, called cross-dock operations. Modified X, I, and L plans were occasionally used. For the most part, the terminals were unadorned architectural ensembles. One of their most essential elements was the heights of the loading platforms. Local delivery trucks had floor heights six to eight inches lower than long-haul trucks; the differences were bridged by various dock arrangements, such as ramps or elevators beneath truck wheels and plates to connect the truck floor and the dock. The docks were surrounded by yard that customarily offered twice as much room as the length of the biggest trucks pulling into and backing up to the docks.[66] Various combinations of manpower, dollies, and conveyor systems moved loads to and from the waiting trucks, with the exact configuration depending on the size of the carrier and the period when the work occurred, as technological developments resulted in improvements. These were laboring beehives punctuated by laconic and rude talk or shouting.

Truck stops, far better known than terminals, date from the 1920s and have been classified into four generations. Public visibility, contributing significantly to the common knowledge about truck stops from the outset, was the principal concern of the first generation. Inserted onto less developed land on the outskirts of towns, the first truck stops set up in a variety of buildings—some adapted houses or enlarged gasoline stations—and their sprawl often required that surrounding trees and plants be cleared. Truckers had to be reassured that they had sufficient space to pull off the road and maneuver. Stops combined restaurants and facilities for replenishing fuel and oil. One of the first to extend services beyond the essentials, the stop at McLean, Illinois, beside Route 66 opened in 1928 under the name Dixie Truckers Stop, sought to emulate something of the autoist's coveted feeling of home on the road by having overnight lodging and discounts for large fuel purchases. On Saturday nights during the Great Depression, an estimated one thousand truckers, tourists, and locals mingled there, listening to bands. Associated Oil's version in Sacramento, California, embodied the most up-to-date features in 1936 when it included a driver's clubroom furnished with showers, sleeping/resting facilities, and card tables. A lubrication facility offered fast service twenty-four hours a day. Like the gas stations known as "service stations" that added garage work to the sale of gas and oil, these most advanced truck stops were called "super service stations" in the trade literature, demonstrating the expanding consumer consciousness about motoring. The accelerated amount of trucking after World War II gave birth to a second generation of stops that pushed services even farther. Quarando's Texaco Terminal Service outside New Brunswick, New Jersey, for example, held truckers' paychecks forwarded by freight companies and offered wrecking service anywhere within fifty miles of the stop. Continuing the improvised site planning of the first-generation stops, the newer ones allowed automobiles and trucks to use the same entrances. Whatever fears autoists may have harbored about giant trucks did not matter to the owners of the new sites: customers were motoring in what was strictly a truckers' world. The scattering of parking spaces throughout the lot and between buildings, another identifying trait of the second-generation stops,[67] must only have heightened the tension for the mingling autoists.

With the rapid growth of interstate traffic by the early 1960s, the newest truck stops began to be more deliberately planned. Pure Oil's J. V. Sanner, who entered the truck stop business in 1934, led the way. In the latest iteration of truck stops, designers decided that private cars could be parked only "where they are safe from

Figure 9.4. A Third-Generation Truck Stop, the Deck Plaza at the Intersection of I-80 and Illinois 82 outside Geneseo, Illinois, c. 1965. Authors' collection.

the big boys' maneuvers," in the words of one motoring journalist.[68] Although cars and trucks still entered through a common path, parking was divided within the lot, with cars at the front of the main building and trucks at the rear (figure 9.4). Truckers remained the key customers, and services for them included the latest considerations. Parking lot size was maximized, partly by consolidating the buildings on each site. Decreasing profit margins, especially because of the rising cost of diesel fuel, an oversupply of truck stops, and rampant tax cheating, magnified considerations long present, resulting in a fourth generation of truck stops, known generally as travel stops or travel plazas. The relationship between truckers and tourists began to shift toward equality with these new facilities no longer principally the truckers' domain. The latest truck stops added the features of common roadside convenience stores for passenger car customers but retained the spacious aisles and inventories familiar to truckers, who took more time to shop than their car-driving counterparts. Museums, included at truck stops since the second generation, became more common. In late 2002, the world's largest truck stop, the TA Truckstop located on Iowa 80, created a standalone museum featuring the antique trucks collected by the facility's late manager, Bill Moon. Several motel chains "branded up," adding their lodging on site. Thus, diversification, a conventional means of achieving economic vitality, came into play. The fourth generation also included efforts to refurbish the truck stop's image as entrepreneurs such as Mapco Express sought locations close to small towns that would attract local as well as truckers' business. To demonstrate to its prospective small-town neighbors that it would be a desirable addition to the community, Mapco Express videotaped the convenience stores introduced into its travel centers.[69]

Truck stops thus continued to present new opportunities for the public to come into contact with truckers. Seeing did not mean greeting, however; travel centers largely perpetuated the separation of the two motoring worlds of blue-collar labor and white-collar recreation or work. Both types of motorists alighted at the same place after navigating safely around one another but refueled at different pumps and shopped at different stores, one sustaining the autoists' hectic pace and the other giving truckers rest. Would the truck stops' new small-town shoppers come to peer more thoughtfully into the truckers' world?

The Trucker's Experience

The specifics of the trucker's work experience have varied with the time and type of service they expedited. Few reliable treatments have examined specific cases, but a rare description of the typical ice truck driver in Detroit in 1919 reveals some of the difficulties of early intracity cartage. Driving a residential route that numbered between 180 and 220 customers, the amount of ice delivered each ten-hour day, six days a week, ranged between four thousand pounds in May and six thousand pounds in July. At each house, the driver cut, sawed, or picked hundred-pound blocks into halves or quarters and carried the ice at least to the residential doorstep and sometimes up stairways to apartment dwellers. Because iceboxes varied in shape, effective truckers remembered their customers' special capacities and shaped the ice outside, where splattered and melting ice chips caused fewer problems than inside customers' kitchens. Because work was based on commission, better incomes depended on satisfying customers' individual expectations while simultaneously querying new residents about their ice needs, since each trucker was expected to build his own customer base. Those who failed to build routes with two hundred stops were fired. At the end of each day, the deliveryman returned to the office to reconcile accounts, and any shortages were subtracted from the trucker's wages.[70]

Long-haul drivers especially are taken to be a cultural Other. Journalists' standard technique of traveling with a driver for a day or longer to report on the experience in a newspaper or magazine attests to this perception. Bryan Di Salvatore has written one of the most empathetic accounts of a contemporary long-haul driver, offering extensive details about truckers' tough work and consequent tough life. Lonnie Umphlett, an independent trucker who drove a flatbed truck throughout the country, shared with his guest a "five-thousand shift road" (trucker's

vernacular for a poorly paved, winding, and slow secondary road), sleeping overnight in the small provision behind the truck cab, carrying enough money to purchase a hundred gallons of gas at each refueling, calculating when best to arrive at
his destination to avoid congested city traffic, and keeping time at stops en route
to between thirty and forty-five minutes, including eating and refueling.[71] Truck
stops, however well they cater to truckers' dining, financial, and spiritual needs,
can offer at best "a faint—sincere, but faint—simulacrum of home."[72] Family, loved
ones, and domestic routines, however much the trucker might like them, seldom
claim his or her time. Daryl Wyckoff's study of 9,630 long-haul truckers in the
late 1970s found that they perceived the worst aspects of their work as monotony,
boredom, loneliness, lack of exercise, irregular hours, and separation from home.[73]
Conditioned by their work, relatively few truckers joined voluntary associations
except churches, in which only 15 percent acknowledged active membership.[74] In
Di Salvatore's words, "Oh, the open road! More than permanent transience, more
than constant anonymity, the defining aspect of the job of the American trucker is
loneliness. Separation."[75]

In 1953, *Nation* magazine concluded that long-haul truckers in Alabama "were
no better off than a share-cropper, being held in similar peonage" by their employers. Contracts required truckers to work exclusively for a particular company,
although the companies were not obligated to provide truckers with minimum
amounts of work.[76] Also in 1953, *Popular Science* luridly described cases of truck
hijacking, concluding with a trucker's six-point checklist for preventing a hijacking.[77] Seven years earlier, however, another trucker had claimed that hijacking was
far less common than had been the case during the 1930s.[78]

What could outweigh the disadvantages of separation? Wyckoff's study characterized truckers as "one of the largest indirectly supervised workforces in the
United States."[79] That independence attracted recruits. Detroit's ice truck drivers
in 1919, for example, often refused to wear the uniforms issued to them, drove their
routes differently each day, and put out of operation various monitoring devices
employers attempted to impose.[80] Magazines periodically spurred the admission of
novices through the allure of rising as far as one's talents permitted.[81] One trucker
told a magazine writer in 1947 that "there's a lot of responsibility, but it's all our
own—nobody else's."[82] Another survey in the late 1960s disclosed some conditions
underlying these buoyant exhortations: new truckers rarely ever considered professional occupations but clearly aspired to blue-collar employment. Most of them
had fathers who worked in the blue-collar trades or agriculture. They earned substantially more than was possible from other work, given their average 11.1 years of
education, and unlike other blue-collar workers felt their jobs to be comparatively
secure. They earned good and steady incomes, expected to remain truckers, and
believed that trucking would change little.[83]

Without constant surveillance, some truckers took advantage of their unusual working conditions. Driving too long without sleep was the most common liability of being one's own boss. As early as the 1940 Hollywood movie *They Drive by Night,* popular culture stoked the common perception of truckers as habitually tired. Teamsters president Frank Fitzsimmons cited a 1979 *New York Times* study in opposition to trucking deregulation, stereotyping the nonunion trucker as a thirty-eight-year-old man, overworked, overmortgaged, and misusing the CB radio to avoid detection while driving as fast as possible six days a week. Members of the public began to worry about truckers' using drugs to fight drowsiness—in the 1950s, Benzedrine and coffee. But Wyckoff's data from the 1970s showed that only 2 percent of truckers had dozed once or more at the wheel and that older drivers preferred to fight sleep by stopping, walking, washing their faces, and driving with the windows down, while younger drivers sang or talked to themselves, listened to the radio, or used the CB radio. Wyckoff concluded that truckers abused drugs, alcohol, and other substances far less than the "folklore of the road" indicated. Those who violated safe-driving practices did not feel proud and feared for themselves and others but also felt they had no choice because they needed to pay their debts and make their livings.[84]

Truckers were also far more careful of autoists than the latter may have thought. Umphlett's explanation of how he and other truckers viewed the highway surprised his passenger-writer. When the trucker asked Di Salvatore what he saw on the road, his answer was vague. Umphlett responded with a lecture: "I see a line of cars up the road. I'm concentrating on the eighth car ahead. And the sixth car. And on the fifth and the third and the rest. I'm lookin' at 'em all. The car that's just ahead, that's important, 'cause it's the one that's gonna get squarshed underneath this bad boy if something happens, but there's only so much I can do about that."[85] Another journalist aboard a truck for an article perceived that passenger cars dashed in front of trucks, pulling in too sharply and then "lazing along senselessly."[86]

Were truckers' and autoists' motoring experiences so fully engulfing that those aboard invariably had predispositions about each other? Writers traveling on assignment with truckers seem to have emerged with considerable respect for their courtesy, compassion, hard work, law-abiding tendency, and, most important, driving skills.[87]

The Imagined Trucker's Experience

Myth veiled trucking from its realities soon after the industry developed. In the 1930s, Teamsters president Daniel J. Tobin promoted a popular faith in truckers as good—decent, masculine, faithfully married family men. Nevertheless, outlawry of the worst sort—that is, association with organized crime—long tainted the public opinion of trucking. Teamsters president Jimmy Hoffa disappeared in 1975 and is widely believed to have been murdered by the Genovese crime family. In 1985, a presidential commission released a report, "The Edge: Organized Crime, Business, and the Labor Unions," that raised to national attention the claims that the Teamsters were the most mob-controlled union in the nation and that its leaders had been under mob domination since the 1950s. A succession of Teamster presidents imprisoned variously for income tax evasion, jury tampering, and attempted bribery of a U.S. senator magnified the union's notoriety. Teamsters' private lives bore a similar image.[88]

Lawrence Ouelett's monograph on trucking explains the personal dimensions of the trucker's mystique. Trucking offers a chance to stand out from modern society's crowd, to be the "last American cowboy," a "knight of the road," a "gypsy," or an "outlaw." *A Portrait of the Last American Cowboy,* as one of the first lengthy descriptions of trucking intended for a popular audience was subtitled, only burnished the mystique with hints of its decline. The highway can be likened to a stage, which truckers mount while wearing bold hats and driving customized vehicles. Seated above the mass of auto motorists, truckers command attention because of their vehicles' size, sound, and distinctive look. The development of "freightliners," fashioned after the streamliner railroad locomotives of the 1930s, when truckers condemned most of their vehicles as ungainly, illustrates how trucking became caught up in its image. According to Ouelett, autoists reinforce the belief that truckers are special because they are skilled at what they do, not amateurs at play or light work, like autoists. Autoists willingly assume second rank when they follow behind truckers in poor driving conditions. Truckers feed this aura of superiority, with many new recruits to the industry believing that trucking is manly and heroic. A study of behavior at one Oklahoma rest stop shows that some male truckers take up the theme of masculinity in CB conversations, approaching female drivers for sexual encounters, and that female prostitutes cater primarily to long-haul truckers, who are perceived as homogenous and available not only because of their work's facts (boredom and loneliness) but because of their masculine reputation. Some people see male truckers as sex objects. Ouelett records cases of women motorists who exposed themselves while driving beside trucks and on rare occasions offered sex.[89]

Popular culture infuses the myth. In 1946, for example, the *Saturday Evening Post* titled an article about the drivers of the big diesels in the West "Glamour Boys of the Highway."[90] Country and western musicians have contributed persuasively. One of the most popular early trucker songs, "Convoy" (1976), reflects the approved lawlessness and fundamental intelligence of the trucker image. Singer C. W. McCall describes a group of truckers using CB radios to evade the newly imposed and unfair fifty-five-mile-per-hour interstate speed limit.[91] Truckers had used CBS since the late 1960s, when transistors made them practical, but many people adopted the new technology when it offered assistance in evading the lower speed limit imposed as a consequence of the oil crisis of the early 1970s.[92] Yet the CB only came into wide use after its association with trucking was publicized. Truckers' vehicles were regularly upgraded to install the latest conveniences. Special Kenworth trucks, for example, were manufactured for the 1976 U.S. bicentennial celebration with the goal of attracting husband-and-wife trucking teams through such lures as a larger-than-average sleeping compartment with windows, 110-volt alternating current electrical hookups, chemical toilets, and bicentennial seals.[93]

In the last quarter of the twentieth century, the automobile motorist's ambivalent relationship with trucking led to increased interest in a comparatively new class of vehicles, pickups, minivans, and sport-utility vehicles, which became marketing sensations in the 1990s. The earliest variants date from Chevrolet's Cameo Carrier, a pickup for play, in 1957. Their future cannot be predicted, but they unquestionably have enabled motorists to co-opt many of the appealing traits of motoring by truck: their higher seats than cars, which fostered drivers' sense of control of the motoring environment; their heavier weights than cars, believed beneficial in case of an accident; and their perception as statements of drivers' personal styles. The white-collar consumers of those hybrids wanted the best of both their and the blue-collar truckers' lifestyles, the truck referencing the self-reliant and resilient cowboy and the car referencing the suburban sophisticate. The demand for greater fuel efficiency in these trucklike vehicles thus turned manufacturers to the production of vehicles handling more like cars but looking more like trucks.[94]

◆ ▼ ●

Motoring by truck is unique. Trucking is a highly visible medium with tremendous impact on lowering commodity costs, expanding inventories, diffusing products widely, and delivering them speedily. Americans have become dependent on all forms of motoring, but trucks have become especially vital. Trucking strikes induce panic among customers, who begin hoarding groceries and other necessities. Trains and planes only supplement.

The American way of life would not exist without motor trucks, but Americans know comparatively little of trucks and truckers. The absence of a reliable history of the trucking industry in America demonstrates the academic oversight. Trucks and truckers remain in many ways an invisible realm. Trucking is hard work, often threatening because of accidents on the road but also periodically because of criminal involvement, less from the standpoint of hijacking and more with regard to organized crime. Many Americans might guess those liabilities but know little of how daily motoring by truck is conducted. They know far more about motoring by car, RV, or trailer because the public in general goes motoring in these vehicles. Trucking is a blue-collar activity whose lifestyle implications most Americans want to escape or avoid altogether in favor of what they believe to be the elevated condition of the middle class, and people consequently feel comfortable substituting trucking folklore for trucking fact. Trucking is thereby transformed into another expression of motoring as play.

In fact, however, motoring by truck is foremost a way of working. It limits and defines its participants, not only while at work but in their time after work. Still, a trucker's daily bread and life off the road is not entirely doleful. As Wyckoff quoted a trucker saying insightfully, "I really like to drive trucks. It's a great life. I'd work for nothing as long as I had a good truck and trailer and a good run. But don't tell my boss about being willing to work for nothing."[95] Trucking is his livelihood, yet something of the romantic open road still appeals to this man.

motoring by bus

Out of motoring came the motor bus. Literally—early buses were luxury sedans enlarged to carry passengers. The precise origins of these motor buses are difficult to determine. Many early bus companies were started by taxi and jitney operators. Taxis were hired as need arose, although as early as 1907 a scheduled taxi service was initiated daily to connect Snyder, Texas, with nearby Colorado City.[1] Jitney drivers intercepted their customers—usually people waiting for streetcars—at curbside. The first jitney appeared in March 1914 in Long Beach, California, and the idea quickly spread to nearby Los Angeles.[2] Regularly scheduled bus service, involving set points of departure and arrival, may have started at Hibbing, Minnesota, as early as 1913.[3]

Like the jitneys, buses quickly became an alternative to streetcar use, but not because it provided an inherently superior ride. Rather, bus popularity was fostered by the streetcar's declining efficiency and convenience as a consequence of rapidly growing auto use. In the 1920s, the automobile had become the preferred means of travel to work, to shop, and to play. As one electric interurban railroad executive lamented, the private auto offered "comfort; it is easy, roomy, soft-seated. There is the power and speed of the machine. It is subject to the whims of the occupants. They can go as fast or as slow as they please, can go where when they please and come back when they please. They have control. The driver has the additional pleasure of driving and this may be shared. Companions, if any, are selected; there is almost privacy. There is an intimate and personal relationship with owner, driver and vehicle."[4]

The car's popularity negatively affected streetcar as well as electric interurban railway use in two important ways. First, streetcar ridership declined as commuters, shoppers, and other travelers increasingly drove themselves. Second, the resulting traffic congestion, at least in larger cities, slowed streetcar movement. With reduced ridership came declining profits, and transit companies, finding it increasingly difficult to upgrade or even maintain equipment, turned increasingly to motor buses. Buses were cheaper to build and cheaper to operate. Since they did not run on fixed tracks, routes could be readily adjusted to meet demand. Buses relieved congestion, proponents argued, by leaving open the center lanes of streets, unlike streetcars. Also unlike streetcars, buses could pull to the curb, and passengers were not required to board in midstreet, a practice that was becoming increasingly hazardous as traffic volume increased.[5]

Nonetheless, early buses were less comfortable than streetcars. Buses were smaller, with seats spaced closer together. Aisles were very narrow. "The bus is rougher to ride in and is more poorly ventilated," admitted one journalist. "It has an easier step because it loads at the curb, but hardly as comfortable a seat. It is harder for the strap hanger to keep his feet in a bus. The bus is perhaps not so easily nor so well heated. It is a lighter vehicle and therefore not so good a protection against injury to its passengers." Buses definitely offered less comfort than autos as well, he said. The bus did not share the "native attractiveness and desirability of the private auto." Nonetheless, economics, he predicted, would mandate that both streetcars and interurban cars would eventually be replaced by buses. Buses would continue to transport those without cars, that diminishing minority of Americans who would continue to rely on public transit.[6]

Bus Company Origins

In 1916, H. E. Jahn, in the delivery business in the northern Indiana town of Hanna, population 410, initiated a scheduled taxi service into La Porte, a larger town some sixteen miles distant. Service began with a single sedan customized to hold ten passengers. Six years later, the firm was covering 185 miles of highway with a fleet of fifteen motor buses (figure 10.1). Bus bodies were custom-built by Champion Auto Equipment of Hammond, Indiana, and were mounted on truck chassis built by various manufacturers. A compartment below the floor of each coach enabled Jahn to expand his package freight business. In 1922, the line carried 265,500 passengers. The operation was geared to the benefit of small-town residents wanting access to larger places: service began each day with buses running into rather than out of La Porte.[7]

Bus lines evolved quickly in response to perceived need. In Florida, buses catered to tourists, giving them access to resorts, especially those poorly served by railroad. In 1919, Florida Motor Transportation was formed through the merger of two pioneering bus lines centered on Miami: the White Star Auto Line, which connected to West Palm Beach, sixty-eight miles to the north, and the Clyde Passenger Express, which connected to Homestead, thirty-two miles to the south. Two years later, the company's northern terminal moved to Jacksonville. Demand

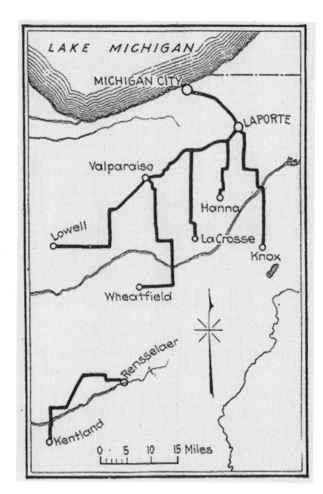

Figure 10.1. Map of Jahn Bus Company Routes, 1922. *Bus Transportation* 1 (September 1922): 469.

varied by season, with the company's buses carrying upward of fifty thousand passengers during the winter months but only twelve thousand during the summer. Since the company also owned a bus operation centered on Asheville, North Carolina, a summer tourist destination, officials shifted equipment seasonally, making the company what the industry came to call a migratory operation.[8]

The quality of an area's roads was an important enabling factor. Where highways were hard surfaced, travel by bus was more reliable, more comfortable, and accordingly more attractive. The declining popularity of electric railway travel also contributed to the growth of bus ridership. In 1928, the Detroit Union Railway, whose lines radiated out of Detroit, created a subsidiary, Eastern Michigan Motorbus, by purchasing and merging eleven previously independent bus companies. The railroad, owned by public utility interests, thereby accelerated abandonment of its unprofitable routes and set the stage for big business to dominant the state's intercity bus operations.[9] Although every American city of size had bus lines radiating out across the surrounding hinterland, bus connections between metropolitan regions remained tenuous, with long-distance passenger travel still dominated by the steam railroads.

Early Bus Technology

Operator success with customized automobiles fostered evolution of the motor bus as a distinctive vehicle. Bus manufacturers tended to be companies reoriented from other activities. Some firms—primarily former carriage and wagon makers—built only bus bodies. Manufactured to fit standard truck chassis, bodies were sent off to one or another truck maker for final assembly into buses. Other companies not only built bodies but also purchased truck chassis and performed the final assembly work themselves. And finally, some truck manufacturers built bodies and chassis and did the final assembly work. McKay Bus of Grove City, Pennsylvania, built nothing except bus bodies, one style provisioned with cross seats and another with side seats. With the latter, passengers sat facing one another, an arrangement satisfactory for short-distance commuting or other travel, such as transporting children to school (figure 10.2).

More practical for long-distance travel was the "parlor-style" coach. The one made initially by Fitzjohn Manufacturing of Muskegon, Michigan, was designed to fit a Reo Model FB 143-inch wheelbase chassis (figure 10.3). This bus could carry twelve passengers: six in front-facing seats (four on the left and two on the right, separated by a fourteen-inch aisle), two on small side benches placed over the rear wheel housings, and four on a bench placed across the back of the coach. There were two doors, the main one up front on the right opposite the driver and an emergency door in the back on the left. Windows, arranged five to a side, could be opened for ventilation. Luggage was carried on a rail-enclosed roof rack at the rear of each coach that was accessed via an outside ladder.[10]

Besides Reo, other leading truck manufacturers that assembled buses early on included Garford Motor Truck of Lima, Ohio; International Harvester of Chicago; Packard of Detroit, and White of Cleveland. In 1927, 105 coach builders and nine vehicle assemblers combined to produce 7,770 coach bodies. Most—an estimated 2,770 (36 percent of the total)—were for school buses. Intercity motor buses came next, with an estimated 2,470 (32 percent).[11]

The sedan-style motor bus or "motor stage" evolved on the Pacific Coast. The inside was divided into four compartments separated by partitions, the upper portions of which were made of plate glass. The first compartment contained the

Figure 10.2. Advertisement for McKay Bus with Side Seating. *Power Wagon Reference Book 1920* (Chicago: Power Wagon, 1920), 514.

Figure 10.3. Advertisement for Fitzjohn Coach with Cross-Seating. *Bus Transportation* 6 (February 1927): 4.

driver's seat, while the second was for baggage. The third contained two front-facing bench seats, each with doors on either side. The fourth compartment contained two rear-facing benches (reserved for smokers), and had doors that "gave an unobstructed view as from the rear platform of [a railroad] observation car."[12] Running boards helped the eighteen passengers access their seats. By 1926, larger deck-and-a-half and double-decker motor coaches were common, at least on bus routes from California north to Oregon and Washington. Pacific Northwest Traction of Everett, Washington, expanded its train service with deck-and-a-half buses between Vancouver, British Columbia, and Seattle. An elevated "observation deck" at the rear, positioned over an enclosed luggage compartment, enabled twelve passengers facing forward to look out over the roof of the lower forward section, where the driver and seventeen passengers sat.[13] By 1930, Pickwick Bus placed into

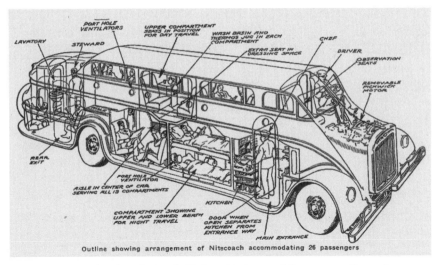

Outline showing arrangement of Nitecoach accommodating 26 passengers

Figure 10.4. The Pickwick Night Coach. *Highway Engineer and Contractor* 19 (September 1928): 67.

service "duplexes," buses with two complete decks capable of carrying more than fifty passengers.

Night Coaches

The most impressive duplex buses were the night coaches or motor sleepers, also introduced by Pickwick and manufactured, like the company's day-coach duplexes, at its Los Angeles shop (figure 10.4). Pickwick was among the nation's earliest intercity bus operators. In 1912, the company began transporting passengers along a 124-mile route connecting towns in California's Imperial Valley with San Diego. In San Diego, customers boarded coaches in front of the landmark Pickwick Theater, from which the bus line took its name. The company expanded to the north and in 1922 offered five-times-a-day, seventeen-hour service between Los Angeles and San Francisco over a 455-mile route. By 1926, routes had been extended even further north to Seattle by way of Portland and east to El Paso by way of Phoenix and Tucson.[14]

One journalist described Pickwick's motor sleeper as looking something like a "gleaming submarine on pneumatic tires," a reference to the small portholes that complemented the bus's large windows. The bus was also fully streamlined. "There is no hood as on an ordinary stage," he observed, "the portion of the body containing the driver's compartment being built directly over the motor." From its tapered nose to the rounded rear section, which cantilevered out behind the rear axle, the bus appeared "graceful as a yacht." Passengers, the writer noted, entered on the right side at the front and stepped up into a compact kitchen or galley before entering a narrow center aisle. Thirteen compartments arrayed on two levels could then be entered by either stepping up or stepping down. With curtains drawn aside, each compartment was revealed to be a "little stateroom" with wide cushioned chairs facing one other. At night the chairs folded down and the addition of a thin mattress created a bed. A lavatory/dressing room was located at the rear of the bus. The bus was thirty-four feet long, eight feet wide, and ten feet tall and carried twenty-six passengers plus a crew of three: a driver, a steward, and a porter. "It will doubtless mean in highway transportation what the Pullman has meant to railroad travel, and will remove the last objection to motor stage travel between far distant parts," the article concluded.[15]

The early twentieth century was a time of very rapid technological development, and perhaps it is not surprising that buses evolved so rapidly both in size and in mechanical sophistication. By 1930, gasoline-electric buses operated, and diesel-electric buses were in the planning stage. Coaches were heated, and some even had crude air-conditioning. Edward Motor Transit ran a route from Williamsport, Pennsylvania, to New York City on which it equipped buses with ice bunkers from which cold air was blown into the coach. One filling of a bunker was sufficient for a three-hour run in the hottest of weather.[16] A few bus companies experimented with radio, not for dispatch purposes but to entertain passengers, with a receiver at each seat. The bus trailer was another innovation. When demand exceeded bus capacity—for example, on weekends in tourist areas—trailers capable of seating as many as twenty additional passengers could be attached, a more economical approach than adding an extra bus.

Government Regulation

In 1929, roughly 6,200 motor carriers operated some 35,250 buses over approximately 719,000 miles of route. Steam railroads, in comparison, ran 55,000 passenger cars over 350,000 miles of line. In addition, electric railroads operated about 80,000 transit cars over 40,000 miles of track.[17] Although many bus routes paralleled and thus duplicated rail lines, these statistics suggest that bus routes also extended well beyond areas served by rail. Although common carrier buses accounted for four billion passenger miles in 1929, the bus industry's share of the nation's passenger business remained less than 15 percent of what the railroads carried.[18] Bus routes connected most parts of the country, and route patterns were quite dense in many states, especially in southern New England, parts of the Lower Midwest, and parts of the Upper South.

The rapid improvement of public highways, providing bus operators with ready-made "roadbeds," coupled with the relatively low capital investment that buses required, fostered a scramble of small entrepreneurs into the bus business nearly everywhere. An oversupply of service quickly resulted in most localities. Brisk competition drove operators to reduce costs by putting into service unsafe vehicles, overworking drivers, and otherwise jeopardizing public safety. When bus companies were threatened with insolvency, service might be curtailed or abruptly abandoned and the public greatly inconvenienced. In 1925, thirty-five states regulated bus operators to reduce excessive competition and thereby encourage more stable service. Most state regulating commissions assigned intercity routes, approved schedules, set fares, imposed safety standards, and even mandated the kind of equipment that could be used. Most states required operators to file annual business reports, imposing uniform accounting practices in the process. States oversaw company incorporation and of course licensing as well as the licensing of drivers and vehicles.[19] State governments also imposed taxes—for example, sales taxes on both the fuel that buses consumed and the tickets that customers purchased. Some states required periodic vehicle inspections. Many states required bus operators to be bonded or to carry liability insurance.

Largely in response to government regulation, bus operators banded together in state trade associations. In 1922, for example, operators formed the Kentucky Bus Owners Association, whose members operated thirty-nine buses over 565 route miles centered largely on Lexington. The association's president, J. E. Kittrell, also served as head of the Lexington Automotive Trades Association; in addition to owning a bus company, he also owned part of Lexington's Reo Motor Car, a sales and service garage.[20] Most importantly, trade associations lobbied for legislation favorable to the bus industry and opposed unfavorable legislation. Most associations held annual meetings and published newsletters and other materials; some also organized self-insurance programs.[21] National organizations also existed, among them the National Association of Bus Operators and the National Bus Traffic Association, which established uniform nationwide ticketing and baggage-handling practices.

Railroad Bus Operations

America's steam railroads were lucky to break even in the passenger business given the Interstate Commerce Commission's requirement that the railroads provide service even on poorly traveled branch lines. However, as with the electric interurban railroads, substituting buses for trains promised substantially to reduce railroad operating costs. By 1928, U.S. operating costs stood at an average of $1.10 per passenger mile for passenger trains but $0.25 per mile for buses.[22] Routing of motor coaches was of course highly flexible, which was not the case for passenger trains. Unlike trains, buses moved through the main streets of towns and cities and did not suffer from smoke, cinders, and noise. Trains moved only between stations, but motor buses could pick up passengers at intervening locations.

Railroads entered the bus business either by operating buses themselves or more commonly by creating bus subsidiaries that operated independently. In a very few instances, the parent railroad owned the bus equipment and the bus subsidiary merely represented an operating organization with nominal capitalization. In 1929, thirty railroads or their subsidiaries carried a total of 50 million bus passengers over twenty-five thousand miles of route.[23] Railroads in the densely populated Northeast led the way: the New York, New Haven, and Hartford carried 4.3 million bus passengers, the Boston and Maine carried 1.4 million, and the Reading carried 910,000.[24] Many western railroads also came to rely on busing. Northland Transportation, a subsidiary of the Great Northern Railroad, extended passenger service away from its parent company's Minnesota lines. The Southern Pacific Railroad organized Southern Pacific Transport around its purchase of Pickwick Stages. In 1936, the Interstate Commerce Commission adopted the "Barker doctrine," which dictated that railroad motor bus operations must be strictly auxiliary or supplementary to railroad operations and must be confined to areas immediately adjacent to railroad lines. The rule substantially dampened railroad enthusiasm for direct rail-bus linkage and encouraged the railroads to foster an independent bus industry. Indeed, if bus companies replaced all passenger service, or so the thinking went, railroads could concentrate solely on profitable freight haulage.

Consolidation

Early in the 1920s, bus company mergers largely involved routes radiating outward from given urban centers. By 1929, however, when 161 companies were merged to form 44 new bus systems, consolidation tended more toward end-to-end combinations, thus fostering long-distance bus travel between metropolitan areas. Consolidation also linked regions by encouraging transcontinental bus routes. The Greyhound bus system was born through the affiliation of three already large bus systems: Southern Pacific Transport (which included Pickwick), the Yelloway System, and Greyhound of Chicago (both of which were owned by Motor Transit, itself controlled by the Great Northern Railroad). Yelloway had offered the first transcontinental bus service after absorbing, a year earlier, both Pioneer Stages and Pioneer-Eastern Stages.[25]

The origins of the Greyhound Corporation stretch well back into busing's earliest history. In 1913, Carl Wickman, an auto dealer, initiated scheduled bus service between Hibbing and Alice in Minnesota's Mesabi Range mining district. Three years later, he incorporated as Mesaba Transportation. In 1922, Wickman sold out to the Great Northern Railway but remained with the firm to direct its reorganization as Northland Transportation. Five years later, a holding company, Motor Transit, was formed, embracing both Northland and western Michigan's Safety Motor Coach, a line that operated its buses under the Greyhound name. Motor Transit absorbed other firms, including bus lines owned by various of Samuel Insull's public utility companies, giving Motor Transit substantial control of bus routes in and out of Chicago.[26] Motor Transit, the primary holding company, became Northland Greyhound, but a year later that name was simplified to just Greyhound.

A host of Greyhound affiliates were rapidly established (including Pickwick-Greyhound, Pacific Greyhound, Southland Greyhound, Eastern Greyhound, Capitol Greyhound, and Richmond Greyhound), some with their own subsidiaries operated under one or another Greyhound name. Pennsylvania General Transit, the bus subsidiary of the Pennsylvania Railroad, affiliated as Pennsylvania Greyhound.[27] Dixie Greyhound was formed through merger of several previously independent companies focused on St. Louis, Memphis, and Jackson, Tennessee (figure 10.5). Ownership of the Greyhound system was, to say the least, quite complex. In 1933, the combined system operated 844 buses with seating capacity for 27,000 passengers.[28]

National Trailways was organized in 1935, with forty-six members affiliating to form another bus system offering transcontinental service. Bus subsidiaries of the Atchison, Topeka, and Santa Fe and Chicago, Burlington, and Quincy railroads formed its two principal segments. A year later, they, along with twenty-eight other Trailways partners, merged under the ownership of the Continental Bus System, with Trailways affiliation continuing. The Interstate Commerce Commission also certified All-American Bus Lines as a transcontinental carrier. In 1941, it became a subsidiary of the Burlington Railroad and consequently a member of the National Trailways Bus System as well.[29]

Tour Buses

By 1950, Greyhound and Trailways together controlled nearly half of the nation's intercity bus market as measured in terms of miles driven.[30] However, small bus companies continued to thrive, especially those that connected major cities, filling gaps in the two national systems. One such company, Illini Swallow Lines, linked Indianapolis; Peoria, Illinois; and Davenport, Iowa. Many small companies, like Illini Swallow, committed heavily to the excursion business, providing guided-tour services as well as fulfilling charter or contract work. Through a subsidiary, Parkhill Tours, Illini Swallow even opened a dude ranch in Montana to serve as a

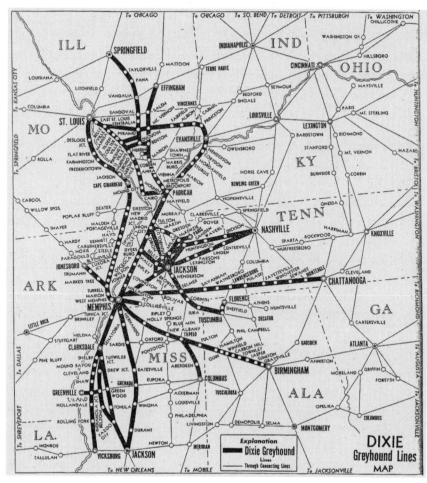

Figure 10.5. Dixie Greyhound Lines Map. *Russell's Official National Motor Coach Guide* (Cedar Rapids, Iowa: Russell's Guides, 1949), 156.

Figure 10.6. Parkhill Tour Departing for the West, Champaign, Illinois, c. 1935. Courtesy of the Illini Swallow Bus Lines.

destination for bus tours (figure 10.6). In 1925, the United States had twenty-five hundred "sightseeing, tourist and contract buses" in operation, most of them on city tour routes. Buses also were very important in the national parks. At Yellowstone in 1926, for example, 275 tour buses carried sightseers.[31]

A sightseeing tour was usually circular in that it began and ended at the same point. The Santa Fe Railroad, however, developed the travel "detour," diverting passengers off of its trains at either Las Vegas or Albuquerque in New Mexico for a three-day excursion through Indian country. The railroad's Fred Harvey subsidiary purchased and operated New Mexico Motorways, which eventually became Santa Fe Trailways. Excursionists stayed at Fred Harvey hotels, including the La Fonda in Santa Fe.[32] As the editors of *Bus Transportation* reported, "Light, heavily upholstered leather swivel chairs placed four on each side of a central aisle, together with a similarly upholstered cross-seat at the rear, accommodate the eleven passengers. The swivel chair permits the passenger a view out of all windows of the bus."[33]

Bus Terminals

In the early years, passengers on most bus lines boarded and unloaded at curbside—for example, in front of a landmark building or along the side of a public square. In 1926, Lewis Freeman described his bus travels: "In La Fayette Square, Buffalo, a starter employed by the line to Rochester kindly stored my bags in a waiting bus while I sought information as to service on my next jump westward. In Cleveland, I was dropped on one side of the big public square and had to carry my luggage three blocks to where a starter, with voice and methods of a Coney Island barker, was drumming up passengers for the bus which runs to a point in Ohio." In Chicago he was dropped off in front of one hotel but left for St. Louis from another location blocks away.[34] Many bus lines had ticket offices in hotels, with hotel lounges doubling as passenger waiting rooms. On long trips, passengers needed periodic access to restrooms. At first, many bus operators simply stopped at railroad stations so that passengers could use public toilets. One step up in bus operations was the bus terminal housed in a rented storefront; passengers continued to board buses at the curb in the open air (figure 10.7).

Not only did makeshift facilities prove inadequate with increased bus popularity, but hotels—especially higher-class establishments—became increasingly reluctant to accommodate bus passengers, who tended to be of modest income. And many bus passengers of all social classes, in turn, felt uncomfortable in formal hotel settings. Travelers often arrived tired and disheveled, as Freeman described: "Men and women tumbling out at a rest stop . . . are not comfortable entering a lobby full of comparatively well-groomed people such as would be found in the leading small city hotels all over the country. If there is any worse snob then the under clerk of a small town hotel, it is the bell-hop of the same institution."[35] What was really needed, certainly in the larger places, were purpose-built bus terminals where passengers would feel at home and where the logistics of loading and unloading could be efficiently accomplished off the street and under cover. Bus interests, chambers of commerce, and municipal governments vigorously advocated the creation of combined "union" bus depots.

Through the 1930s, four types of bus terminals evolved, differentiated by how buses came and went. At the Union Stage Depot in Los Angeles, opened in 1922, passengers entered through the front door, bought their tickets at a counter in the large waiting room, and then stepped outside through a side door to the street to board buses (figure 10.8). Concessions included a lunchroom, a drugstore, a cigar and notions store, and a bootblack stand. The terminal was run as a not-for-profit operation, with the eight participating companies paying a percentage of their gross ticket receipts toward the building's maintenance and debt reduction.[36] At the Union Bus Station in Madison, Wisconsin, opened in 1928 by Wisconsin Power and Light, passengers bought tickets and waited on an upper level. As buses were announced by gate, travelers descended on the appropriate stairways to loading platforms below. Each bus had a separate lane and passed through the terminal, with no backing or other maneuvering necessary.[37] By far the most frequently used terminal layout was the stub type, where buses angled into loading slots either inside a building or outside under shed roofs. However, New York

Figure 10.7. Intermountain Transportation Bus Depot at Anaconda, Montana, 1930. *Bus Transportation* 9 (September 1930): 488.

Figure 10.8. Union Stage Depot, Los Angeles, 1922. *Bus Transportation* 1 (May 1922): 275.

City's Central Union Bus Terminal, opened in 1931, was located in the basement of the Dixie Hotel and used a turntable. "Buses enter and leave by separate ramps, to and from a turntable," observed one reporter. "This swings the bus then in line with the loading stalls which radiate from the turn table like spokes from a wheel hub. Passengers reach the buses from the adjacent waiting room through two sets of doors. These lead to concourses which form the rim of the wheel."[38]

Pickwick Stages did not relish sharing its terminals, at least in the largest cities it served. In San Diego in 1928, the company bought a three-hundred-room hotel and renamed it the Pickwick, intending to use part of the building as a terminal. The company then began constructing wholly new hotel/bus station complexes, first in San Francisco and then in Portland and Phoenix. The grandest project of all opened in Kansas City in 1930. According to one reporter, "The terminal itself consists of two levels flanked on one side by a commodious waiting room where passengers can satisfy their every need. Entrances lead directly to Kansas City's newest and largest hotel, the Pickwick, a hostelry of 500 rooms, fitted up in 1930 style. To the left of the terminal proper is an 800-car storage garage, with drive-in entrances separate and distinct from those used by the buses." One hundred thousand people toured the facility the day it was dedicated.[39]

Pickwick's building of hotel-oriented terminals ended when the company became part of Greyhound. All across the nation, Greyhound built new terminals intended to echo in architectural styling the streamlining of its buses. The buildings, with art deco and streamlined modern decor, featured low silhouettes, extensive areas of window coursed horizontally, facades curved at main entrances, signs integrated into the facades, and facades brightly colored with the company's signature blue, gray, and white (figure 10.9). Greyhound thus adopted place-product-packaging as a means of establishing a clear corporate identity. Not only did the buildings look alike on the outside, but inside they were similarly programmed—that is, arranged, furnished, decorated, signed, and staffed more or less the same everywhere.

Greyhound also established a system of look-alike Post House Restaurants, at first with lunch counters and table service and then with cafeteria lines. Self-service speeded up eating, which was essential to keeping buses running on schedule. Post Houses were decorated in knotty-pine paneling. Those located in small towns, usually at important junction points in the Greyhound route network, were configured both inside and out to resemble stagecoach stops, with buildings tending to follow a standard format: 1½ stories, gable roofs with front-facing dormers, windows with shutters, and front porches. The restaurant's city locations bore a kind of early American styling that owed much to Colonial Williamsburg's 1930s restoration. In 1955, 147 Post Houses operated.[40]

Figure 10.9. Greyhound Bus Depot, Minneapolis, 1937. Lake County, Illinois, Museum, Curt Teich Postcard Archives.

Bus Innovation

Numerous manufacturers remained in the bus-building business as late as 1950, including Aerocoach, Beck, Crown, Fitzjohn, Flexible (sometimes spelled Flxible), Mack, and White. However, General Motors's GMC Coach Division accounted for 51 percent of the market thanks both to its dominance of the city transit business and to its lucrative relationship with Greyhound. But five years later, when GMC controlled 81 percent of the market, it faced antitrust litigation. The company was charged with buying or buying control of competitors, coercing bus companies to accept GM employees as board members (thus influencing bus purchases), and denying competing manufacturers access to improved technologies (for example, diesel engines and automatic transmissions).[41]

GM collaborated with Greyhound in the design of buses, delivering two thousand new Silversides in 1947 and 1948.[42] Of all of the company's models, however, the Scenicruiser, introduced in 1954, dominated Greyhound service into the 1980s (figure 10.10). The bus was described as having a spacious rear passenger deck elevated above the forward seating area, thus providing "unequaled sightseeing opportunities." A wide windshield curved around the entire forward section of this upper level, giving an unobstructed view of the road ahead. "The degree of visibility from all angles," a Greyhound annual report claimed, "is unmatched by any other public transportation vehicle, and greatly increases the passengers' view of passing scenery—one of the major attractions of bus travel."[43]

Figure 10.10. The Scenicruiser's Observation Deck. Greyhound, *Annual Report* (Chicago: Greyhound, 1955): front cover.

One journalist rode a Scenicruiser specifically to write for a popular magazine (in which Greyhound was an important advertiser). "From the glassed-in observation deck of a fabulous new superbus, known to its drivers as 'the Mighty Monster,' I enjoyed a ringside seat at one of the greatest shows on earth—my fellow Americans at work and play amidst the glorious scenery of the Eastern Seaboard," he wrote. The driver, who sat with his feet on a level with the rooftops of passing cars, easily scanned the road ahead. "At his finger tips were power steering, power brakes, and an electrically controlled, 8-speed, push-button gear shift. Just behind him was a 10-passenger forward deck and then a short flight of steps leading to a glassed-in observation deck, where 33 more of us travelers reclined in foam-rubber contour chairs gazing out at the sights through tinted picture windows, overhead skylights, and a panoramic windshield."[44] By the end of 1960, more than thirty-two hundred of these buses were in service.[45]

The Flexible Company designed the Vistaliner for Continental Trailways, delivering 208 of the buses.[46] Trailways also imported buses from Kassbohrer Fahrzenwerke in Ulm, Germany, and in 1962 set up a factory in Belgium (later moved to Texas) to produce its luxurious Golden Eagle and its toned-down Silver Eagle buses. According to one journalist, "Both silver and gold coaches have comfortable reclining seats; footrests; rest rooms with washbasins, mirrors, and electrical outlets; wide windows; blankets and pillows for passenger rest." But the Golden Eagle coaches had only fifteen seats to the Silver Eagle's twenty-nine and therefore offered greater leg room. In addition, the Golden Eagle featured two lounges for card games and letter writing and a galley with "a red-and-golden uniformed hostess to run it, ready to offer coffee, tea, or snacks at the wave of a hand."[47]

Bus Travelers

Who rode the nation's intercity buses? By and large, bus travelers came not from the upper class or even the middle class but from among those people who, for whatever reason, lacked cars or did not wish to drive or who could not afford to fly or even take a train. Cost constituted the bus's most attractive feature. Intercity buses became the preferred mode of travel for Americans on limited incomes: students going to college, soldiers and sailors reporting for duty or returning home on leave, workers searching for employment. In the late 1970s, bus travelers paid approximately five cents per mile, train passengers paid ten cents per mile, and motoring in a private car cost between fifteen and eighteen cents per mile. In 1974, Trailways offered a $149 Eagle Pass, which offered unlimited travel throughout the United States for thirty days.[48] Observed one writer, "Senior citizens, long canny about stretching limited retirement income and with sufficient time for leisurely travel, have been bus buffs for years. School teachers with flexible summer schedules and foreign visitors with their economical unlimited travel passes also are enthusiasts. And recently, as inflation soars, more and more families have discovered that *seeing* America by bus is really seeing America, not flying *over* it."[49]

Other reasons for motoring by bus also existed, of course. It allowed travelers to see the real United States, the fundamental aspects of the nation comprised of its "real" people and places. Relishing the success of *On the Road*, Jack Kerouac wrote in *Esquire* in 1970, "Exhausting or not, there's no better way to see the [country] than to take a good old bus and go battling along on regular roads and come to all kinds of towns and cities where you can get out and walk sometimes a whole hour and see the world and come back to your bus and drive on." At Butte, Montana, he did just that. "Arriving, I stored my bag in a locker while some young Indian cat asked me to go drinking with him; he looked too crazy. I walked the sloping streets in super below-zero weather with my handkerchief tied tight around my leather collar, and saw that everybody in Butte was drunk. It was Sunday night. I had hoped the saloons would stay open long enough for me to see them. They never even closed. In a great old-time saloon I had a giant beer."[50]

More than just prowling around terminals or, for that matter, looking out of bus windows put travelers in touch with America. America could be experienced inside the buses as well. "Save for a soldier from Fort Bliss and myself," Freeman wrote of a 1926 bus trip across Arizona, "the passengers filling all the rest of the seats were Mexican peons and their families on their way to pick cotton in the Salt River reclamation project near Phoenix." The people and their personal effects, including bedrolls, made for a colorful sight.[51] Of course, bus travelers also commented on what they saw of the road and the roadside. In 1935, Bertram Fowler observed that during the daytime, buses slowly twisted and turned through Connecticut's villages and towns and shot along the straightaways outside the cities. "Filling stations splash their arresting hues against dull backgrounds, the 'hot-dog stand' and the roadside shop flaunt their stiff banners of commercial appeal," he wrote. But at night Connecticut seemed a different place. One by one the filling stations snapped off their lights, retiring into darkness. And the midnight express, the "king of the highway," took over the road: "It booms up a long grade. Ahead, twin red lights blink and the high, wide back of a lumbering truck looms hugely in the headlights. The probing finger of a searchlight shoots out from the bus. . . . The truck edges toward the side of the road with a muted blast of the horn. The bus roars past."[52]

Bus travelers could socialize; indeed, it was almost impossible not to interact with one's fellow passengers. In Mary Day Winn's opinion, buses featured a "spirit of *camaraderie* . . . such as one seldom finds on a train." Trains, she thought, were formal. Buses were not. "People in the little, self-contained unit are within sight and hearing of each other; all bump through the same mud hole at the same time, swallow the same cloud of dust from a passing car, look out simultaneously to thrill and exclaim over the same view." At rest stops, invariably everyone got out "to stand around the huge vehicle like a flock of chickens round a mother hen, smoking, gossiping, and munching chocolate bars."[53] Perhaps passengers socialized the most while eating at rest stops. "We all quickly became friends," wrote Nathan Asch of a western bus trip in 1934. "The little girl who with her mother was going back to Texas acquired many almost-fathers and many packages of chewing gum and peanuts. The German boy, university saber-cuts bright upon his cheeks . . . asked questions [and] was told stories of the West. A truckman said that when he had been working on a pipe line in Oklahoma, for an eye-opener he and the others had drunk mixed gasoline and buttermilk." The student did not believe him.[54]

Those who traveled to collect experiences for articles and books boarded buses largely to validate expectations. "I expected to be crowded and elbowed, overcome by carbon monoxide, and overrun by screaming little people with sticky hands and bubble gum," confessed Don Eddy after a 1956 bus trip. "I can report now that not one of those things happened. I was never uncomfortable, never shoved around, never too cold or too warm, never annoyed."[55] Writing for *Holiday,* Kerouac was less flattering. "There's hardly anything in the world, or at least in America, more miserable than a transcontinental bus trip with limited means. More than three days and nights wearing the same clothes, bouncing around into town after town; even at three in the morning when you've finally fallen asleep, there you are being bounced over the railroad track of a town, and all the lights are turned on bright to reveal your raggedness and weariness in the seat." Then there were the dreadful stretches, especially lonely at night, between equally dreadful cities, "all of them looking the same when seen from the bus of woes, the never-get-there bus stopping everywhere, and worst of all the string of fresh enthusiastic drivers every two or three hundred miles warning everyone to relax and be happy."[56]

◆ ▼ ●

America's love affair with the automobile fostered rapid development of the nation's roads. Highway improvement, in turn, encouraged travel by bus. In 1956, two thousand bus companies engaged in the intercity passenger business, half of them in interstate service. They operated more than twenty thousand buses, servicing an estimated forty thousand communities. Bus travel accounted for approximately 30 percent of all intercity passenger miles by public carrier and about 4 percent of the total estimated intercity travel, including that by automobile.[57] In 1963, airlines had come to account for some 42 percent of all intercity travel handled by public carriers, with buses handling about 25 percent and trains about 18 percent.[58] Deregulation of the airlines in 1978, followed by deregulation of trucking and busing in 1980, started a downward spiral for Greyhound and Trailways, and both companies eliminated service to much of rural and small-town America. However, the continued popularity of the automobile and of motoring by car constituted the bus industry's most perplexing problem. As more and more Americans owned and drove automobiles, the industry's customer base dwindled. Cars were simply too comfortable, too convenient, and fundamentally too empowering.

convenience
in store

Some of the cultural values considered fundamental in America might include the intense privileging of individual prerogative, the sustained embrace of mobility and change, the mechanistic vision of a substantially utilitarian world, and an almost messianic drive for perfection.[1] The United States has traditionally defined such phenomena as opportunity, success, and progress largely in personal terms. Community, for its part, has been thought of principally in political terms, with the role of government calculated mainly to enhance individual liberties and freedoms. Based on an essentially capitalistic economy, American society has embraced still other values, impulses undoubtedly rooted in those listed earlier but nonetheless commonly expressed in other terms. The word *convenience* frequently crops up.[2] The concept is closely related to speed and efficiency as well as to cost and to price. In our highly materialistic world, identity rests substantially on what individuals consume. And what they consume often as not involves getting as much as possible for the dollar and getting it as quickly as possible and whenever need arises.

Perhaps not the embrace of convenience as much as the avoidance of inconvenience defines the American character. It has been said that convenience is like oxygen: only its absence truly arouses attention.[3] As consumers, Americans have come to prize quick efficiency. As a result, retailers have sped up the buying process with self-serve counters, pay-as-you-exit cashiers, and bar-code scanning and computerized credit card processing, innovations originally intended to reduce labor costs that have also made purchasing more customer friendly and therefore faster. In the auto age, convenience has also come in the form of off-street parking close to store entrances and drive-in, drive-up, and later drive-through facilities for certain kinds of retailing. Motorists today make many purchases without even leaving their cars.

These developments resulted from the same "time and motion" thinking that revolutionized industrial production through such labor-saving innovations as standardization of parts and moving assembly lines. In retailing, however, customers became part of the production process. The customer picked up and carried intended purchases to the cashier. The customer ordered, perhaps through a speaker, and then drove to a window to pay for and receive sandwiches, clean shirts, or prescription drugs. The customer pumped gas, even paying for it at the pump with a credit card. Employing customers in the delivery of goods and services enabled retailers to reduce labor costs, as fewer employees translated into fewer paychecks. But such changes also had empowering implications for the customer. Customers shared in determining the pace of delivery and often found their efforts rewarded through lower prices.

Convenience, especially through automation, promised time savings. When automatic teller machines were located along driveways, bank customers no longer had to park, walk into a building, and queue at a teller's window just to cash checks. Drive-up windows at banks originally required the filling out of forms and the awkward passing of money, often by pneumatic tube. Today, from inside the car, one merely inserts a bank card and punches in a numerical code, and the cash comes tumbling out. Such convenience is very much a modern imperative, the belief that life's activities ought to be fully rationalized for efficiency and that accordingly everyday occurrences ought fully to reflect functionality.[4] Modernity is part and parcel of capitalism's constant "creative destruction," whereby market competition fosters, through ever-present technological change, repeated rounds of investment and profit taking.[5]

The act of motoring fostered substantial change, of course, although much of it, at least as far as the built environment was concerned, was makeshift and ephemeral. Early on, roadside commercial buildings were very ordinary, built of cheap materials and with shoddy workmanship. They used flashy color schemes and large signs, mostly to gain as much customer attention as possible at minimal cost. Such exuberance, critics charged, rarely masked the mundane but only symbolized the vulgar. Although some Americans found the nation's new commercial roadsides unpleasant, most did not. And nearly everyone, irrespective of aesthetic sensitivity, used the nation's new car-oriented facilities on an ever-increasing basis. Motoring's convenience became intoxicating, perhaps too intoxicating for most Americans to think deeply about the motor car's landscape implications.

Fast Food and Drive-ins

The clock closely regulated the lives of factory workers, clerical workers, and retail clerks. Time for eating at noon, when rural Americans had traditionally taken their heaviest meal, was very short. Thus evolved the lunch, a light repast to be eaten very much on the run. Restaurants featuring "quick service," especially by frying eggs, meat, and potatoes, became popular, largely in the form of lunchrooms located along business streets and especially near streetcar stops and factory gates.

With the coming of Prohibition, confectionary stores, drugstores, and five-and-ten stores such as Woolworth's and Kresge's added soda fountains to emphasize ice cream concoctions. When customers began using automobiles, however, quick-service eating began to change. In 1920, the operators of the Pig Stand Restaurant in Dallas, Texas, pioneered curb service. Motorists had only to stop in front of the store and honk the horn. A waiter, soon dubbed a carhop, came to take orders and then delivered the food on trays. Motorists could eat in their cars. Pig Stand Number 2, established two years later in a Dallas suburb, may have been the first drive-in. It was a cheaply erected roadside stand positioned back from the street and surrounded by a parking lot. Pig Stand Number 21, opened in California in 1931, pioneered the drive-up (later called the drive-through) window. Orders were taken, money exchanged, and food handed out of a window in sacks.[6] After World War II, drive-ins with carhop service became the rage, especially among teenagers with their first cars.

The McDonald brothers pioneered what they called the "self-service drive-in" during the 1950s.[7] Motorists parked but walked up to service windows and ordered hamburgers, french fries, and milk shakes. The production of food on a highly mechanized assembly line enabled the delivery of orders almost immediately. Through television and other advertising, the McDonald's chain, with Ray Kroc at the helm, sold itself as a family restaurant, especially for those with young children. Teenagers were discouraged from stopping. Through franchising, McDonald's spread rapidly nationwide and then globally. By 2002, the United States had more than thirteen thousand stores, part of a global empire that included thirty thousand stores in 121 countries.[8] The typical American had come to consume three hamburgers and four orders of french fries every week: on any given day, roughly a quarter of the nation's population bought fast food of some kind.[9] In 2002, fast food sales in the United States topped $105 billion.[10] McDonald's remained the industry giant, accounting for 43 percent of all the quick-service hamburgers sold in the country and outselling its next four competitors combined.[11] McDonald's had been a pioneer, quickening the pace of food delivery. Front-end cash registers at counters and drive-through windows, for example, were connected electronically with production lines, so that when clerks punched in customer orders, food preparation began immediately. McDonald's also experimented with self-service kiosks that enabled customers to order without clerk intervention.[12]

Drive-up Convenience

Few lines of retailing lacked at least some experiments with the drive-in idea. All marketing at the retail level felt the impact of automobility, if only through the convenience of customer parking, necessarily placed close to stores.[13] By the end of the twentieth century, the vast majority of the nation's retailers were located in shopping centers well provisioned with parking lots or garages or were stand-alone businesses with their own off-street parking. Such self-contained establishments, strung along major thoroughfares, form the basic element of the nation's increasingly ubiquitous commercial strips. But drive-up or drive-through service gained widespread acceptance only where merchandise came in small packages that could easily be handed directly to motorists in their cars. The sales transaction had to be simple and easy, readily handled by motorists cramped behind the steering wheels of their cars.

For example, drive-up service substantially facilitated banking (at least such common exercises as withdrawing or depositing money or cashing checks). Banks with drive-up windows appeared just before World War II, the first on record opening in 1937 in Vernon, California, an industrial suburb of Los Angeles. Motorists drove up to a gate that, when opened, allowed them to drive into a garagelike space. There they stopped beside a small bulletproof-glass partition inserted into a wall. Business was transacted through a stainless steel rotary container activated by a teller standing behind the glass.[14] After World War II, outdoor teller booths came to the fore, prefabricated and ready to install. They represented a substantial improvement over the prewar version, with drawers that could be extended to waiting cars and electronic voice amplifiers that enabled tellers to converse with customers. Teller windows greatly increased in size, enabling bank employees to survey adjacent driveways and motorists to look directly into bank offices. Drive-up bank windows were manufactured by the same companies that sold safes, bank vaults, and bank alarm systems.

At first, bankers adopted drive-up convenience as a means of combating downtown traffic congestion. Where customers found on-street parking in short supply and where banks could not provide off-street parking, drive-up facilities could counter motoring inconvenience, even if the remedy initially was intended as only a temporary solution. Very quickly, however, motoring convenience ruled the day. Given a taste of "dashboard banking," motorists came to expect and demand it, rendering obsolete bank locations without drive-up windows. After 1950, newly chartered banks in new city suburbs or suburban branches of downtown banks (in states where branch banking was allowed) were invariably constructed with both large parking lots and several drive-up windows (figure 11.1). Automated teller machines (ATMs) arrived during the 1980s. ATMs could be positioned anywhere, not just at bank locations or in parking lots and along driveways for autoists' convenience but also in strictly pedestrian spaces.[15]

The drive-up idea spread to other areas of retailing. Druggists adopted drive-up windows to dispense prescriptions. Dry cleaning shops added drive-up service as customers easily became habituated to both dropping off and picking up garments

Figure 11.1. Advertisement Showing Drive-In Banking as a Convenience. *Banking* 53 (September 1960): 17.

without leaving their cars. In some localities, dairy stores and discount bread outlets used the windows. But the idea was not universally accepted. Grocers, for example, generally rejected drive-up windows, with chains opting for the supermarket model and the mom-and-pop stores sticking to traditional storefront selling. A few small markets took orders by phone and then allowed customers to pick up their purchases, often by driving right into a portion of the store itself. One variant was the drive-in beer or liquor store.

Of course, the outdoor movie theater won widespread acceptance. The idea was patented by Richard Hollingshead Jr., who, with his cousin, Willis Smith, opened the first such theater in Camden, New Jersey, in 1933. As architectural historian Chester Liebs recounts, the patent covered all of the theater's basic elements: "a location in a field 'preferably by a highway,' a screen facing the field and shielded by a large wind-resistant 'screen house' (later called a screen tower), a series of inclined ramps radiating out in a semicircle around the screen, and a projection booth located at a suitable distance from the screen."[16] After World War II, in-car speak-

EASTER SUNRISE SERVICES
APRIL 18, 1954
Immanuel and Trinity Lutheran Churches
DANVILLE, ILLINOIS

Figure 11.2. Easter Sunrise Services at a Drive-In Movie Theater, Danville, Illinois, Postcard, April 18, 1954. Courtesy Trinity Lutheran Church.

ers complemented loudspeakers, thus improving sound. Today, patrons can listen on their car radios. With such names as the Sunset or the Starlite, drive-in theaters became especially popular with adolescents, including those who turned the privacy of darkened car interiors toward courtship. After marriage, these couples later returned with their children, often pajama-clad, strapped into the backseats.[17] Drive-in movie theaters proliferated immediately after World War II. By 1950, seventeen hundred screens operated nationwide, a number that had grown to three thousand by 1986.[18]

Drive-in movies offer more than convenience, argue psychologists Peter Marsh and Peter Collett. "People do not go to drive-in movies because it is more convenient; they go to drive-ins because they like sitting in their cars, where they can watch the film from their own territory, not from an impersonal seat in someone else's space. Because it is their little living room on wheels they can do what they like inside it: talk, smoke, eat, kick their shoes, have sex or go to sleep." Drive-in theaters provide opportunities for people to engage in a variety of social activities in their cars, with the film simply providing a rationale for doing so. People enjoy being in their stationary cars, viewing the "world, and all its dangers, in womb-like security" or taking advantage of a chance to be seen "inside a personal display of taste, affluence and power."[19]

Many drive-in theaters hosted Sunday-morning church services (figure 11.2). Some congregations eventually built drive-in churches. The Reverend Robert H.

Schuller, who began preaching in 1956 at a drive-in theater, moved into the mammoth Crystal Cathedral in 1980, located in the Los Angeles suburb of Garden Grove. Designed by architect Philip Johnson, the church seats three thousand worshipers inside a giant glass-enclosed narthex, but huge doors swing open to allow thousands more to participate while sitting in cars outside.[20]

Americans, enthralled as they are with automobiles, have accepted the drive-in church. But will they accept the drive-in mortuary? At least one enterprising funeral director thought they would. Gatling's Funeral Home in Chicago introduced "Drive-Thru Visitation." "The convenience and high technology of drive-through banks and hamburger places has come to the funeral world," reported the *New York Times*. Those wishing to pay their respects to a deceased friend or relative had only to drive up, punch in an appropriate code, and view the remains on a television screen. Visitors could also sign a register before departing. The service was available twenty-fours a day. Although the television image lasted only three seconds, the push of a button would bring it back over and over again. "Visitors have become so accustomed to the idea," the *Times* reported, "they now know to ask 'Will Mr. So-and-So be on the drive-through?'"[21]

Of all the new businesses to appear across America on the roadside, the motel was quintessentially auto convenient. The term, combining as it did the two stem words *motor* and *hotel,* was suggestive. A derivation of the auto camp, the cabin court, and even the tourist home, motels thrived by providing motorists with privacy, informality, and, more to the point, parking immediately adjacent to guest rooms.[22] Guests arrived, checked in at an office, and then drove to their accommodations. Nothing could be simpler than loading and unloading the car directly at one's door, and no tipping of door or bell staff was required. A few motel chains, like the Cross-Country Inns of Ohio, introduced drive-up windows for check-in and check-out purposes, with advertising that emphasized quick service. By 1970, suburban motels had largely replaced the traditional downtown hotels as the auto traveler's overnight stop of choice. During the 1980s, however, the suburban motels came to look more like hotels: multistory buildings with extensive lobbies, dining rooms, and conference rooms, among other amenities. Downtown hotels, for their part, necessarily became more automobile convenient, if not with parking lots adjacent then with parking garages.

Gas Stations and Convenience Stores

Perhaps nothing today epitomizes automobile convenience quite like the convenience store. Having come to fore only since the mid-1970s, they are now everywhere in ever-increasing numbers. Americans may persist in calling them gas stations, but they have their origin in two distinct retail activities, not only the selling of gasoline but also the retailing of convenience groceries, whence these establishments obtained their names. Today, most but not all convenience stores sell gasoline, but all sell convenience goods such as cigarettes, soft drinks, bread, milk, and other sundries. Profit originally came mainly from the grocery line, with gasoline largely serving as a loss leader to attract grocery customers. The bundling of formerly separate product lines has made convenience stores "one-stop" shops for various high-demand consumer goods and services.

Gasoline was originally sold packaged in tin cans at hardware stores and even at drugstores. It was also sold from horse-drawn tank wagons. By 1905, however, gasoline was also widely available at the nation's new garages, both where cars were stored and where cars were repaired and even sold. The first gasoline stations appeared about 1909. To reduce their dependence on independently owned garages, where quality could not always be controlled, petroleum companies created chains of look-alike filling stations. Through place-product-packaging, they sought to build heightened brand loyalty among customers.[23] Gasoline was cheap, and price mattered little as a competitive variable from company to company. Quick service, which most garages were poorly equipped to provide but which filling stations did quite well, became the important variable in gasoline retailing. In the 1920s, however, car lubrication, washing, light engine repair, and tire, battery, and accessory sales also came to the fore in what were popularly called service stations. Gasoline stations now sported enclosed service bays and enlarged offices for merchandise display. In 1932, the United States had more than 318,000 gas stations.[24] In 1940, the nation's 1.5 million gasoline pumps—3 for every mile of state highway—accounted for 12 percent of the nation's total retail sales by dollar value.[25] In 1970, there were some 236,000 gas stations, but by 1994 the number had fallen to 125,000.[26] Today, relatively few traditional gas stations survive.

First came substantive petroleum price increases, engendered initially by the Arab oil boycott of 1973 but sustained by the Organization of Petroleum Exporting Countries. Price suddenly became the most important competitive factor, forcing the industry to cut costs through such innovations as self-service as well as through larger-scale facilities than had ever before existed. These "big pumpers" increased profits through economies of scale. A second change involved the automobile itself. As cars became increasingly computerized and otherwise technically sophisticated, the costs of garage diagnostic and repair equipment soared. Car repair increasingly became the province of highly trained specialists. Such specialization came to characterize car servicing in general, with national chains of "lube shops" as well as muffler, brake, and transmission shops. The days of the jack-of-all-trades gas station mechanic had come to an end. A third change involved new Environmental Protection Agency regulations. In 1984, amendments to the Resource Conservation and Recovery Act required gas station operators to meet stringent corrosion-prevention and leak-detection requirements no later than 1998. December of that year thus saw the closure of about twenty thousand of the nation's remaining older gas stations. In light of anticipated earnings, the small-scale operations simply could not afford the mandated upgrades such as tank replacement.[27]

The first convenience store, in the modern sense of the word, originated in 1927 when a Dallas ice-dock manager added grocery items to help boost his sales during the winter months. Customers who drove in for ice would, he hoped, return for convenience groceries even when ice was not needed. So began Southland Ice's nationwide grocery business. The company eventually became the Southland Corporation and branded its stores under the name 7–11. In 1939, however, Southland operated sixty little open-air stores called Tote'ms. Refrigeration diminished the demand for ice, and Southland responded by turning more and more to groceries and by adding gasoline at many locations. In 1988, Southland operated more than 6,900 7–11 stores, 2,100 of them selling gasoline. Circle K, the next-largest chain, which originated in 1951 in El Paso, Texas, had about 1,200 outlets, 759 of which sold gasoline.[28]

Numerous convenience store chains quickly evolved, emulating one another. In 1970, 252 chains operated roughly sixteen thousand convenience stores nationwide.[29] Everywhere merchandise was expanded well beyond basic food and beverages to include health and beauty aids and even some hardware and auto supplies. Chains began to cash checks and to sell money orders. They began to rent household equipment such as floor polishers and carpet cleaners. Customers could buy magazines and newspapers. They could test their old radio and television tubes. They could rent videotapes. By 1988, the United States had more than sixty-nine thousand convenience stores.[30] Operators had begun adding deli counters and automatic teller machines, and a few added car washes, helping the industry grow to generate $1.4 billion per year.[31] As traditional gasoline stations declined in number, convenience store gasoline retailing boomed. By 2001, more than 124,000 U.S. convenience stores sold gasoline, more than double the number a decade earlier.[32]

Land purchase, building construction, equipment installation, and inventory for a new store required an average of $1.8 million in 2001.[33] With an investment of that scale, quality design, quality materials, and even quality workmanship were very much required. Unlike the nation's gasoline stations of the previous century, convenience stores in the twenty-first century were not built to be ephemeral. Aesthetics inside and out became important considerations. Design innovation had come to fore to enhance not only store functionality but store image. Gasoline brands no longer screamed at motorists through giant signs, bright light-reflective porcelain enamel facades, or fluttering pennants, streamers, and other eye-catching devices. Convenience stores spoke in more refined terms. They needed to be inviting yet also reassuring. They needed not only to look clean but to be clean, not only to look convenient but to be convenient. They needed to look up to date but perhaps not avant-garde.

Store canopies played an important role in this perception. Canopies, at least small ones, had been very much a part of traditional gasoline retailing, especially in the southeastern and southwestern United States, where customers and gas station attendants alike valued protection from the sun.[34] Roadside buildings, traditional gas stations included, tended to be single-story affairs. Low in profile, they often were not easily or readily noticed by motorists, pushed back from the road behind driveways and parking lots. Roadside buildings by themselves were, for the most part, anything but visually impressive, and many of them consequently had to be festooned with oversized signs and other garish eye-catching devices. Gas stations relied on exaggerated curbside signs to attract motorists' attention to driveway entrances. Convenience stores, however, solved the problem of poor visual impression primarily by covering pump islands with large canopies, which became the convenience store's prime architectural expression (figure 11.3). Lit at night and often during the day, canopies created a bright, attractive outdoor space, a kind of outdoor room, readily noticed and readily understood.[35]

Building facades, for their part, also needed to be inviting to reinforce the motorist's decision to stop. Fully glazed "open fronts" came to dominate, making store interiors easily visible from the pumps (figure 11.4). Interior layout needed to be readily comprehensible.[36] Customers had to be able instantly to orient themselves. Convenience stores thus featured wide aisles, high ceilings, and enhanced lighting. "We think of ourselves, our facility, as a store and not a [gas] station," the owner of a Los Angeles convenience store commented, explaining his enterprise's all-glass facade; skylights; and smooth stuccolike, dryvit surrounds in "soft earth" colors. As one customer commented at the store's opening, the store represented the Planet Hollywood of gasoline retailing. With an arcade-style layout, the store's interior featured hand-cut ceramic tile, carpeting, pine-slat walls with original graphics, split-level ceilings, indirect lighting, and granite countertops. "The visibility from inside the store, coupled with the bright lighting throughout, strengthens the sense of safety and security," the owner confided.[37]

Two technical innovations greatly facilitated gasoline sales at convenience stores: self-service pumps and pumps equipped to handle electronic payment by credit card. Self-service first appeared in the 1930s as a means of lowering labor costs.

Figure 11.3. Convenience Store, Lake Buena Vista, Florida, 2003. Authors' collection.

Figure 11.4. Convenience Store, Lake Buena Vista, Florida, 2003. Authors' collection.

However, legislatures in one state after another outlawed self-service, principally because of the perceived fire hazard. Pump attendants remained nearly universal nationwide until the late 1960s. In 1970, only 1 percent of U.S. gasoline was sold at self-service pumps. However, in the wake of the increases in gas prices caused by the Arab oil embargo of the early 1970s, many retailers switched to self-service, which enabled them to operate with fewer employees, thus cutting labor costs and permitting them to pass on to customers a savings of several cents a gallon. In 1975, 35 percent of the country's gas sales were self-service, and in 1982, that number had more than doubled to 72 percent.[38] At-the-pump credit card payment greatly reduced cashier workloads, reducing employee turnover and thereby the time and effort managers devoted to hiring and training new employees.

During the 1990s, fast food arrived on the convenience store scene. Although deli food had previously been available, customers could now purchase nationally branded, quick-service restaurant fare. Groceries and gasoline thus were bundled together with still another product line. Many larger convenience stores featured two or more fast food brands, such as Dairy Queen coupled with Dunkin' Donuts or Pizza Hut combined with Taco Bell and/or KFC. Over the decades, the convenience store had come of age through much trial and error. When grocery retailers added gasoline, few of them knew anything about pumps, tanks, or canopies. Gasoline retailers, for their part, knew little about merchandising packaged food. The arrival of fast food brought a third set of marketing requirements. The eateries consequently installed and maintained their own operations. Even McDonald's, a relative latecomer, had five hundred convenience store locations in the United States by 2003. In that year, the fast food sold in convenience stores accounted for about 13 percent of total industry sales nationwide.[39]

◆ ▼ ●

America's commercial roadsides clearly reflect the nation's embrace of automobile convenience. Contemporary retailing takes the drive-in, drive-up, or drive-through form. More importantly, to prosper, retail stores must now carry clear "park-at" implications. The nation's commercial roadsides thus have come to look pretty much the same everywhere, prompting more than a little criticism for their uniformity. Indeed, critics see the automobile as having exerted a kind of tyranny that has planed down the American scene to levels of bland homogeneity if not crass insensibility. One architectural critic has called America's new suburban landscapes "interminable wastelands dotted with millions of monotonous little houses on monotonous little lots and crisscrossed by highways lined with billboards, jazzed-up diners, used-car lots, drive-in movies, beflagged gas stations, and garish motels."[40] Gas stations have certainly come in for their share of negative attention. Wrote one geographer, "There is nothing in the essential chemistry of petroleum products . . . which requires motor fuel to be sold amid whirling plastic signs, foil-wrapped multi-colored tires, cannibalized cars, half an acre of ill-tended asphalt, and the syndrome of *schlock* that we have come to associate with gas stations across America." The same held true for hamburger stands and other "like emporia," he continued. "It is hard to believe that the marketing of sandwiches which happen to be made of meat (mostly) requires an environment reminiscent of a defective . . . Wurlitzer juke box, but American fast food restaurants are nearly always built that way."[41]

There is certainly nothing intrinsic in the chemistry of gasoline or, for that matter, the chemistry of hamburger meat that produces what many critics still see as a national disgrace: America's commercial roadsides. But the social physics of automobility can, at least in part, explain this roadside appearance. Americans widely share such cultural values as speed, efficiency, and convenience. Early in the twentieth century, Americans accepted the motor car as the one device best able to enhance individual mobility, not just because it permitted people to get places quickly but because it empowered individuals. Motorists could choose not only their travel destinations but their routes for getting there. They could move cocooned in reasonably comfortable and highly personalized vehicles. The commercial roadside evolved as a linear array of conveniently accessed places, positioned and designed specifically to entice. In America's highly materialistic society, the commercial roadside now looms as a consumer's paradise, merchants competing through product and service as well as through the seduction of convenience, defined as easy access and quick transaction. In the future, America and Americans will undoubtedly find only more convenience in store. Whether the places produced will be comely—whether the landscapes will seem blighted—is perhaps irrelevant. Roadside business has not necessarily required attractiveness but has only needed to attract. For most Americans, the nation's roadsides work. They do not need fixing. That does not mean, of course, that changes will not occur, as they always have.

the highway experience

Highway motoring changed how America functioned and how Americans came to think about themselves and their nation. By tremendously exaggerating mobility, motoring inflated, to quote writer Kris Lackey, the nation's "sense of individual power, will and significance."[1] Early on, the automobile enhanced human physicality by fostering geographical mobility and by doing so in ways that seemed fundamentally liberating. Motorists decided when as well as where to go. They could stop at will to take advantage of opportunities along the way. They could interact with types of people and in types of places little encountered previously. Nonetheless, speed was of the essence. When under personal control, speed proved especially exhilarating. At issue among society's elites, however, was social display, with car ownership and use becoming signs of wealth and social status. Following the mass production and mass marketing of motor cars, even America's middling classes would embrace this stance.

The pleasure trip, as with all forms of auto trip taking, also came to privilege human visuality. Seeing served very much as the primary means by which to assess surroundings. Motoring changed the seeing of landscape and place by quickening the pace, a rapid kaleidoscopic seeing of things overwhelming slower, more studied apprehension. High-speed freeway driving in particular condensed landscapes into limited sets of visual quick takes. Scenes rapidly emerged and occluded, although fast driving at times could make the motorist, as Mitchell Schwarzer puts it, seem the "fixed monument" around which landscapes often seemed to swirl.[2]

Travel by motor car certainly reduced what Paul Adams dubs the "peripatetic sense of place."[3] Today, Americans mainly drive places. Little do they walk, even after arriving at a destination. Newer landscapes—places built for automobility—tend not to encourage the coming and going of pedestrians but are fully scaled to motoring. Old landscapes—places specifically designed to be experienced on foot—are much reduced in visual impact when motored through and certainly when motored around. Cocooned in the modern car, motorists hear little of the world outside and feel little save the occasional bump in the road. Surroundings are very much reduced to generalized visual tableaux. Detachment occurs, Adams argues, when surrounding landscape is reduced to mere scenery and when the seeing of things becomes fully equated with experience.[4] The "open road" in America today involves not only straightened, widened, and flattened-out highways but straightened, widened, and flattened-out ways of viewing the world.

About 1900, pleasure motoring became an American ideal. The notion that one could pleasure across country in one's own car became compelling. Motoring for pleasure lay an important political base for the nation's highway development. Congress at first rationalized federal involvement in highway building largely in terms of national defense, as evidenced by dubbing of the nation's new interstate roads "defense highways." But what enabled passage of the key 1921 Highway Act and the other legislation that followed over subsequent decades was less the potential to move military equipment and personnel than the potential to move pleasure-seeking motorists. Travel by train declined 22 percent between 1921 and 1941, but travel by car increased sixfold.[5] In 1935, 85 percent of all vacation travel took place by automobile, with the amount spent on pleasure motoring accounting for half of all the U.S. money spent on recreation.[6] By the mid-1980s, more than three-quarters of all vacation travel occurred via private motor vehicle.[7]

Pleasure Motoring

When Arthur Eddy drove from Chicago to New York City in 1902, he sat high up on his vehicle very much in athletic relationship with his surroundings. "Going 20 to 25 miles per hour on a machine . . . with 32-inch wheels and short wheel-base," he wrote, "gives about the same exercise one gets on a horse; one is lifted from the seat and thrown from side to side until you learn to ride the machine as you would a trotter and take the bumps accordingly." No sport since Roman chariot racing, Eddy asserted, afforded so much excitement. Early motoring was in many ways an exercise in risk avoidance, requiring, according to Eddy, "nerve, dash, and daring." "It constantly offers something to overcome; as in golf, you start out each time to beat your record. The machine is your tricky and resourceful opponent."[8] Primitive roads, of course, were very much part of the equation. But so also were the often highly personalized connections with people and places under novel circumstances, the piloting of a primitive machine not just across the country but in the country.

A quarter century later, Americans traveled in much more sophisticated cars that were not only comfortable but dependable. People could drive on roads both smooth and safe, certainly in comparison to those that Eddy navigated. Cars were enclosed, the passing scene framed through windshields with landscape made into a series of moving pictures. Even cars sold to the masses sported the self-starters that negated arm-wrenching acrobatics in getting under way. Even modestly priced cars had engines capable of high speeds and of negotiating the most distasteful road conditions. Of course, most main highways were hard surfaced; even those that lacked such surfaces tended to be graded and graveled and thus reasonably well drained.

Quickness in travel enabled motorists to drive very long distances without stopping. By 1930, a motor trip from Chicago to New York City took two days rather than the two weeks that Eddy had required. In 1916, a motorist was lucky to travel 125 miles in a day, but average daily distances increased to 170 miles in 1920, 200 miles in 1925, 300 miles in 1931, and 400 miles in 1936.[9] Indeed, improved highways wrought an obsession with covering long distances, providing proof not only of driver endurance but of a prized automobile's dependability. Driving came to impose a momentum all its own, with the distance traveled in a single day becoming an important source of pride. True, motoring was no longer reserved for the select few, the doers of stunts or the seekers of thrills. Motoring's pioneer phase was past. But adventure was still to be found, if only in breaking one's own performance records. Anyone who owned an automobile could do so with little or no preparation or special paraphernalia.

Highway travel was not totally devoid of hazard. Carelessness was born of inattention to the road and passing scene. Look-alike highways produced fatigue-inducing monotony. Traffic accidents remained a constant possibility. But mechanical breakdowns came less often. Little risk remained of being stranded without food, water, or a place to spend the night. Garages, gas stations, cabin courts, and cafés lined most highways. Highly personalized interactions not just with strangers but also with locals were available in these places close at hand. Highway associations and automobile clubs provided maps and guidebooks. Named highways were signposted, and highway numbering had come to the fore. Roadside business had spawned a signage epidemic, informative and thus comforting to the traveler but also visually distracting.[10] Of one highway in the American South, a traveler noted, "There was only the unending literature of the roadside to divert us: 'Gas. Beer. Coke. . . . Jumbo Milk Shakes . . . Live Bait . . . Don't be a Litterbug. . . . "Tiny" Condon for Sheriff.'"[11]

Today, most Americans drive long distances mainly on the nation's freeways. In many localities, traffic volumes are extremely high, making for what one journalist termed "brutal" driving. With traffic along I-35 between Austin and San Antonio up to 220,000 vehicles a day, average speed dropped to a mere thirty-five miles per hour; between the early 1980s and the late 1990s, freeway traffic in Austin had increased by 165 percent.[12] Near Greenwich, Connecticut, an average of 80,000 vehicles used I-95 every day, producing what another journalist described as a "culture of congestion."[13] Increased truck traffic greatly added to the crowding of roads everywhere: freight carried in trucks nationwide increased by 80 percent during the 1990s; by the turn of the twenty-first century, 65 percent of all shipped freight went by truck. Especially disconcerting were the eighteen-wheelers. In 2001, three hundred of these trucks passed the I-40 weigh station at El Reno, Oklahoma, each hour.[14] In many western states, motorists additionally confronted long combination vehicles, rigs with as many as three trailers that could reach the total length of a football field.[15] In 2000, the number of car crashes on roads of all kinds had increased to 6.3 million per year.[16]

Today's motor cars provide greater protection from road hazards than ever before. But they also more fully insulate or isolate motorists. In the realm of safety, cars now come with computerized power brakes, power-assisted steering, improved headlights, seat belts, padded dashboards, and front and side air bags. In the realm of comfort, cars now come with sophisticated computer-assisted suspension systems, and passenger compartments are better insulated against road noise. Tinted glass reduces glare. With sophisticated sound systems, however, it is no longer the passing scene that offers ready entertainment. Cell phones further distract. Many cars now come equipped with global positioning systems. Drivers no longer need to pay close attention to their locations. The car orients. In 1997, the first "automated road" in the United States opened in San Diego, a stretch of I-15 where computers controlled cars specially equipped with video cameras, magnetic resonators, and radar. After the computer took over, the driver had only to sit back and let his or her mind wander. But as even the project's director admitted, "It really is exciting for about the first 15 seconds, [but] then it gets really dull."[17]

Through pleasure motoring, Americans had found that they could break life's routines in personally empowering ways. Implicit was a sense of independence through freedom of action as well as a new kind of novel and thus exhilarating spectatorship. Perhaps this sense of independence largely represented a fantasy, but Americans nonetheless succumbed to the siren song of the open road. D. H. Lawrence sensed that a "new great doctrine" for the world had been created, America's true "heroic message." This doctrine reaffirmed what Walt Whitman had once celebrated with important amplification provided by the motor car. Motoring produced the "true rhythm of the American continent."[18] With increased car ownership, of course, other kinds of travel by car, especially the journey to work and the journey to shop, came rapidly to the fore. Perhaps today, car use most affects American character in these sorts of travel. By 1960, most Americans viewed car ownership as very much an everyday necessity rather than an amenity.

Motoring Necessity

Driving to work and to shop brought unanticipated change. The number of commuters grew faster than road mileage could be increased or improved to service them.[19] Downtown traffic congestion and the lack of convenient downtown parking had for decades encouraged suburban decentralization. By 1980, big-city suburbs contained 60 percent of the nation's jobs, and between 1960 and 1980, two-thirds of all new jobs were created there. Some 60 percent of the nation's commuting took place from suburb to suburb rather than from suburb to central city.[20] The journey to shop also took place almost entirely by car and substantially in the suburbs. In 1983, the average American household made 39 percent more shopping trips and 40 percent more family business trips by private car than had been the case in 1969: over the same period, the average length of trip increased 20 percent for shopping and 3 percent for other travel.[21]

Automobile use changed the American family, especially in regard to women's roles. In the suburbs, women moved to the forefront of car use as part of their responsibility for household logistics. But women also entered the workforce as never before. By 2000, two-thirds of all women in the United States were employed outside the home, up from only one-third a half century earlier; like men, the vast majority of women drove to work. Women served as the principal decision makers in half of all motor car purchases.[22]

Automobility impacted more than just how men and women lived their lives. At the end of the twentieth century, the United States, with less than 5 percent of the world's population, consumed more than 25 percent of the world's petroleum— 9 million barrels each day fueling motor vehicles.[23] Automobile use and all that attended and supported it, including highway development, had become the keystone of American capitalism, the cornerstone of the nation's expendable-goods economy, in which things manufactured were marketed, distributed, bought, and consumed in cycles of capital reinvestment. Cars and highways had become ever more central to the nation's economic health, to the seeming prosperity of the American people, and to their sense of overall well-being.

The fantasy of the open road took on a life of its own that even the most ardent early twentieth-century auto enthusiasts had generally not foreseen. Critics accused the fantasy of spawning something of a monster, an octopus with tentacles that touched every aspect of American life. To the automobile and the nation's growing petroleum dependence could be tied many environmental, health and safety, and social problems from air pollution to traffic deaths and injuries to class segregation based on geographical mobility or lack thereof. Petroleum dependence influenced not only government domestic policy but foreign policy as well.

For most Americans today, the nation's dependence on automobiles remains an acceptable if not necessarily desirable condition of life. Widespread doubt has not existed since well before 1920. Early on, motoring was perceived as threatening the livelihoods of many people: horse breeders, wagon makers, livery stable operators, and others whose interests were very much vested in horse power. Also negatively inclined were the nation's farmers—for example, those who feared the auto's impact on hay cultivation, one of the nation's most important crops, and those who feared for their or their animals' safety on rural roads turned into speedways by city people. The image of the frightened horse, bolting with the approach of a motor car, was based in reality. The initial rural opposition to motoring carried clear class implications.[24]

Beginning in the 1920s, a few planners began to question an emergent transportation system that favored only car and truck use. But even the most insightful critics, observers such as Lewis Mumford, a writer widely admired not only for his vision but for his use of language, were largely ignored.[25] Mumford's encouragement to caution (like a slow-moving car on a country highway) was rapidly overtaken (like a car speeding in the passing lane) by the very real accomplishments of the highway builders—for example, the accomplishments of Mumford's fellow New Yorker, Robert Moses.[26]

Criticism grew, however, after the nation's planners and politicians adopted the superhighway as an ideal, applying it not just to rural locales but also to urban places. With their limited-access traffic lanes, parkways, toll roads, and freeways came to sweep around small towns, leaving them isolated, and cut through and disrupted big-city neighborhoods. The new highways were capable, observers said, of turning traditional business districts into economic "ghost towns."[27] They were capable of much, reducing neighborhood livability and of substantially destroying property values. Opposition developed among laypeople but primarily only among those negatively affected. Threatened communities coalesced to challenge the highway engineers, but for most localities, such efforts marked but a final phase in community life, as the bulldozers ultimately had their way.[28] Urban freeways promised much to affluent suburban commuters, the constituency favored by Congress, but little to inner-city residents save the demolishing of houses and the uprooting of businesses.[29]

Highway opponents, whoever they were, did not by and large dislike motoring per se. Most were motorists themselves, not about to give up their automobiles. Members of this cohort opposed only the manner in which vested highway interests ran roughshod over the American landscape and thereby the American people.[30] Highway building had come to epitomize modernist thinking, they argued, defining modernism as the ideology that intertwined newness and progress as impelling action. Human landscapes required careful articulation. They could not simply be wiped away and then totally replaced without causing social trauma. One could not raze the built environment with impunity. The past did count, they asserted, and the best of the past needed to be preserved as cultural resource. In addition, highway travel needed to be coordinated with other modes of transportation, which in turn needed to be carefully related to land use. Highway builders, acting alone, could not produce high-quality, livable places; nor, for that matter, could they even satisfy the nation's pressing transportation needs.

Highway advocates, of course, continued to argue otherwise, although the airlines, operating from federally subsidized airports, had come to dominate passenger travel over very long distances. In air travel, speed was more than ever the impelling attribute. Commuting via mass transit and traveling between cities by train (held to a minimum, of course) might be expected to service Americans traveling short distances or at least those not affluent enough to own cars and those physically unable to drive. But the bulk of the nation's transportation needs—both for people and freight—would always primarily involve cars and trucks. Motor transport was, after all, what Americans wanted. Widened streets, enlarged highways, and, most importantly, new highways would always solve traffic problems. Unfortunately, a kind of Parkinson's Law was at work. Roads did not relieve as much as invite congestion; motoring always increased to fit road capacity. Road improvements sped motorists along, but only in the short term.[31]

By the 1980s, potholes and rough pavement could be found nearly everywhere, evidence of the problem. Astronaut James Lovell said that he felt safer catapulting toward the moon than driving down the dilapidated Gulf Freeway between Houston and Galveston.[32] Repairing the pavement could present temporary problems. On the Northwest Tollway in Chicagoland, reconstruction during the summer of 1984 expanded the commute into and out of the city from fifty to eighty minutes.[33] By the 1990s, commuters nationwide were spending an estimated 14.5 million hours each day just sitting in their cars.[34] The federal government took some steps to balance the nation's transportation system, including token subsidies for public transit in the Federal Highway Act of 1973, the Surface Transportation Assistance Act of 1982, and the Intermodal Surface Transportation Efficiency Act of 1991. But most of the nation's commuters continued to prefer their own cars and to drive themselves. They preferred to drive alone all the way to work, rejecting shared or public transit for even part of the journey.[35]

Americans accepted not only the increased taxes but also the heightened stress that accompanied everyday motoring. Rush hour traffic at the fringes of many American cities might once have moved at speeds as high as fifty or sixty miles per hour, slowing to a crawl, of course, at city centers. By the 1990s, however, traffic was becoming congested in many outlying areas as well, especially around major freeway interchanges. The term *road rage* was coined to cover a number of aggressive behaviors prompted by the frustration induced by motoring.[36] On American highways today, traveling is less a matter of speed, the car fully responsive to human will, than a matter of slowing to a crawl and often to a stop. Motoring has taken on clear territorial implication. If the "open road" once symbolized liberation and freedom, then what of the overcrowded road? What of the road not fully open? Might a social pathology of motoring be evolving? And, if so, what might it symbolize for America's future?

The Highway Experience

Assessing the highway narrative as a kind of literature, most commentators have found motoring much like personal autonomy. Motoring has meant escape from or at the very least partial release from the tyranny of commonplaces and everyday life. Accordingly, observers likened the highway to a sort of malleable frontier space, awaiting exploration and definition. But cocooned from others, the passing scene at a distance, the motoring experience may have turned most contemporary motorists to introspection. True, the automobile makes people mobile in that it takes them places. However, as a medium of isolation, it also makes for self-absorption and even self-indulgence. Today's motorists live in a fleeting, distanced, and largely visual world where social interaction with others is highly impersonal.

Has motoring made Americans increasingly self-referential? Is that what motoring offers today by way of discovery? Popular film has commonly used America's vast open spaces to locate and explore situations of profound inner conflict. The lonely highway frequently appears as metaphor, standing as a means to an end rather than an end in itself.[37] The highway is thus portrayed as a purgatory zone, a place of no importance save as someplace to get through, to leave behind. Have Americans as motorists come to relish or at least to accept suspension between here and there? And in that suspension are they in fact becoming more inner-directed? Has the highway experience become a kind of blind spot in the American psyche that reduces our ability critically to assess our automobile-dominated culture?[38]

Novelist John Steinbeck portrays mobility as part of a dialectic, a persisting rivalry between the deep-seated human need for ownership of immovable things, requiring degrees of rootedness, and what may be the stronger opposing need to constantly keep on moving. Daryl Zanuck's production of Steinbeck's *The Grapes of Wrath*, now a classic road movie, brought this thinking into clear focus.[39] For the Joad family, life in Oklahoma was impossible, but along the road (on the way west to California along Route 66), they assessed and acted on every encounter in terms of the home they had left behind. Their movement occurred by serendipity but always with the purpose of ultimately finding a new home. Until that time, the highway was home.

Perhaps Americans will continue to make themselves at home on the road. Protected rather than isolated from their surroundings, they may even find reassurance in being on the road again. Roland Barthes, a founding student of semiology, wrote that the car was the supreme creation of its era, conceived with passion by largely unknown artists and consumed by people as image (as well as relied on through use) as if a "purely magical object."[40] The same was true of the highway. According to Peter Marsh and Peter Collett, motorists readily appropriated the road as an extension of their homes.[41] But the car rather than the highway played the central role. Adoring owners celebrated their cars, fittingly naming them like people. "For our Lydia is not business, she is pleasure. She is joy, if you please, of the open road," in the words of travel writer Edward Hungerford.[42] His was the stuff of romance. Conversely, Jean Baudrillard traveled by car across the Desert Southwest in search of an "astral America."[43] Personal introspection was best done, he argued, on America's desert highways, the roads that shot straight as arrows across seemingly limitless spaces. In the desert, speed totally voided the few surrounding references. Perhaps under such circumstances, love of car could actually become love of self.

Motoring Nostalgia

Special effort must now be expended to experience motoring as once it was. Doing so may even require the indulgence of the antique car buff. At the very least, it involves the deliberate seeking out of what writer Least Heat Moon termed "blue highways."[44] Moon set out to visit small American communities that had strange and funny names, accessing these places mainly by following back roads. There he engaged people directly, making his travels highly personalized and indeed centered on other people. Everywhere across the United States are relics of bypassed or abandoned highway over which, with the right kind of thinking if not the right kind of old car, a kind of time travel is possible. In recent years, certain old highways have become important tourist attractions: for example, the fabled Route 66 from Chicago to Los Angeles and the older Lincoln Highway from New York City to San Francisco. Travelers come looking for more personalized connections with people and place, the sorts of connections that early motoring encouraged.

Route 66 reverberates in popular consciousness, having been memorialized in song, featured in a television series, and celebrated in a spate of guide and photography books.[45] Historical preservationists, both professionals and lay, have worked all along the highway to save old buildings and stretches of road alignment. In Illinois, work began when members of the state's newly formed Route 66 Association realized that if future motorists were to have a highway experience fully reminiscent of the past, tangible evidence would be required.[46] Today tourists flock the "mother road" to stop at old cafés, motor courts, and even tourist attractions and drive at least short stretches of renumbered "heritage highway." Foreigners' curiosity (there are Route 66 enthusiasts throughout the world) and Americans' personal quests to rediscover family motoring roots rank high among the rationales commonly cited. A roadside museum in Oklahoma and a state park in Missouri celebrate not just the road but America's era of "classic" motoring—roughly 1915 to 1960.

The Lincoln Highway too has generated affection.[47] The Lincoln Highway Association has been revived with members drawn from across the nation. Brian Butko, author of a popular travel guide to the road in Pennsylvania, wrote, "Real aficionados of historic highways try to find long-abandoned stretches. They drive them in pickups or jeeps. But vast lengths are open to the casual traveler as well, with numerous artifacts and monuments."[48] Much like military reenactors, this breed of tourists, especially the antique car buffs, motor to relive earlier times.

But most of America's once significant auto roads are beyond preservation. They are largely unrecognizable for what they once were. Many original rights-of-way simply no longer exist. Indeed, most highways from before World War II have been repeatedly upgraded and remain integral to the nation's contemporary highway system. Along the original stretch of the Pennsylvania Turnpike, for example, traffic lanes have been added, bridges replaced, on- and off-ramps reengineered, and even tunnels replaced by new road alignments through deep road cuts. Over extensive stretches, the turnpike has been relocated from north-facing mountain slopes to south-facing slopes, cutting down on winter snow and ice. Piecemeal upgrades of highways occur so constantly and so extensively across the nation that the detour sign has once again become a motoring constant. Nonetheless, as least some Americans have developed a nostalgia for classic motoring, for the kind of road trip that people might have taken before the nation's interstate freeways fully changed the driving experience. Perhaps they wish again to indulge passing landscape. Freeways may be *in* the landscape, but only rarely do they seem to be *of* the landscape—too many things, once visible close at hand, are now pushed to a distance.

◆ ▼ ●

For travel over very long distances, contemporary Americans prefer flying. On commercial airliners, stereo music, cinema, and even television completely divert traveler attention. Who looks out of airplane windows any more? But congestion in terminals, on runways, and on roads leading to and from airports has so increased in recent years that air travel now requires an enormous amount of extra time. Perhaps high-speed trains will become America's long-distance travel mode of choice. Maybe something other than motoring will come to dominate commuting. The number of Americans opting for mass transit grows at least incrementally every year. Many of our largest and in many respects most viable cities never gave up their subways, their elevated railroads, or even their streetcars.

Might motoring someday go the way of the dinosaurs? Unlikely. Americans have for a century maintained a love affair with the motor car. As a way of getting there and as a thing to own, nothing has ever surpassed the automobile. Cars were not thrust on the American people. Americans were not dragged kicking and screaming onto auto-dealer sales floors. Americans adopted the motor car very much of their own volition. Other modes of transportation may challenge for certain kinds of travel or for travel by certain kinds of people, but automobiles will not be totally replaced. Americans use their cars with pride. Most Americans keep their cars close at hand, transferring to them many of the feelings otherwise reserved for home and even for people. Americans build lifestyles around their cars; consequently, they readily symbolize the self. Motoring can still be fun or at least conceived as fun despite the tyranny of congested freeway driving. Motoring clearly continues to challenge, although it does so in ways very different from the days of early motoring. Automakers place on the market sports cars and sport-utility vehicles, including those with off-road capabilities, continuing to appeal to excitement and human playfulness.

Motoring still excites Americans in ways fundamental to being American. Many Americans believe that individual effort will enable them to live lives of relative independence, that individuals can and should experience the world in highly personal terms. Many Americans also believe that individuals, in pursuing their own self-interests, produce a healthier society. The highway experience in America speaks to both propositions. American highways, whether measured by the resources committed or by the time and human energy required for their construction and maintenance, stand as the nation's most substantial public works. Highways represent a predominant expression of national will. They constitute an expression of national being translated solidly into landscape, tangible evidence of both individual and communal intent. The federal government was relatively insignificant in the everyday lives of Americans prior to the twentieth century, save perhaps during the years of the Civil War. But the motoring-induced highway system has come to substantially affect American lives every day and in every place. In America, cars and highways have become a powerful cultural engine indeed.

NOTES

Prologue

1. F. F. R., "I Am the Motor," *The Highwayman* 2 (November 1922): 1.

2. Many of the ideas in this section were previously expressed in a special issue of the *Bulletin of the Illinois Geographical Society* edited by Jill Freund Thomas and Keith A. Sculle. See John A. Jakle, "The Highway in America," *Bulletin of the Illinois Geographical Society* 38 (Fall 1996): 5–10. An abridged version appeared as "America's Highways," in *The Great American Road* ([Dearborn, Mich.]: Henry Ford Museum and Greenfield Village, [2001]), 23.

1. Motoring: An Introduction

1. "Misuse of the Word 'Motor,'" *Literary Digest* 76 (January 6, 1923): 63.

2. *Webster's New International Dictionary of the English Language,* 2nd ed. (Springfield, Mass.: Merriam, 1949), 1600.

3. Lee Goeller, letter to the editor, *New York Times,* October 23, 1997, A-20.

4. "The Pioneer Motor State," *Literary Digest* 48 (June 27, 1914): 1552.

5. Christopher Finch, *Highways to Heaven: The Auto Biography of America* (New York: HarperCollins, 1992), 36.

6. "Gasoline and Electricity Harnessed Together in Woods Dual Power Car," *Hoosier Motorist* 4 (September 1910): 56.

7. Finch, *Highways to Heaven,* 43.

8. See Peter J. Hugill, "Technology and Geography in the Emergence of the Automobile Industry, 1895–1915," in *Roadside America: The Automobile in Design and Culture,* ed. Jan Jennings (Ames: Iowa State University Press, 1990), 29–39; James J. Flink, *America Adopts the Automobile, 1895–1910* (Cambridge: MIT Press, 1970).

9. Peter J. Hugill, "Good Roads and the Automobile in the United States, 1880–1929," *Geographical Review* 72 (July 1982): 335.

10. Harry Wilkin Perry, "What Kind of an Automobile?" *Suburban Life* 6 (May 1908): 277.

11. Virginia Scharff, *Taking the Wheel: Women and the Coming of the Motor Age* (Albuquerque: University of New Mexico Press, 1992), 18.

12. Sandy McCreery, "Come Together," in *Autopia: Cars and Culture,* ed. Peter Wollen and Joe Kerr (London: Reaktion, 2002), 385.

13. Chris Batchelder, "Yesterday's Races Made Today's Cars," *Hoosier Motorist* 26 (May 1928): 7.

14. "Reliability Tours," *Buffalo Motorist* 43 (June 1950): 41–42.

15. James M. Rubenstein, *Making and Selling Cars: Innovation and Change in the U.S. Automotive Industry* (Baltimore: Johns Hopkins University Press, 2001), 262.

16. Peter Marsh and Peter Collett, *Driving for Passion: The Psychology of the Car* (Boston: Faber and Faber, 1986), 84–87.

17. Rubenstein, *Making and Selling Cars*, 246.

18. David Beecroft, "The Progress of 25 Years," *Automobile Trade Journal* 29 (December 1, 1924): 293.

19. David T. Wells, "The Growth of the Automobile Industry in America," *Outing* 11 (November 1907): 207.

20. "The International Harvester Company," *Automobile Trade Journal* 29 (December 1, 1924): 338.

21. "The Studebaker Corporation," *Automobile Trade Journal* 29 (December 1, 1924): 91.

22. "What America Pays for Motoring and the People's Motor Support," *Buffalo Motorist* 12 (February 1919): 110.

23. "The Ford Motor Company," *Automobile Trade Journal* 29 (December 1, 1924): 85.

24. Rubenstein, *Making and Selling Cars*, 10.

25. "Facts about the Ford and Its Makers," *Ford Times* 7 (December 1913): 142.

26. Ibid.

27. Marsh and Collett, *Driving for Passion*, 34.

28. Scharff, *Taking the Wheel*, 55.

29. Walter McComes, "My Sturdy Ford," *Ford Times* 7 (February 1914): 263.

30. Hugill, "Good Roads," 337.

31. "A Visit to the World's Great Automobile Factory," *Ford Times* 6 (June 1913): 370.

32. Ibid., 371.

33. Rubenstein, *Making and Selling Cars*, 58.

34. "Visit to the World's Great Automobile Factory," 372.

35. Rubenstein, *Making and Selling Cars*, 188–89.

36. "The General Motors Corporation," *Automobile Trade Journal* 29 (December 1, 1924): 289.

37. Douglas Brinkley, *Wheels for the World: Henry Ford, His Company, and a Century of Progress, 1903–2003* (New York: Viking, 2003), 340.

38. Rubenstein, *Making and Selling Cars*, 187.

39. Brinkley, *Wheels for the World*, 295.

40. Rubenstein, *Making and Selling Cars*, 186.

41. Alfred Reeves, "Preliminary Facts and Figures: Automobile Industry, 1929," *Highway Engineer and Contractor* 36 (January 1930): 75.

42. Norman G. Shidle, "Livelihood of 20,000 People in the U.S. Census Comes from the Automobile Business," *National Petroleum News* 18 (February 5, 1926): 109.

43. "U.S. Automobile Registrations," *National Petroleum News* 94 (Mid-July 2002): 16.

44. "Who Owns a Motor Car?" *Literary Digest* 75 (November 11, 1922): 78.

45. Robert Lynd and Helen Lynd, *Middletown: A Study in Modern American Culture* (New York: Harcourt, Brace, 1929).

46. "Small Town Car Owners in Majority," *Motor Travel* 15 (November 1923): 23.

47. "The Life of an Automobile," *Literary Digest* 92 (January 8, 1927): 67.

48. "The Mistakes of Beginners," *Literary Digest* 45 (August 10, 1912): 232.

49. Minna Irving, "My Lady of the Car: Motoring as a Recreation for Women—A Personal Experience and a Bit of Romance," *Suburban Life* 9 (November 1909): 234.

50. Charles L. Sanford, "'Woman's Place' in American Car Culture," in *The Automobile and American Culture,* ed. David L. Lewis and Laurence Goldstein (Ann Arbor: University of Michigan Press, 1983), 139.

51. Hilda Ward, "The Automobile in the Suburb from a Woman's Point of View," *Suburban Life* 5 (November 1907): 1.

52. Scharff, *Taking the Wheel,* 113.

53. See Alice H. Ramsey, *Veil, Duster, and Tire Iron* (Covina, Calif.: Castle, 1961).

54. Quoted in "The Feminine Influence on the Car," *Literary Digest* 72 (March 18, 1922): 64.

55. Scharff, *Taking the Wheel,* 113.

56. Stephen Bayley, *Sex, Drink, and Fast Cars* (New York: Pantheon, 1986), 16.

57. Finch, *Highways to Heaven,* 276.

58. Bayley, *Sex, Drink, and Fast Cars,* 77.

59. "Now—Radio Motoring," *Studebaker Wheel,* July 1931, 6–7.

60. Michael Bull, "Soundscapes of the Car: A Critical Study of Automobile Habitation," in *Car Cultures,* ed. Daniel Miller (Oxford: Berg, 2001), 185.

61. *Webster's New International Dictionary,* 2696.

62. Karl Grenville Baker, "Why They 'Commute' by Automobile," *Suburban Life* 15 (July 1912): 11.

63. C. Bailey Sanderson, "The Awakening of a City Man," *Suburban Life* 16 (June 1913): 398.

64. Alexander Johnston, "The Delights of Motoring during the Winter Time," *Countryside Magazine and Suburban Life* 19 (December 1917): 293.

65. "Motorist's Creed," *American Motorist* 9 (June 1917): 27.

66. Ralph D. Paine, "Discovering America by Motor," *Scribner's* 53 (February 1913): 137.

67. Arthur Jerome Eddy, "Eddy's 2,900-Mile Tour," *Good Roads,* November 1901, 19–20.

68. M. Worth Colwell, "Motoring through the Mountains," *Travel* 14 (August 1908): 507, 509.

69. Carlos Arnaldo Schwantes, *Going Places: Transportation Redefines the Twentieth Century West* (Bloomington: Indiana University Press, 2003), 129–30.

70. Quoted in Day Allen Willey, "Long Distance Runs by Automobile," *Travel* 14 (May 1909): 356.

71. "Touring to the Exposition," *Ford Times* 9 (October 1915): 117.

72. Vernon Gill, *Diary of a Motor Journey from Chicago to Los Angeles* (Los Angeles: Grafton, 1922), 92–93.

73. A. W. Seaman, "Some Real Facts on Coast to Coast Touring," *American Motorist* 7 (April 1915): 214.

74. See, for example, "What to Take on a Trip," *Official Automobile Blue Book, 1919* (New York: Automobile Blue Book, 1919), insert at 576.

75. Jan Gordon and Cora J. Gordon, *On Wandering Wheels: Through Roadside Camps from Maine to Georgia in an Old Sedan Car* (New York: Dodd, Mead, 1928), 83.

76. Ibid., 51.

77. For a fuller discussion of auto tourism, see John A. Jakle, *The Tourist: Travel in Twentieth-Century North America* (Lincoln: University of Nebraska Press, 1985).

78. "More than Forty-four Million People Will Take Vacation Motor Trips this Year," *Buffalo Motorist* 21 (February 1928): 29.

79. Samuel Crowther, "Automobiles: Carriers of Progress," *World's Work* 50 (May 1930): 41.

80. Clyde Haberman, "100 Years of Death on the Road," *New York Times,* September 14, 1999, A-23.

81. "New York Autos Vie with War—Creating Casualty Lists," *Literary Digest* 66 (August 14, 1920): 86.

82. "The Cost of Highway Accidents," *Good Roads,* March 1928, 157.

83. John B. Rae, *The Road and the Car in American Life* (Cambridge: MIT Press, 1996), 344.

84. J. G. Ballard, *A User's Guide to the Millennium* (New York: HarperCollins, 1996), 233.

85. Silas Bent, "Collapsing Time and Space," *World's Work* 59 (November 1929): 67.

86. P. E. Vaughn, "The Song of the Open Road," *Studebaker Wheel,* August 1932, 13.

87. "The Open Road," *Texaco Star* 16 (June 1929): inside cover.

88. Quoted in Gerald Silk, *Automobiles and Culture* (New York: 1984), 101.

2. America's Good Roads Search

1. See M. G. Lay, *Ways of the World: A History of the World's Roads and the Vehicles That Used Them* (New Brunswick, N.J.: Rutgers University Press, 1992), 238.

2. "Roads and Streets," in *Power Wagon Reference Book, 1920* (Chicago: Power Wagon, 1920), 771.

3. "Networks of Roads Will Release Locked-Up Riches of the Nation Says the President of the United States," *American Motorist* 8 (November 1916): 12, 54.

4. Theodore Roosevelt, "National Development and Good Roads," *Good Roads,* June 1903, 227.

5. W. Pierrepont White, "Good Roads for the People," *Outing* 11 (November 1907): 227.

6. See David V. Herlihy, "The Bicycle Story," *Invention and Technology* 8 (Spring 1992): 48–59.

7. "Twentieth Anniversary of the Automobile Club of Buffalo," *Buffalo Motorist* 20 (June 1927): 36, 38.

8. "Club History: Fifty Years of Service," *Buffalo Motorist* 43 (June 1950): 8–13.

9. See "Its Our Fortieth Anniversary," *Motor News* 39 (July 1956): 8–11, 29.

10. William J. Trepagnier, "AAA Golden Jubilee Begins," *Motor News* 39 (March 1952): 32.

11. Andy Newman, "First Came the Car; Then the Wrong Turn. Voila: The Map," *New York Times,* October 11, 2000, C-22.

12. Trepagnier, "AAA Golden Jubilee Begins," 33.

13. Paul S. Sutter, "Paved with Good Intentions: Good Roads, the Automobile, and the Rhetoric of Rural Improvement in the *Kansas Farmer,* 1890–1914," *Kansas History* 18 (Winter 1995–96): 288.

14. "Twentieth Anniversary of the Automobile Club of Buffalo," 41–42.

15. "Old Time Driving," *Buffalo Motorist* 43 (June 1950): 59.

16. Vernon McGill, *Diary of a Motor Journey from Chicago to Los Angeles* (Los Angeles: Grafton, 1927), 47.

17. William Kaszynski, *The American Highway: The History and Culture of Roads in the United States* (Jefferson, N.C.: McFarland, 2000), 28.

18. Ibid., 32.

19. Bruce E. Seely, *Building the American Highway System: Engineers as Policy Makers* (Philadelphia: Temple University Press, 1987), 25.

20. Carl Arnaldo Schwantes, *Transportation Redefines the Twentieth-Century West* (Bloomington: Indiana University Press, 2003), 122–23.

21. "Arkansas Roads Hampered by Archaic System," *American Motorist* 7 (March 1915): 105.

22. "'Good Road Day' in Pennsylvania," *Good Roads*, May 6, 1916, 208–10.

23. D. W. Smith, "The Road Movement in Illinois," *Good Roads*, August 1905, 516.

24. "Highway Work in Illinois," *Good Roads*, December 5, 1914, 205.

25. "Vermilion County, Illinois," *Good Roads*, July 29, 1916, 1.

26. "Four Thousand Miles of Hard Road; Not One Cent of Taxes," *Illinois Highways* 14 (July 1917): 67.

27. An earlier version of this discussion appeared as John A. Jakle, "Pioneer Roads: America's Early Twentieth-Century Named Highways," *Material Culture* 32 (Summer 2000): 1–22.

28. See James R. Akerman, "Blazing a Well-Worn Path," *Cartographica* 30 (Spring 1993): 10–20.

29. Emily Post, *By Motor to the Golden Gate* (New York: Appleton, 1916), 246.

30. Harold Meeks, *On the Road to Yellowstone: The Yellowstone Trail and American Highways, 1900–1930* (Missoula, Mont.: Pictorial, 2000), 35–36.

31. Harold Meeks, "The Lincoln Highway and the Yellowstone Trail," *Lincoln Highway Forum* 4 (Spring 1997): 11.

32. For a detailed discussion of the Lincoln Highway, see Drake Hokanson, *The Lincoln Highway: Main Street across America* (Iowa City: University of Iowa Press, 1988).

33. Newton A. Fuessle, "The Lincoln Highway: A National Road," *Travel* 14 (February 1915): 26.

34. Effie Price Gladding, *Across the Continent by the Lincoln Highway* (New York: Brentano's, 1915), 111.

35. Roy D. Chapin, "Across the Continent on the Lincoln Highway," *Countryside and Suburban Life* 23 (August 1916): 88.

36. Hokanson, *Lincoln Highway*, 94.

37. A. F. Bennett, "Lincoln Highway Nears Tenth Birthday," *Good Roads*, March 21, 1923, 107.

38. Arline B. N. Moss, "Report of National Committee on National Old Trails Road," in *Proceedings, Thirty-Eighth Continental, National Society, DAR* (Washington, D.C.: Daughters of the American Revolution, 1929), 10.

39. R. H. Johnston, "A Winter Tour from New York to Savannah," *Travel* 13 (May 1908): 368.

40. Winifred Hawkridge Dixon, *Westward Hoboes: Ups and Downs of Frontier Motoring* (New York: Scribner's, 1921), 213.

41. Victor Eubank, "Log of an Auto Pioneer Schooner," *Sunset* 28 (February 1912): 188.

42. "How Sparks (Kan.) Won the Pikes Peak Highway," *Modern Highway*, June 1921, 12–13.

43. "Follow the Red and White Marks," *Appian Way of America* 1 (September 1923): 4–5.

44. "Kansas Road Celebration," *Modern Highway*, August 1922, 11–12.

45. "The 'Good Roads Woman' behind the Jackson Highway," *Literary Digest* 67 (November 6, 1920): 61.

46. Alma Rittenberry, "The Jackson Highway, Chicago to New Orleans," *American Motorist* 7 (October 1915): 605.

47. Martha Carver, "Driving the Dixie: The Development of the Dixie Highway Corridor," *Society of Commercial Archeology Journal* 13 (Fall–Winter 1994–95): 13.

48. Eugene Brown, "The Trail," *Modern Highways,* August 1, 1925, 1.

49. Schwantes, *Transportation Redefines the Twentieth-Century West,* 142.

50. Ibid., 144.

51. Charles A. Taff, *Commercial Motor Transportation* (Homewood, Ill.: Irwin, 1969): 16.

52. Quoted in Lincoln Highway Association, *The Lincoln Highway: The Story of a Crusade That Made Transportation History* (New York: Dodd, Mead, 1935), 228.

3. Detour Ahead: Rebuilding America's Roads

1. John A. McDonald, "Detours and Maintenance of Traffic during Construction," *Good Roads,* April 1928, 235.

2. W. A. Van Duzer, "Economics of Highway Detours," *Roads and Streets* 70 (June 1930): 233.

3. Vernon McGill, *Diary of a Motor Journey from Chicago to Los Angeles* (Los Angeles: Grafton, 1922), 40–41.

4. C. Wiles Hallock, "The Men Who Make the Roads," *Good Roads,* January 11, 1922, 22.

5. B. E. Gray, "The Story of One Gravel Road," *Good Roads,* August 31, 1921, 108–9.

6. W. L. Spoon, "Burnt Clay Roads," *Good Roads,* October 1906, 789.

7. J. M. Wise, "Shell Roads," *Good Roads,* September 1, 1920, 104.

8. "Straw Roads," *Good Roads,* June 1905, 376.

9. Laurence Isley Hewes, *American Highway Practice* (New York: Wiley, 1942), 291.

10. "Bitumens and Their Use in Paving and Road Making," *Good Roads,* July 1909, 232.

11. Hewes, *American Highway Practice,* 89–90.

12. C. R. Stokes, "Asphaltic Surfacing of Gravel Roads," *Highway Engineer and Contractor* 40 (June 1932): 17.

13. Ibid., 19.

14. Arthur G. Bruce and John Clarkeson, *Highway Design and Construction* (Scranton: International Textbook, 1951), 459.

15. Ibid., 389.

16. George M. Mullins, "Road Oils," *National Petroleum News* 23 (August 12 1931): 45.

17. Bruce and Clarkeson, *Highway Design and Construction,* 560; see also William D. Walters Jr., "The American Shale Paver: Its Origin, Evolution, and Role in Landscape Preservation," *Pioneer America Society Transactions* 10 (1987): 59–65.

18. Hewes, *American Highway Practice,* 337.

19. Ibid., 338.

20. Maurice O. Eldridge, "Brick Roads," *Good Roads,* March 1905, 123.

21. Hewes, *American Highway Practice,* 354.

22. "Accidental Discovery Led to First Concrete Roadway," *Good Roads,* October 1909, 347.

23. Edward N. Hines, "A Michigan Concrete Road," *Good Roads,* October 1909, 347.

24. Hewes, *American Highway Practice,* 138.

25. See Fay Rowley, "The Ideal Section 'Today,'" *Highway* 39 (January 1948): 20–22.

26. Don Charles, "Motorists Drive by Instinct," *Highway* 22 (September 1931): 235.

27. Frederick W. Cron, "Highway Design for Motor Vehicles—A Historical Review, Part 3: The Interaction of the Driver, the Vehicle, and the Highway," *Public Roads* 39 (September 1975): 69.

28. Frederick W. Cron, "Highway Design for Motor Vehicles—A Historical Review, Part 7: The Evolution of Highway Grade Design," *Public Roads* 40 (September 1976): 79.

29. Ibid., 81.

30. "Scheduling Highway Maintenance Operations," *Highways* 37 (May 1946): 116.

31. "Pennsylvania Set Good Example for the Empire State," *Buffalo Motorist* 11 (February 1918): 17.

32. "Roadside Trash," *California Highways and Public Works* 32 (May–June 1953): 41.

33. "Using Convict Labor," *American Motoring* 9 (April 1917): 18.

34. Mrs. Gino Ratti, "The Alluring Road," *Hoosier Motorist* 13 (May 1925): 5.

35. C. S. Lee, "Three Hundred Thousand Miles of Surfaced Thoroughfares Constructed since 1880," *Motor Travel* 13 (July 1921): 37.

36. *America's Highways: Accelerating the Search for Innovation* (Washington, D.C.: Transportation Research Board, National Research Council, 1984), 16.

4. Highways as Public Prerogative

1. Robert Bruce, "Twenty Years' Road Development: Highway Improvement in New York State since 1898 Epitomized," *American Motorist* 10 (April 1918): 11.

2. U.S. Bureau of the Census, *Historical Statistics of the United States, Colonial Times to 1970, Bicentennial Edition, Part 2* (Washington, D.C.: U.S. Department of Commerce, Bureau of the Census, 1975), 710.

3. Rudi Volti, "Essay: A Century of Automobility," *Technology and Culture* 37 (October 1996): 667, attributes this feeling to the automobile itself, but this feeling was not to be achieved without motion on a road.

4. J. Malcolm Bird, "Tours and Detours: Impressions of the through Automobile Highways of the Eastern and Central States," *Scientific American* 125 (November 1921): 7.

5. Emily Post, *By Motor to the Golden Gate* (New York: Appleton, 1916), 67.

6. Bruce, "Twenty Years' Road Development," 7.

7. Edward Hungerford, "What of the American Highway?" *Saturday Evening Post,* September 13, 1924, 54.

8. Bruce E. Seely, *Building the American Highway System: Engineers as Policy Makers* (Philadelphia: Temple University Press, 1987), 51.

9. John B. Rae, *The American Automobile: A Brief History* (Chicago: University of Chicago Press, 1965), 52; John B. Rae, "Coleman du Pont and His Road," *Delaware History* 16 (Spring–Summer 1975): 181.

10. Thomas H. MacDonald, "The Present System of Federal Control and Aid for Highways: Its Results, Merits, and Limitations," *Good Roads,* January 14, 1920, 15.

11. A. R. Hirst, "The American Highway Problem," *Good Roads,* January 7, 1920, 1.

12. Seely, *Building the American Highway System,* 46–65, 67–69.

13. D. W. Meinig, *The Shaping of America: A Geographical Perspective on 500 Years of History,* vol. 4, *Global America, 1915–2000* (New Haven: Yale University Press, 2004), 11–18.

14. John Chynoweth Burnham, "The Gasoline Tax and the Automobile Revolution," *Mississippi Valley Historical Review* 48 (December 1961): 436.

15. Charles M. Upham, "Highway Finance," *Highway Engineer and Contractor* 20 (May 1929): 43.

16. "State Highway System for Virginia," *American Motorist* 10 (March 1918): 28.

17. Thomas H. MacDonald, "The Sources of Highway Income and Present Status of Highway Finance," *Roads and Streets* 70 (February 1930): 55–56.

18. Burnham, "Gasoline Tax," 442–44, 456; Abdel M. Fawzy, James W. Martin, and Mark Frishe, "Development of the Motor-Fuels Tax in the United States," *Southwestern Social Science Quarterly* 35 (December 1954): 209.

19. Norman A. Blaney, "A Review of Highway Financing," *Roads and Streets* 71 (May 1931): 185.

20. Ibid., 187. Regarding an earlier but unadopted system, see John B. Rae, "Coleman du Pont and His Road," 171–83.

21. Burnham, "Gasoline Tax," 447.

22. J. N. Mackall, "'Metering' Highway Transportation to Public," *Good Roads,* February 7, 1923, 55.

23. Burnham, "Gasoline Tax," 448–49.

24. Lawrence Leslie Waters, *Use Taxes and Their Legal and Economic Background* (Lawrence: University of Kansas, Department of Journalism, 1940), 9–33.

25. Ernest Ludlow Bogart and John Mabry Mathews, *The Modern Commonwealth, 1893–1918* (Springfield: Illinois Centennial Commission, 1920), 150–51; Clifford Older, "Survey of Road Work in Illinois," *Good Roads,* January 11, 1922, 11–12; Frank T. Sheets, "The Status of Road Construction in Illinois," *Blue Book of the State of Illinois, 1925–1926,* 336.

26. Frank T. Sheets, "Illinois Road Building and the Proposed One Hundred Million Dollar Bond Issue," *Blue Book of the State of Illinois, 1923–1924,* 255; Donald F. Tingley, *The Structuring of a State: The History of Illinois, 1899 to 1928* (Urbana: University of Illinois Press, 1980), 241; Frank T. Sheets, "Highway Construction in Illinois," *Blue Book of the State of Illinois, 1929–1930,* 454; Robert P. Howard, *Illinois: A History of the Prairie State* (Grand Rapids, Mich.: Eerdmans, 1972), 490–91.

27. Howard, *Illinois,* 490; Tingley, *Structuring of a State,* 242.

28. Gordon M. Sessions, *Traffic Devices: Historical Aspects Thereof* (Washington, D.C.: Institute of Traffic Engineers, 1971), 81. For a description of the Wisconsin program, see J. T. Donaghey, "Maintenance of State Trunk Highway System This Year," *Wisconsin Motorist* 9 (June 1918): 25–29; "Numbering Wisconsin Trunk Highways," *Wisconsin Motorist* 9 (June 1918): 31.

29. A. H. Hinkle, "Standard Highway Signs," *Good Roads,* April 1924, 95; Sessions, *Traffic Devices,* 82, 84.

30. Seely, *Building the American Highway System,* 41–42.

31. Sessions, *Traffic Devices,* 90.

32. Ibid., 90–91.

33. Cited in Sessions, *Traffic Devices,* 89.

34. Ibid. For the events leading up to and including the work of the Joint Board of Interstate Highways, see John A. Jakle and Keith A. Sculle, *Signs in America's Auto Age: Signatures of Landscape and Place* (Iowa City: University of Iowa Press, 2004), 60–62.

35. Numerous publications publicized the new sign system; see, for example, William Ullman, "Shielding the Nation's Highways," *Buffalo Motorist* 18 (December 1925): 15–17, 36–38.

36. Ibid., 15.

37. Ernest McGaffey, "Numbering the Highways of the United States," *Highway Engineer and Contractor* 18 (February 1928): 32.

38. Quinta Scott and Susan Croce Kelly, *Route 66: The Highway and Its People* (Norman: University of Oklahoma Press, 1988), 12, 14–15; Arthur Krim, "Highway Reports: First Numbering of Route 66 Discovered in Missouri," *SCA NewsJournal* 11 (Summer 1990): 10–11; Arthur Krim, "Mapping Route 66: A Cultural Cartography," in *Roadside America: The Automobile in Design and Culture,* ed. Jan Jennings (Ames: Iowa State University Press, 1990), 201–4; Arthur Krim, "'Get Your Kicks on Route 66!' A Song Map of Postwar Migration," *Journal of Cultural Geography* 18 (Fall–Winter 1998): 49–60; Arthur Krim, *Route 66: Iconography of the American Highway,* ed. Denis Wood (Santa Fe, N.M.: Center for American Places, 2005), 59–198.

39. Baynard Kendrick, *Florida Trails to Turnpikes, 1914–1964* (Gainesville: University of Florida Press, 1964), 173–77; Charles M. Upham, "Analysis of Causes and Methods for Prevention of Highway Accidents," *Highway Engineer and Contractor* 17 (October 1927): 68. Regarding the development of warning signs, also see Jakle and Sculle, *Signs in America's Auto Age,* 65–68.

40. Herbert A. Rowe, "The Crossing Crash," *Buffalo Motorist* 21 (August 1928): 14–16.

41. For example, see "Nearly Twenty Thousand Killed or Injured at Grade Crossings—Seventy Percent Were Motorists—Elimination of Grade Crossings Must Continue," *Buffalo Motorist* 13 (December 1920): 46.

42. Rowe, "Crossing Crash," 16.

43. Robert L. Meyer, "A Look at the First Congress," *Safety and Health* 135 (February 1987): 23; Robert L. Meyer, "The Pyle Years: Washington Enters the Safety Scene," *Safety and Health* 135 (July 1987): 26–27.

44. Frederick W. Cron, "Highway Design for Motor Vehicles—A Historical Review," *Public Roads* 38 (December 1974): 87–88.

45. Frederick W. Cron, "The Interaction of the Driver, the Vehicle, and the Highway," *Public Roads* 39 (September 1975): 68–79.

46. Peter J. Hugill, "Good Roads and the Automobile in the United States, 1880–1929," *Geographical Review* 72 (July 1982): 349.

47. Richard O. Davies, *The Age of Asphalt: The Automobile, the Freeway, and the Condition of Metropolitan America* (Philadelphia: Lippincott, 1975), 11.

48. Frederic L. Paxson, "The Highway Movement, 1916–1935," *American Historical Review* 51 (January 1946): 239.

49. Henry Earle Riggs, "The Highway in National Transportation," *Highway Engineer and Contractor* 36 (January 1930): 72.

50. Tom Lewis, *Divided Highways: Building the Interstate Highways, Transforming American Life* (New York: Viking Penguin, 1997), 51–53, 84; Seely, *Building the American Highway System,* 26–28; James J. Flink, *The Automobile Age* (Cambridge: MIT Press, 1988), 371; Mark H. Rose, *Interstate: Express Highway Politics, 1941–1956* (Lawrence: Regents Press of Kansas, 1979), 9–10.

51. Ilya Ilf and Eugene Petrov, *Little Golden America: Two Famous Soviet Humorists Survey the United States* (London: Routledge, 1946), 61–62.

5. Dealerships and Garages

1. Joseph J. Corn, "Work and Vehicles: A Comment and a Note," in *The Car and the City: The Automobile, the Built Environment, and Daily Urban Life,* ed. Martin Wachs and Margaret Crawford (Ann Arbor: University of Michigan Press, 1992), 25, 32.

2. For example, see "From $25,000 to $600,000 . . . ," *American Garage and Auto Sales*, March 1920, 13.

3. For a popular outline, see Robert Genat, *The American Car Dealership* (Osceola, Wis.: MBI, 1999). That automobile lovers' passion runs not only to the vehicles in use but to the architecture and settings where they are sold can be sampled in Jay Ketelle, *The American Automobile Dealership: A Picture Postcard History* (Amarillo, Tex.: Ketelle Collectibles, [1980]).

4. Thomas S. Dicke, *Franchising in America: The Development of a Business Method, 1840–1980* (Chapel Hill: University of North Carolina Press, 1992), 56; Thomas G. Marx, "The Development of the Franchise Distribution System in the U.S. Automobile Industry," *Business History Review* 59 (Autumn 1985): 465–68, 471–72; James M. Rubenstein, *Making and Selling Cars: Innovation and Change in the U.S. Automotive Industry* (Baltimore: Johns Hopkins University Press, 2001), 267–69; Genat, *American Car Dealership*, 18–19; James J. Flink, *The Automobile Age* (Cambridge: MIT Press, 1988), 217.

5. Gerald L. Bloomfield, "Coils of the Commercial Serpent: A Geography of the Ford Branch Distribution System, 1904–33," in *Roadside America: The Automobile in Design and Culture,* ed. Jan Jennings (Ames: Iowa State University Press, 1990), 40; Rubenstein, *Making and Selling Cars,* 265.

6. Dicke, *Franchising in America,* 8.

7. Bloomfield, "Coils of the Serpent," 42, 49; Rubenstein, *Making and Selling Cars,* 266; John B. Rae, *The American Automobile: A Brief History* (Chicago: University of Chicago Press, 1965), 62–63.

8. Dicke, *Franchising in America,* 54, 71, 75; Flink, *Automobile Age,* 191.

9. Rubenstein, *Making and Selling Cars,* 288–90.

10. Chester H. Liebs, *Main Street to Miracle Mile: American Roadside Architecture* (Boston: Little, Brown, 1985), 76, 80, 83; Rubenstein, *Making and Selling Cars,* 253; Flink, *Automobile Age,* 193; Commission on Chicago Landmarks, "Motor Row District: Michigan Avenue, Primarily between Cermak Road and the Stevenson Expressway," Preliminary Landmark Recommendation, approved April 3, 2000, 11, City of Chicago, Department of Planning and Development, Commission on Chicago Landmarks.

11. See especially the discussion of the psychology of dealership and showroom aesthetics in Genat, *American Car Dealership,* 44–63.

12. Liebs, *Main Street to Miracle Mile,* 92.

13. "Supermarkets: Dealers in Surplus Cars Go Big Time," *Business Week,* October 1, 1955, 105; Hubert W. Kelley Jr., "Mutiny of the Car Dealers," *Harper's,* August 1956, 70–71; William E. Holler, *The Automobile Dealer . . . Yesterday, Today, and Tomorrow* (Mt. Dora, Fla.: Holler, 1957), 22; "Dealers Take the Offensive," *Business Week,* June 17, 1950, 31–32; "The Auto Dealer: Old, Tired, and Baffled," *Business Week,* May 22, 1954, 44; "Why People Aren't Buying Cars," *U.S. News and World Report,* May 2, 1958, 37; Flink, *Automobile Age,* 282; Rubenstein, *Making and Selling Cars,* 286.

14. Alcarcilus Shelton-Boodram, "Auto Dealerships," in *Encyclopedia of African American Business History,* ed. Juliet E. K. Walker (Westport, Conn.: Greenwood, 1999), 45–50; Rubenstein, *Making and Selling Cars,* 279, 282, 284; Arlena Sawyers, "Study: Good Service Builds Buyer Loyalty," *Automotive News,* July 20, 1998, 6.

15. James J. Flink, *America Adopts the Automobile, 1893–1910* (Cambridge: MIT Press, 1970), 222.

16. "Up to the Ford Standard," *Ford Times,* February 1916, 311; "Maintenance Development," *Automobile Trade Journal* 29 (December 1, 1924): 296.

17. Clifton Egert, "Selecting Tools, Supplies, and Equipment for the Private Garage," *Automobile Dealer and Repairer* 24 (December 1917): 46.

18. Flink, *America Adopts the Automobile,* 217; Stephen L. McIntyre, "'The Repair Man Will Gyp You': Mechanics, Managers, and Customers in the Automobile Repair Industry, 1896–1940" (Ph.D. diss., University of Missouri-Columbia, 1995), 56, 60.

19. Emily Post, *By Motor to the Golden Gate* (New York: Appleton, 1916), 249.

20. Ralph Chamberlain, "'Over the Hills and Far Away,'" *Automobile Dealer and Repairer* 29 (August 1920): 41–44.

21. Egert, "Selecting Tools, Supplies, and Equipment," 46; Marguerite S. Shaffer, *See America First: Tourism and National Identity, 1880–1940* (Washington, D.C.: Smithsonian Institution Press, 2001), 251.

22. Virginia Scharff, *Taking the Wheel: Women and the Coming of the Motor Age* (Albuquerque: University of New Mexico Press, 1992), 47.

23. "Confessions of an Oil-Starved Car," *Literary Digest* 68 (January 8, 1921): 70.

24. Donald M. Smith, "Why Jobbers Should Consider Tune-Up Shops for Diversifying," *National Petroleum News* 81 (April 1989): 40; Donald M. Smith, "Car Care Center Growth Slows, but Developers See Bright Future," *National Petroleum News* 83 (May 1991): 32.

25. Flink, *America Adopts the Automobile,* 145, 149; "Philadelphia Auto Club Open Garage to A.A.A. Members," *American Motorist* 8 (June 1916): 44. For a history of the multipurpose storage garage, see John A. Jakle and Keith A. Sculle, *Lots of Parking: Land Use in a Car Culture* (Charlottesville: University of Virginia Press, 2004), 114–34.

26. See, for example, "Parking Pioneer Retires," *Parking,* July 1970, 29; National Steel Joists advertisement, *Building Age* 44 (May 1922): 85.

27. William Phillips Comstock, *Garages and Motor Boat Houses* (New York: Comstock, 1911), 63.

28. See, for example, the series by Tom Wilder, "Planning Your New Building," *Motor Age,* March 5, 1925, 25; March 26, 1925, 25; May 7, 1925, 25; February 11, 1926, 27.

29. William Ullman, "Speeding Up Auto Repairs," *Buffalo Motorist* 18 (September 1925): 25.

30. J. P. Gruet, "Filling Stations," *Texaco Star* 3 (February 1916): 10.

31. R. A. Knight, "The Modern Filling Station," *Texaco Star* 3 (April 1916): 10.

32. C. R. McCarty, "The Development of the Gasoline Filling Stations," *Texaco Star* 3 (March 1916): 11.

33. A. S. Kennedy, "Filling Stations," *Texaco Star* 3 (March 1916): 13.

34. Ullman, "Speeding Up Auto Repairs," 25.

35. Joseph E. Mills, *Garage Management and Control* (Chicago: Shaw, 1928), 79.

36. C. P. Shattuck, "Catch Them Early; Train Them Right," *American Garage and Auto Dealer* 27 (July 1927): 15.

37. Ibid., 15.

38. McIntyre, "'The Repair Man Will Gyp You,'" 334.

39. Mary Day Winn, *The Macadam Trail: Ten Thousand Miles by Motor Coach* (New York: Knopf, 1931), 292.

40. "Auto Repair Ripoffs: Study by AAA," *Road and Track,* July 1978, 119.

41. "Ralph Nader Reports," *Ladies' Home Journal,* April 1972, 50.

42. Carol Schwalberg, "An Opinion on Driving Auto Mechanics Crazy (or Honest)," *Mademoiselle,* October 1975, 20; "Ways They Can Cheat You When They Service Your Car," *Changing Times* 28 (June 1974): 11–14.

43. Schwalberg, "Opinion on Driving Auto Mechanics Crazy," 20.

44. McIntyre, "'The Repair Man Will Gyp You,'" 20, 31, 476, 537–38, 552, 558.

45. "How Important Is the Color of a Man's Collar?" *Good Housekeeping,* November 1967, 26, 30; Ernst H. Suerken, "Auto Mechanics as an Occupation," *Industrial Arts and Vocational Education* 48 (October 1959): 252; B. Richard, "Auto Mechanics—Highly Skilled Specialists Needed for Today's Cars," *Popular Mechanics,* January 1961, 48, 50.

46. Winifred Hawkridge Dixon, *Westward Hobos: Ups and Downs of Frontier Motoring* (New York: Scribner's, 1921), 190.

47. "Women Customers—They're in Every Market Now," *Business Week,* December 25, 1954, 34–36.

48. Andrew O. Shapiro, "Auto Suggestions: How to Deal with Those Repair Shops," *New York,* April 21, 1980, 73.

49. Bill Kilpatrick, "It's Not Worth a Damn If It Doesn't Run," *Field and Stream,* November 1977, 106.

50. Ray Hill, "Certified Auto Mechanics—Will They Do a Better Job on Your Car?" *Popular Science,* January 1974, 74–75.

51. Kevin Borg, "The 'Chauffeur Problem' in the Early Auto Era: Structuration Theory and the Users of Technology," *Technology and Culture* 40 (October 1999): 797–832.

52. See, for example, "Ways They Can Cheat You When They Service Your Car," 14.

53. For an example of the claim that combinations of garage work represented poor business practices, see J. H. Moore, "The Garage—A Paying Proposition," *Automobile Dealer and Repairer* 30 (January 1921): 30.

54. McIntyre, "'The Repair Man Will Gyp You,'" 13, 143.

55. Ibid., 310–11.

56. C. H. Thomas, "A Pennsylvania General Service Shop," *American Blacksmith and Motor Shop* 23 (March 1924): 14.

57. Keith A. Sculle, "Just a Garage," *Historic Illinois* 1 (December 1978): 9.

58. Charles W. Seiger, "Another Complete Sales-Service Plant," *American Garage and Auto Dealer* 24 (January 1925): 17–18.

59. "Building Up a Brake Service," *Accessory and Garage Journal* 18 (February 1929): 18; Ruel McDaniel, "Here Is a Brake Service That Is Different—And Very Profitable," *American Garage and Auto Dealer* 27 (November 1927): 12–13, 38; Paul W. Matthews, "The Curriculum Is Car Washing," *Highway User* 30 (September 1965): 22–23. For an example of an early car wash specialty, see K. H. Lansing, "Bring 'Em in Dirty, Take 'Em Out Clean!" *American Garage and Auto Dealer* 27 (July 1927): 12.

60. "At Your Service," *Hoosier Motorist* 14 (September 1926): 11; Ruel McDaniel, "'You Wreck 'Em, We Fix 'Em,' Says Doc," *American Garage and Auto Dealer* 27 (June 1927): 9; William J. Trepagnier, "The Automobile Club Is Twenty-one Years Old," *Motor News* 20 (July 1927): 9, 33.

61. James L. Creasy, "Evolution of the Road Map," *Highway Magazine* 48 (June 1957): 116; "Service Station Charlie," *American Garage and Auto Dealer* 25 (January 1926): 21; Jan Gordon and Cora J. Gordon, *On Wandering Wheels: Through Roadside Camps from Maine to Georgia in an Old Sedan Car* (New York: Dodd, Mead, 1928), 281; James R. Akerman, "Blazing a Well-Worn Path: Cartographic Commercialism, Highway Promotion,

and Automobile Tourism in the United States, 1880–1930," *Cartographica* 30 (Spring 1983): 10–20; Douglas A. Yorke Jr. and John Margolies, *Hitting the Road: The Art of the American Road Map* (San Francisco: Chronicle Books, 1996), 44–45, 114; "Free Road Maps Fading from the Scene," *National Petroleum News* 66 (July 1974): 25; Barbara Bradley, "A Map You Don't Have to Fold," *Christian Science Monitor,* November 2, 1987, 18, 20. For an excellent history of Rand McNally's influential "Blazed Trails" series of highway maps, see James R. Akerman, "Selling Maps, Selling Highways: Rand McNally's 'Blazed Trails' Program," *Imago Mundi* 45 (1993): 77–89.

62. John A. Jakle and Keith A. Sculle, *The Gas Station in America* (Baltimore: Johns Hopkins University Press, 1994), 66; Marvin Reid, "America Enters the Gasoline Era," *National Petroleum News* 76 (February 1984): 51; "Cities Service Standardized Station," *National Petroleum News* 22 (November 19, 1930), 102; K. H. Lansing, "Super-Service Brings Profit," *Accessory and Garage Journal* 18 (May 1929): 15, 19. For an example of a "one-stop" gasoline station, see Roger B. Stafford, "Utah Refiner Predicts One-Stops Will Be Stations of Future," *National Petroleum News* 23 (November 25, 1931): 50, 52.

63. Jakle and Sculle, *Gas Station in America,* 39–40, 45, 191–98. In contrast to the Quality Oil's use of a quirky seashell, Atlantic Refining used architecture with classical allusions to establish a positive reputation among motorists and the civic-minded elite; see Keith A. Sculle, "Atlantic Refining Company's Monumental Service Stations in Philadelphia, 1917– 1919," *Journal of American and Comparative Cultures* 23 (Summer 2000): 39–52; Keith A. Sculle, "Pittsburgh's Monuments to Motoring: Atlantic's Fabulous Stations," *Western Pennsylvania History* 83 (Fall 2000): 122–35.

64. "More Profits from Tires for Oil Companies This Depression Year," *National Petroleum News* 30 (August 17, 1938): 25–26, 28; Roger B. Stafford, "Tire Dealers to Develop One-Stop Service Stations Individually," *National Petroleum News* 21 (November 20, 1929): 29; M. S. Sullivan, "How Firestone Sells 600,000 Gallons a Year at Two Stations," *National Petroleum News* 22 (June 4, 1930): 107–8.

65. Keith Reid, "Fading from the Scene," *National Petroleum News* 80 (July 2002): 20; Roger Field, "Self-Service Gas Stations," *Science Digest,* June 1976, 87–89; Mark Edmond, "Why Quick Lube Outlets Are Grabbing Market Share," *National Petroleum News* 80 (May 1988): 52–56; Mark Edmond, "Fast Lubes and Lookalikes Dominate Lubricants Business," *National Petroleum News* 87 (August 1995): 40, 42–43; McIntyre, "'The Repair Man Will Gyp You,'" 428; Smith, "Why Jobbers Should Consider Tune-Up Shops," 40; Smith, "Car Care Center Growth Slows," 32.

6. The Tourist's Roadside

1. Roger William Riis, "Song of the Open Road," *Reader's Digest,* August 1941, 5.

2. George W. Sutton, "Rolling Vacations," *Collier's,* August 6, 1921, 13; "Save Money by Spinning from Coast to Coast," *Literary Digest,* November 7, 1925, 74.

3. "Save Money by Spinning," 76.

4. Ibid., 75.

5. "Author's Hobby Takes Him through 45 States," *Hobbies* 49 (March 1944): 23.

6. Marilyn Murphy, "Roam Sweet Home," *Ms.,* May–June 1992, 43.

7. Ibid., 45.

8. Emily Rose Burt, "Motoritis: An Agreeable Malady," *Delineator* 97 (October 1920): 110.

9. Elon Jessup, "The Flight of the Tin Can Tourists," *Outlook,* May 25, 1921, 167.

10. Sutton, "Rolling Vacations," 13.

11. Frank E. Brimmer, "Following the Open Road in Your Car," *Woman's Home Companion* 52 (June 1925): 42.

12. F[rank] E. Brimmer, "Home Away *from* Home," *Woman's Home Companion* 50 (May 1923): 48.

13. John D. Long, "A Vacation on Wheels," *Delineator* 107 (July 1925): 14.

14. Brimmer, "Home Away *from* Home," 47–48, 64.

15. Osma Palmer Couch, "When We Go Traveling," *American Home* 6 (June 1931): 197.

16. Frank E. Brimmer, "Nomadic America's Changing Spending Habits," *Magazine of Business* 53 (April 1928): 445.

17. Ibid., 446–47.

18. Ibid., 446.

19. Virginia Scharff, *Taking the Wheel: Women and the Coming of the Motor Age* (Albuquerque: University of New Mexico Press, 1992), 25–26.

20. Marguerite S. Shaffer, *See America First: Tourism and National Identity, 1880–1940* (Washington, D.C.: Smithsonian Institution Press, 2001), 256.

21. Long, "Vacation on Wheels," 63.

22. "A Woman's Advice on Motor Camping," *Literary Digest* 85 (April 4, 1925): 86.

23. "Lucky Ladies Who Motor Alone," *Literary Digest* 78 (August 11, 1923): 50.

24. Helen M. Mann, "May Day Motorists," *Overland Monthly* 75 (May 1920): 419.

25. "Lucky Ladies Who Motor Alone," 52.

26. Charlotte Montgomery, "The Woman and Her Car," *Good Housekeeping,* December 1954, 26, 171.

27. Bertha Streeter, "Vacations by Motor," *Parent's Magazine* 4 (July 1929): 24.

28. Charlotte Montgomery, "When the Children Go Along," *Good Housekeeping,* June 1951, 161.

29. Bob Trebilcock, "Not Too Big for Little Ones," *Yankee* 59 (June 1995): 54.

30. Nancy Richardson, "Believe It or Not, a Trip in the Car *with* Children and *without* Tears Is Altogether Possible—If You Plan Well," *Woman's Home Companion* 74 (July 1947): 110.

31. Streeter, "Vacations by Motor," 48.

32. Dorothy J. Curd, "When Baby Motors," *Woman's Home Companion* 61 (June 1934): 117.

33. A. B. Schwartz, "Baby Takes a Motor Trip," *Hygeia* 9 (June 1931): 540.

34. Curd, "When Baby Motors," 118.

35. Jean LaGrone Smith, "Vacationing with Baby," *Parent's Magazine* 15 (August 1940): 23, 30.

36. Montgomery, "When the Children Go Along," 162.

37. Florence C. Budd, "Traveling with a Dog," *American Home* 34 (November 1945): 85–87; Richardson, "Believe It or Not," 110.

38. Warren James Belasco, *Americans on the Road: From Autocamp to Motel, 1910–1945* (Cambridge: MIT Press, 1981).

39. *Automobile Dealer and Repairer* 37 (May 1924): 17.

40. Jan Gordon and Cora J. Gordon, *On Wandering Wheels: Through Roadside Camps from Maine to Georgia in an Old Sedan Car* (New York: Dodd, Mead, 1928), 83.

41. See, for example, Keith A. Sculle, "'Our Company Feels That the Ozarks Are a Good Investment . . .': The Pierce Pennant Tavern System," *Missouri Historical Review* 43 (April

1999): 293–307; Keith A. Sculle, "Traveling in Style: The Park Plaza Motel Chain," *Journal of the West* 41 (Fall 2002): 63–70.

42. R. Stephen Sennott, "Roadside Luxury: Urban Hotel and Modern Hotel and Modern Streets along the Dixie Highway," in *Looking beyond the Highway: Dixie Roads and Culture*, ed. Claudette Stager and Martha Carver (Knoxville: University of Tennessee Press, 2006), 114–35, outlines the hotels' niche in the lodging trade for automobile travelers.

43. The literature on this subject demands further attention. For an early installment about African American roadside accommodations nationally, see Lyle Henry, "Accommodations 'for Colored,'" *Society for Commercial Archaeology Journal* 23 (Fall 2005): 12–19.

44. Virginia Moore, "Who's Driving It Now?—Or, the Open Road and Hamburgers," *Christian Science Monitor,* June 11, 1949, 11.

45. Philip Langdon, *Orange Roofs, Golden Arches: The Architecture of American Chain Restaurants* (New York: Knopf, 1986), 41–47; John A. Jakle and Keith A. Sculle, *Fast Food: Roadside Restaurants in the Automobile Age* (Baltimore: Johns Hopkins University Press, 1999), 42–44; Keith A. Sculle, "Outlining Dutchland Farms, a Founder of Automobile Highway Travel in America," *Pioneer America Society Transactions* 22 (1999): 39–50.

46. "Cooking Your Own Motel Breakfast," *Sunset* 122 (June 1959): 151, 153–54.

47. "Eating Out . . . When You're on the Road," *Glamour,* July 1987, 192.

48. See especially Jane Stern and Michael Stern, *Roadfood* (New York: Random House/ Obst, 1978; revised 1980, 1986, 1992, and 2002).

49. "Eating Right on the Road," *Better Homes and Gardens,* August 1993, 94, 100.

50. George Ade, "Do You Run a Motor-Car or a Moveable Madhouse?" *American Magazine,* September 1921, 53.

51. Ibid., 55.

52. Florence M. Bauer and W. W. Bauer, "The Martin Family Vacation Episode V: Hot Weather; Speed or Relaxation?" *Hygeia* 14 (July 1936): 608–11.

53. John T. Flynn, "Dirty Work at the Crossroads," *Collier's,* April 24, 1926, 26, 41.

54. Ilya Ilf and Eugene Petrov, *Little Golden America: Two Famous Soviet Humorists Survey the United States* (London: Routledge, 1936), 71–72; Frederic F. Van de Water, "Discovering America in a Flivver," *Ladies' Home Journal,* April 1926, 223; Paul W. Kearney, "How to Drive Hundreds of Miles and Enjoy It," *Better Homes and Gardens,* August 1953, 119; Frank Triplett, "Highway Homicide," *Time,* August 17, 1987, 18; Curtis Billings, "Mishaps on the Tourist Trail," *Hygeia* 10 (August 1932): 690; William Ecenbarger, "America's Most Dangerous Highways," *Reader's Digest,* November 2000, 74–82.

55. Herman G. Morgan, "Health Hints for Motor Tourists," *Hygeia* 4 (July 1925): 361; Alice K. Perkins, "When You Go Touring: Expert Advice on the Clothes to Take and How to Pack Them," *Ladies' Home Journal,* August 1935, 16–17, 48; "Weather Reports for Motorists," *Science Digest* 22 (August 1947): 34.

56. Peter Martin, "Roadside Business: Casualty of War," *Saturday Evening Post,* August 8, 1942, 16–17, 47–48; Richard L. Frey, "Don't Let Death Hitch a Ride with You!" *Cosmopolitan,* August 1953, 82–87; John Pashdag, "Vacation Travel '74," *Motor Trend* 26 (June 1974): 95–97; Timothy Blankenhorn, "The Silver-Haired Set on Tour," *Road and Track* 40 (May 1989): 54–56.

57. Denise McCluggage, "Long-Distance Car Vacations," *Glamour,* August 1983, 204; Jessica Reeves, "Dogma Girl Hits the Road," *Ms.,* March–April 1998, 96; Harold Hinton,

"The Family-Less Car," *New York Times Magazine,* August 20, 1950, 53, 55; L. J. K. Setright, ". . . and Thou beside Me Singing in the Wilderness," *Car and Driver* 25 (July 1979): 138.

58. Erik Cohen, "A Phenomenology of Tourist Experiences," *Sociology* 13 (1979): 185–86; Erik Cohen, "Tourism as Play," *Religion* 15 (1985): 291–304.

59. "The Land of Santa Claus," *Highway Magazine* 40 (December 1949): 279–81; "Santa Claus, Ind.," *Stanolind Record* 13 (December 1931): 29–30; "Santa Claus Land" brochure, ca. 1965, in possession of the authors; John A. Jakle, *The Tourist: Travel in Twentieth-Century North America* (Lincoln: University of Nebraska Press, 1985), 24.

60. Richard B. Starnes, introduction to *Southern Journeys: Tourism, History, and Culture in the Modern South,* ed. Richard D. Starnes (Tuscaloosa: University of Alabama Press, 2003), 2; Delores B. Jeffords, "Shrine of the Indian Water Gods," *Highway Magazine* 42 (August 1951): 172–75; Tim Hollis, *Dixie before Disney: 100 Years of Roadside Fun* (Jackson: University Press of Mississippi, 1999), 145–48, 151–52. On Florida's especially large number of intermediate destinations, see Margot Ammidown, "Edens, Underworlds, and Shrines: Florida's Small Tourist Attractions," *Journal of Decorative and Propaganda Arts* 23 (1998): 238–59.

61. See, for example, "Pioneer in Breeding of Fur Bearing Animals Who Has Helped Win Recognition of Industry," *Lake Placid News,* September 8, 1922, 12; "J. S. Sterling Dies in Miami Beach," *Lake Placid News,* March 20, 1959, n.p.; Emalene Wark, "Gingerbread Castle," *Motor News* 38 (September 1955): 22; E. Ward McCray, "Last Frontier Village," *Motor News* 35 (March 1953): 8–9, 24; Keith A. Sculle, "Roadside Business: The Origins of the 'Indian Village,'" *Kansas History* 14 (Spring 1991): 15–25. John Margolies, *Fun along the Road: American Roadside Attractions* (Boston: Little, Brown, 1998), illustrates many of these intermediate destinations along with their thumbnail histories but, as Margolies declares (6), does so without intending to divine their underlying meanings.

62. Franklin M. Reck, *A Car Traveling People* (Detroit: Automobile Manufacturers Association, 1945), 37.

63. Goldie Shearer, "Popular Garden Stand Features Organic Produce," *Organic Gardening and Farming* 18 (January 1971): 110. See also Elizabeth Frazer, "Roadside Market," *Saturday Evening Post,* December 20, 1924, 63.

64. Molly O'Neill, "Roadside Attractions," *New York Times Magazine,* August 30, 1992, 70.

65. Dan Looker, "Building a Farm on Location Not Acres," *Successful Farming* 94 (January 1996): 62–64.

66. "Roadside Stands," *Americana* 6 (November 1978): 32.

67. Ibid., 31.

68. Ibid., 34; "The Roadside Market," *Hoosier Motorist* 6 (October 1917): 1; Gene Logsdon, "Your Best Cash Crops," *Organic Gardening and Farming* 20 (August 1973): 37.

69. Dorothy Cheney Quinan, "From Cows to Cones," *Farm Journal* 80 (August 1956): 116.

70. J. Wilson McKenney, "Roadside Date Shop on the Desert," *Desert Magazine* 1 (August 1938): 13–15.

71. See, for example, Keith A. Sculle, "A Bit of the South Florida Roadside Transplanted: Allan W. Davis Sea Shells and Souvenirs," *Society for Commercial Archeology Journal* 22 (Fall 2004): 12–16; Keith A. Sculle, "The Thomas Family's Roadside Novelty Shops," *White River Valley Historical Journal* 44 (Summer 2005): 18–21.

72. Hal Burton, "For a Relaxing Vacation, There's Only One Cape Cod," *Better Homes and Gardens,* August 1952, 56, 103, 132–36; Hal Burton, "Lots of Mountains for Your Money," *Better Homes and Gardens,* February 1950, 58.

73. Erving Goffman, *The Presentation of Self in Everyday Life* (Woodstock, N.Y.: Overlook, 1973), 238–55; Dean MacCannell, *The Tourist: A New Theory of the Leisure Class* (New York: Schocken, 1976), 91–99.

74. John B. Jackson, "Other-Directed Houses," *Landscape* 6 (Winter 1956–57): 31–32. Kent MacDonald, "The Commercial Strip: From Main Street to Television Road," *Landscape* 28, no. 2 (1985): 12–19, extends strip architecture's explanation from Main Street in the 1950s–60s through television's influence in the 1970s; the changes are substantial, although the principle remains the same: strip architecture entertains.

75. David Gebhard, introduction to *California Crazy: Roadside Vernacular Architecture,* ed. Jim Heimann and Rip Georges (San Francisco: Chronicle Books, 1980), 11–25. See, for example, H. Roger Grant, "Highway Commercial Architecture: Albia, Iowa's 'Dutch Mill,'" *Palimpsest* 58 (May–June 1977): 84–87; Keith A. Sculle, "Frank Redford's Wigwam Village Chain: A Link in the Modernization of the American Roadside," in *Roadside America: The Automobile in Design and Culture,* ed. Jan Jennings (Ames: Iowa State University Press, 1990), 125–35; Brian A. Butko, "Sleeping in a Ship—Along Pennsylvania's Lincoln Highway," *Image File: A Journal from the Curt Teich Postcard Archives* 6, no. 4 (1991): 3–6.

76. Chester H. Liebs, *Main Street to Miracle Mile: American Roadside Architecture* (Boston: Little, Brown, 1985), 4.

77. Shaffer, *See America First,* 4–5.

78. "Our Natural Playgrounds," *Ford Times* 9 (January 1916): 249–51.

79. Gary Mason and Sara Amy Leach, "The Redwood Highway: Ancient Trees and Tourist Bait," *SCA Journal* 16 (Fall 1998): 4–11.

80. Peter Blodgett, "Selling the Scenery: Advertising and the National Parks, 1916–1933," in *Seeing and Being Seen: Tourism in the American West,* ed. David M. Wrobel and Patrick T. Long (Lawrence: University Press of Kansas, 2001), 271–98.

81. W. H. Spindler, "Grand Canyon National Park Geared to Tourist Traffic," *Highway Magazine* 38 (March 1947): 52.

82. Paul S. Sutter, *Driven Wild: How the Fight against Automobiles Launched the Modern Wilderness Movement* (Seattle: University of Washington Press, 2002).

83. "Californians Urged to Demand Saving Historic Weaverville," *Roadside Bulletin* 2 (October 1934): 23. For examples of highways promoted as historic site destinations, see W. H. Spindler, "Traveling the Lincoln Country of Illinois," *Highway Magazine* 32 (May 1941): 111–15; Felix and Nikki Zelenka, "The Gold Rush Route," *Highway Magazine* 40 (February 1949): 28–30.

84. David Lowenthal, "Past Time, Present Place: Landscape and Memory," *Geographical Review* 65 (January 1975): 11–12.

85. Kenneth L. Roberts, "Roads of Remembrance," *Saturday Evening Post,* December 7, 1929, 24–25, 250–53; Daniel M. Bluestone, "Roadside Blight and the Reform of Roadside Architecture," in *Roadside America,* ed. Jennings, 170–84; John Robinson, *Highways and Our Environment* (New York: McGraw-Hill, 1971), 126–39.

86. Lee Foster, "Your Vacation Guide," *Travel Holiday,* July 1986, 65.

87. Andrew Hurley, *Diners, Bowling Alleys, and Trailer Parks* (New York: Basic Books, 2001), 202–4, 247–51.

88. F. M. Radigan, "The Rise of the Recreational Vehicle," *Highway User,* November 1970, 20–21.

89. James Jones, "Living in a Trailer," *Holiday* 12 (July 1952): 74, 78–82, 120; Hurley, *Diners, Bowling Alleys, and Trailer Parks,* 197; David Meyers, "Trailing the Sun," *Motor News*

35 (January 1953): 31. For an elaborate example of romanticized trailer life, see Edith B. Campaigne and Jameson C. Campaigne, "Edie in Trailerland," *Saturday Evening Post,* May–June 1977, 34–37; September 1977, 38–39, 108, 110; October 1977, 36–37, 102, 104.

90. "After Retirement—What?" *Highway Magazine* 44 (March 1953): 58.

91. John Fraser Hart, Michelle J. Rhodes, and John T. Morgan, *The Unknown World of the Mobile Home* (Baltimore: Johns Hopkins University Press, 2002), 82–83.

92. Ibid., 38; Allan D. Wallis, *Wheel Estate: The Rise and Decline of Mobile Homes* (Baltimore: Johns Hopkins University Press, 1997), 21; Hurley, *Diners, Bowling Alleys, and Trailer Parks,* 268–72. For an excellent case study, see Lee Irby, "Taking Out the Trailer Trash: The Battle over Mobile Homes in St. Petersburg, Florida," *Florida Historical Quarterly* 79 (Fall 2000): 181–200.

93. "The New Gypsies," *Reo Review* 1 (November 1921): 3–4; Roger B. White, *Home on the Road: The Motor Home in America* (Washington, D.C.: Smithsonian Institution Press, 2000).

94. See, for example, Margaret G. Nichols, "Exploring the 50-Mile Limit," *Field and Stream* 78 (April 1974): 162–65; Les Payne, "We Saw the U.S. in Our Motor Home," *Black Enterprise* 12 (June 1982): 240–42.

95. Bill and Jan Moeller, *Full-Time* RVing: A Complete Guide to Life on the Open Road (Camarillo, Calif.: Trailer Life Books, 1993), 17.

96. Ibid., 15–17.

97. Margaret Cerullo and Phyllis Ewen, "'Having a Good Time,'" *Radical America* 16, nos. 1–2 (1986): 13–44.

98. Cindy S. Aron, *Working at Play: A History of Vacations in the United States* (New York: Oxford University Press, 1999).

7. Rejecting the Roadside as Landscaped Landscape

1. J. M. Bennett, *Roadsides: The Front Yard of the Nation* (Boston: Stratford, 1936), 1.

2. Elizabeth Lawton and W. L. Lawton, *The Roadsides of North Carolina: A Report of a Study of the Problem of Roadside Improvement along the Highways of the State* (Washington, D.C.: National Council for the Protection of Landscape Beauty, 1930), 4–6.

3. "Esthetic Considerations in Road and Bridge Work," *Good Roads,* September 22, 1920, 145.

4. A. R. Hirst, "Safety and Beauty as Factors in Road Design and Construction," *Good Roads,* March 8, 1922, 140.

5. [James Agee], "The Great American Roadside," *Fortune,* September 1934, 53.

6. Edmund K. Faltermayer, *Redoing America* (New York: Collier, 1968), 29.

7. See, for example, Peter Blake, *God's Own Junkyard* (New York: Holt, Rinehart, and Winston, 1964); Ian Nairn, *The American Landscape* (New York: Random House, 1965).

8. For a fuller discussion of roadside signage, see John A. Jakle and Keith A. Sculle, *Signs in America's Auto Age: Signatures of Landscape and Place* (Iowa City: University of Iowa Press, 2004).

9. Jan Gordon and Cora J. Gordon, *On Wandering Wheels* (New York: Dodd, Mead, 1928), 41, 124.

10. Rollo W. Brown, *I Travel by Train* (New York: Appleton Century, 1939), 289.

11. Quoted in Lawton and Lawton, *Roadsides of North Carolina,* 8.

12. Kenneth L. Roberts, "Travel in Billboardia," *Saturday Evening Post,* October 13, 1928), 186.

13. "Designing for Appearance as Well as Utility," *Good Roads,* December 28, 1921, 293.

14. Bennett, *Roadsides,* 55.

15. Wilhelm Miller, "The First Roadside Planting along the Lincoln Highway," *American City* 4 (April 1916): 326, 329.

16. John A. Hazelwood, "Beautifying Highways," *Good Roads,* June 21, 1919, 264.

17. John Liska, "The Relation of Improved Highways to Home Life," *Good Roads,* January 29, 1925, 27.

18. John S. Martin, "Shrubs, Vines, and Flowers for the Roadside," *Good Roads,* December 1906, 956.

19. Burton W. Potter, *The Road and the Roadside* (Boston: Little, Brown, 1893), 113.

20. C. F. Boehler, "Beautifying Our Roadsides," *Good Roads,* September 29, 1920, 157.

21. Henry Morrison, "Tree Planting along Roadways," *Good Roads,* December 1903, 496.

22. "Roadside Planting," *Good Roads,* October 5, 1921, 177.

23. F. W. Besley, "Tree Planting along Public Highways," *Good Roads,* November 9, 1921, 217.

24. "That Battered Tree," *Public Safety* 44 (August 1953): 17.

25. James H. MacDonald, "Beautifying the Roadside," *Good Roads,* January 1906, 7.

26. Colin P. Campbell, "Legal Rights in Trees beside Highways," *Good Roads,* January 1907, 18.

27. Besley, "Tree Planting," 217.

28. V. Herbert Sargent, "What May Be Accomplished by Highway Beautification and Scientific Tree Planting," *Highway* 22 (January 1931): 7.

29. C. R. Thomas, "Hints on Roadside Tree Planting," *Highway Engineer and Contractor* 17 (September 1927): 29.

30. "A Report of Progress in Highway Beautification," *Highway Engineer and Contractor* 20 (June 1929): 45.

31. See John A. Harrington, "Survey of Landscape Use of Native Vegetation on Midwest Highway Rights-of-Way," in *Safety, Rest Areas, Roadway Vegetation, and Utility and Highway Issues 1991* (Transportation Research Record 1326; Washington, D.C.: Transportation Research Board, National Research Council, 1991), 141.

32. H. H. Slawson, "Highway Weed Control," *Highway* 28 (June 1937): 141.

33. "Completion of the Northeast Boulevard in Philadelphia, Pennsylvania," *Good Roads,* May 2, 1914, 299.

34. Laurence Isley Hewes, *American Highway Practice,* vol. 1 (New York: Wiley, 1942), 206–7.

35. Quoted in Robert W. Hadlow, "The Columbia River Highway: America's First Scenic Road," *SCA Journal* 18 (Spring 2000): 16.

36. See F. J. Brady, "The Columbia River Highway in Oregon," *Good Roads,* October 6, 1920, 167–71.

37. *A Proposed Program for Scenic Roads and Parkways* (Washington, D.C.: President's Council on Recreation and Natural Beauty, 1966), 109.

38. Sara Amy Leach, "Fifty Years of Parkway Construction in and around the Nation's Capital," in *Roadside America: The Automobile in Design and Culture,* ed. Jan Jennings (Ames: Iowa State University Press, 1990), 186.

39. Bennett, *Roadsides,* 219.

40. Ralph T. Burch, "Today's Natchez Trace," *Highway* 50 (February 1959): 38.

41. Quoted in "The Long Island Motor Parkway," *Good Roads,* July 1908, 224.

42. Gilmore D. Clarke, "The Parkway Idea," in *The Highway and the Landscape,* ed. W. Brewster Snow (New Brunswick, N.J.: Rutgers University Press, 1959), 38.

43. William W. Niles, "The Bronx River Parkway," *Motor Travel* 12 (April 1920): 13.

44. Ibid., 15.

45. See John B. Rae, *The Road and the Car in American Life* (Cambridge: MIT Press, 1971), 71–73.

46. L. G. Holleran, "The Hutchinson River Parkway," *Motor Travel* 20 (February 1929): 7–9.

47. Gilmore D. Clarke, "Gasoline Stations for Highway Freeways and Parkways," *Highway* 26 (May 1935): 4.

48. Clarke, "The Parkway Idea," 44.

49. For a full discussion of Robert Moses, see Robert A. Caro, *The Power Broker: Robert Moses and the Fall of New York* (New York: Vintage, 1975).

50. Robert Moses, "Park and Parkway Improvement in Metropolitan New York," *Motor News* 23 (October 1940): 24.

51. Caro, *Power Broker,* 318.

52. David G. Havlick, *No Place Distant: Roads and Motorized Recreation on America's Public Lands* (Washington, D.C.: Island, 2002), 23–24.

53. E. S. Matheson, "Skyline Drives," *Motor News* 21 (March 1939): 21.

54. Havlick, *No Place Distant,* 25.

55. H. J. Spelman, "Building the Blue Ridge Parkway from Shenandoah to Great Smokies," *Highway* 28 (August 1937): 173.

56. Burch, "Today's Natchez Trace," 38.

57. *Natchez Trace Parkway* (Washington, D.C.: U.S. National Park Service, 1970).

58. Quoted in *The Art and Science of Roadside Development: A Summary of Current Knowledge* (Washington, D.C.: Highway Research Board, National Academy of Sciences/National Research Council, 1966), 1.

59. See Wilbur H. Simonson, "Evolution of Modern Highway Design in the United States: The Complete Highway," in *Landscape Design and Its Relation to the Modern Highway,* ed. J. Curtis Hanes and Charles H. Connors (New Brunswick, N.J.: Rutgers University, College of Engineering, 1952), 10–21.

60. "Roadside Improvement Projects Actively Sponsored by United States Bureau of Public Roads," *American City* 49 (January 1934): 39.

61. Ruth B. Johnson, "Federal Highway Beautification Goals," in *Outdoor Advertising: History and Regulation,* ed. John W. Houck (Notre Dame, Ind.: University of Notre Dame Press, 1969), 128.

62. Clifton W. Enfield, "Federal Highway Beautification: Outdoor Advertising Control, Legislation and Regulation," in *Outdoor Advertising,* ed. Houck, 150.

63. Wallace A. Johnson, "Preserving the Scenic Qualities of the Roadside," in *Highway and the Landscape,* ed. Snow, 124.

64. Lewis L. Gould, "First Lady as Catalyst: Lady Bird Johnson and Highway Beautification in the 1960s," *Environmental Review* 10 (Summer 1986): 77–92.

65. Wilbur J. Gramhausen, "Roadside Parks," *Highway* 49 (May–June 1958): 97–98.

66. William Whyte, *The Last Landscape* (Garden City, N.Y.: Doubleday, 1968), 288.

67. Ibid., 254.

68. Jonathan Daniels, *A Southerner Discovers New England* (New York: Macmillan, 1940), 14.

69. [Volney Hurd], "After Hours," *Harper's,* January 1950, 100–101.

70. Nigel Nicolson and Adam Nicolson, *Two Roads to Dodge City: Two Colorful English Writers, Father and Son, Chronicle Their Wonderful Journeys across America* (New York: Harper and Row, 1987), 68.

8. Limited-Access Highways as Dream Fulfillment

1. David R. Levin, *Public Control of Highway Access and Roadside Development* (Washington, D.C.: U.S. Government Printing Office, 1943), 4.

2. Bruce E. Seely, "Urban Freeway Development and the Bureau of Public Roads, 1930–1950," *SCA Journal* 15 (Spring 1997): 16; Spencer Miller, "History of the Modern Highway in the United States," in *Highways in Our National Life: A Symposium,* ed. Jean Labatut and Wheaton L. Lane (Princeton: Princeton University Press, 1950), 110; Levin, *Public Control* (1943), 18–19; Christopher Tunnard and Boris Pushkarev, *Man-Made America: Chaos or Control?* (New Haven: Yale University Press, 1963), 167; David R. Levin, *Public Control of Highway Access and Roadside Development,* rev. ed. (Washington, D.C.: U.S. Government Printing Office, 1947), 19.

3. Levin, *Public Control* (1943), 9.

4. Ibid., 5.

5. See, for example, Frederick P. Clark, "'Limited Motorways,'" *American City* 51 (January 1936): 56.

6. Tunnard and Pushkarev, *Man-Made America,* 160.

7. M. G. Lay, *Ways of the World: A History of the World's Roads and of the Vehicles That Used Them* (New Brunswick, N.J.: Rutgers University Press, 1992), 314; Spencer Miller, "History of the Modern Highway," 105; Phil Patton, *Open Road: A Celebration of the American Highway* (New York: Simon and Schuster, 1986), 67.

8. Bruce Radde, *The Merritt Parkway* (New Haven: Yale University Press, 1993), ix, 33, 40, 45, 121; E. C. Welden, "The Merritt Parkway," *Highway Magazine* 31 (August 1940): 173–74.

9. Timothy Mark Davis, "Mount Vernon Memorial Highway and the Evolution of the American Parkway" (Ph.D. diss., University of Texas, 1997), 718, 736. Davis's is the definitive history of the Mount Vernon Memorial Highway. For an excellent overview of parkways in Washington, D.C., see Sara Amy Leach, "Fifty Years of Parkway Construction in and around the Nation's Capital," in *Roadside America: The Automobile in Design and Culture,* ed. Jan Jennings (Ames: Iowa State University Press, 1990), 187–89.

10. W. A. Bugge and W. Brewster Snow, "The Complete Highway," in *The Highway and the Landscape,* ed. W. Brewster Snow (New Brunswick, N.J.: Rutgers University Press, 1959), 23–24.

11. A. D. Griffin, "Arroyo Seco," *California Highways and Public Works* 40 (January–February 1961): 60.

12. Radde, *Merritt Parkway,* 7; Caro, *Power Broker,* 162; Seely, "Urban Freeway Development," 14; Lewis Mumford, *The Highway and the City* (New York: Harcourt, Brace, and World, 1963), 236; Kathleen LaFrank, "Real and Imagined Landscapes along the Taconic State Parkway," in *Constructing Image, Identity, and Place,* ed. Alison K. Hoagland and Kenneth A. Breisch (Knoxville: University of Tennessee Press, 2003), 247–63; Patton, *Open*

Road, 70. For an example of the disparagement of Moses's parkways, see Radde, *Merritt Parkway,* 11.

13. Radde, *Merritt Parkway,* 7.

14. Sigfried Gideon, *Space, Time, and Architecture: The Growth of a New Tradition,* 5th ed. (Cambridge: Harvard University Press, 1967), 826, 831.

15. Lay, *Ways of the World,* 110–11; P. K. Schuyler, "Is the Toll Road a Solution?" *Roads and Streets* 70 (April 1930): 129–30; Gilmore D. Clarke, "The Parkway Idea," in *Highway and the Landscape,* ed. Snow, 33; Charles A. Glover, "The Challenge of the New Highway Program," in *Highway and the Landscape,* ed. Snow, 60; John B. Rae, *The Road and the Car in American Life* (Cambridge: MIT Press, 1971), 182.

16. Schuyler, "Is the Toll Road a Solution?" 131.

17. Lester P. Barlow, "Government-Owned Toll Motorways," *Highway Engineer and Contractor* 19 (November 1928): 34.

18. Lester P. Barlow, "Public-Owned Toll Roads," *Highway Engineer and Contractor* 20 (June 1929): 39.

19. Mark H. Rose, *Interstate: Express Highway Politics, 1941–1956* (Lawrence: Regents Press of Kansas, 1979), 11, 17–18, 27.

20. Ibid., 5, 16, 48; Seely, "Urban Freeway Development," 15; Tom Lewis, *Divided Highways: Building the Interstate Highways, Transforming American Life* (New York: Viking, 1997), 53.

21. "Motorists Make Pennsylvania Turnpike an Amateur Speed-Testing Ground," *National Petroleum News* 32 (November 27, 1940): 27–30, 32; E. Willard Miller, "The Pennsylvania Turnpike," in *Geographical Snapshots of North America,* ed. Donald G. Janelle (New York: Guilford, 1992), 428, 430; Patton, *Open Road,* 77–78; J. Herbert Walker, "The Big Road," *Highway Traveler* 23 (Summer 1951): 15; "Novel Service Stations Designed for Pennsylvania's Super Highway," *National Petroleum News* 32 (May 29, 1940): 26; *The Pennsylvania Turnpike System* (brochure) (Harrisburg: Pennsylvania Turnpike Commission, [1952?]), [2].

22. Walker, "Big Road," 16; John B. Rae, *Road and the Car,* 177.

23. E. Willard Miller, "Pennsylvania Turnpike," 431.

24. Walker, "Big Road," 13.

25. John B. Rae, *Road and the Car,* 174–76; Albert J. Wedeking, "Indiana's Toll Road Celebrates a Birthday," *Highway Magazine* 46 (September 1955): 197; W. H. Spindler, "The New York State Thruway," *Highway Magazine* 45 (April 1954): 77; Robert S. Beightler, "A New 'National Road,'" 45 (December 1954): 269.

26. Timothy A. Harrison, "Effect on the Nation of the Federal Highway Program," *Highway Magazine* 48 (March 1957): 43; Glover, "Challenge of the New Highway Program," 62; Henry Moon, "The Interstate Highway System," in *Geographical Snapshots,* ed. Janelle, 425, 427; *Twin Trailer Trucks: Effects on Highways and Highway Safety* (Washington, D.C.: Transportation Research Board, National Research Council, 1986), 219; D. W. Meinig, *The Shaping of America: A Geographical Perspective on 500 Years of History,* vol. 4, *Global America, 1915–2000* (New Haven: Yale University Press, 2004), 22–23; Rose, *Interstate,* 96, 98.

27. Rose, *Interstate,* 47, 86.

28. George A. Dondero, "The Key to a Better Highway System," *Highway Magazine* 45 (July 1945): 148; Herbert Brean, "Dead End for the U.S. Highway," *Life,* May 30, 1955, 105.

29. Carlos Arnaldo Schwantes, *Going Places: Transportation Redefines the Twentieth-Century West* (Bloomington: Indiana University Press, 2003), 285, 288; Lewis, *Divided Highways,* 88–91.

30. Rose, *Interstate,* 93.

31. Cited in ibid.

32. Cited in Lewis, *Divided Highways,* 119–20.

33. Gary T. Schwartz, "Urban Freeways and the Interstate System," *Southern California Law Review* 49 (March 1976): 436–37.

34. Patton, *Open Road,* 92; Lay, *Ways of the World,* 318; Moon, "Interstate Highway System," 425; James J. Flink, *The Automobile Age* (Cambridge: MIT Press, 1988), 175–76; Lewis, *Divided Highways,* ix.

35. Robert Lubar, "Interchange Ahead," *Fortune,* October 1958, 132; Ray Vicker, "What the New Freeways Will Mean to You," *Better Homes and Gardens,* February 1958, 156; "How the Superhighways Are Changing America," *U.S. News and World Report,* August 31, 1950, 45–46, 48; Moon, "Interstate Highway System," 426–27.

36. Darrell A. Norris, "Interstate Highway Exit Morphology: Non-Metropolitan Exit Commerce on I-75," *Professional Geographer* 39 (February 1987): 30.

37. Christopher Sutton and Jeff Engelstad, "Growth in the High Plains: Douglas County and Denver's 470 Beltway," *Bulletin of the Illinois Geographical Society* 41 (Spring 1999): 5–13.

38. Jay J. Dugan, "Watch That Turnpike!" *Coronet* 33 (April 1953): 36; Paul W. Kearney, "I Drive the Turnpikes and Survive," *Saturday Evening Post,* May 5, 1956, 49.

39. Kearney, "I Drive the Turnpikes and Survive," 49.

40. See, for example, ibid.; "How to Drive on a Superhighway," *Changing Times* 10 (June 1956): 14; Dugan, "Watch That Turnpike!" 36.

41. Dugan, "Watch That Turnpike!" 36.

42. Duane L. Gregg, "What You Should Know about Driving the Interstate Highways," *Better Homes and Gardens,* June 1967, 30, 32; "How to Drive on a Superhighway," 14; Michael Lamm, "How to Plan Ahead and Get the Most from the Interstate Highway System," *Popular Mechanics,* June 1971, 83.

43. Gregg, "What You Should Know," 30; Lamm, "How to Plan Ahead," 83; Schwartz, "Urban Freeways and the Interstate System," 20.

44. Joe Weber, "Everyday Places on the American Freeway System," *Journal of Cultural Geography* 21 (Spring–Summer 2004): 1–26.

9. Motoring by Truck

1. Merrill J. Roberts, "The Motor Transportation Revolution," *Land Economics* 32 (August 1956): 228–38, acknowledged the meager attention historians had paid to the trucking industry at the time of his writing, but although Roberts's article provided a good overview up to that time, he did not continue publishing on the subject. Typical among historians' persistent oversight of trucking's considerable contribution to the nation's mobile lifestyle, Quinta Scott and Susan Croce Kelly, *Route 66: The Highway and Its People* (Norman: University of Oklahoma Press, 1988), holds that the miraculous construction of the nation's highway grid "gave automobiles someplace to go" (3) but says nothing about trucks.

2. William R. Childs, *Trucking and the Public Interest: The Emergence of Federal Regulation, 1914–1930* (Knoxville: University of Tennessee Press, 1985), 1; Robert F. Karolevitz, *This Was Trucking: A Pictorial History of the First Quarter Century of Commercial Motor Vehicles* (Seattle: Superior, 1966), 18–19, 42; "The Transcontinental Truck Trip," *Literary Digest*, September 9, 1911, 412–13.

3. John B. Rae, *The Road and the Car in American Life* (Cambridge: MIT Press, 1971), 110.

4. "The Growth of the Commercial-Car Industry," *Literary Digest*, March 9, 1912, 489.

5. "The Horse as an 'Economic Anachronism,'" *Literary Digest*, April 26, 1913, 140–41.

6. Harry Wilkin Perry, "The Motor Car in Its Application," *American Motorist* 4 (November 1912): 863–64.

7. "Automobiles Safer Than Horses," *World's Work* 27 (April 1914): 736.

8. "Do Farmers Want Radial Highways?" *Good Roads*, March 1907, 94–95.

9. James J. Flink, *America Adopts the Automobile, 1895–1910* (Cambridge: MIT Press, 1970), 89–90; Childs, *Trucking and the Public Interest*, 2; Wayne G. Broehl Jr., *Trucks . . . Trouble . . . and Triumph: The Norwalk Truck Line Company* (New York: Arno, 1976), 21.

10. "Selling Trucks on Credit," *Literary Digest*, July 13, 1912, 68; Charles A. Taff, *Operating Rights of Motor Carriers: (Interstate Commerce Commission Policy Regarding Property Carriers)* (Dubuque, Iowa: Brown, 1953), 16; Harry Wilkin Perry, "Present Conditions, and Especially Those Due to the European War," *Literary Digest*, May 27, 1916, 1539; F. Van Z. Lane, "Motor Truck Fits into Short Haul Problem from Every Standpoint," *Freight Transportation Digest*, July 16, 1919, 5–6; "Why Railroads Like Motor-Trucks," *Literary Digest*, December 28, 1919, 85; Childs, *Trucking and the Public Interest*, 19.

11. Childs, *Trucking and the Public Interest*, 20–21.

12. Joe Kelly, "The Rural Motor Express and Return Loads," *Hoosier Motorist* 6 (July 1918): 12, 41.

13. John A. Craig, "Motor Trucks to Solve the Freight Problem," *World's Work* 35 (March 1918): 566.

14. John Benjamin, "They Uphold a Tradition," *Highway User* 29 (January 1964): 7–8.

15. "Motor Truck Parcel Post," *Good Roads*, March 30, 1918, 175–76.

16. "The Rural Motor Express," *Motor Truck Club Bulletin* 6 (June 1918): 11.

17. Craig, "Motor Trucks to Solve the Freight Problem," 566.

18. "Why Railroads Like Motor-Trucks," 85; Craig, "Motor Trucks to Solve the Freight Problem," 567.

19. P. W. Litchfield, "History's Lesson to the Motor Truck," *Wisconsin Motorist* 19 (April 1918): 43–45; A. F. Joy, "The Wingfoot Express," *Highway User*, February 1968, 24–26. For Litchfield's account of the pneumatic tire's development, see P. W. Litchfield, *Industrial Voyage: My Life as an Industrial Lieutenant* (New York: Doubleday, 1954), 141–45.

20. Taff, *Operating Rights of Motor Carriers*, 16.

21. Childs, *Trucking and the Public Interest*, 33, 39–41, 43; Broehl, *Trucks*, 22.

22. Edward Mott Woolley, "Earning a Living in Motor Traffic," *Collier's*, January 28, 1922, 9.

23. Childs, *Trucking and the Public Interest*, 35–36.

24. Ibid., 35.

25. Kenneth D. Durr and Philip L. Cantelon, *Never Stand Still: The History of Consolidated Freightways, Inc. and CNF Transportation Inc., 1929–2000* (Rockville, Md.: Montrose, 1999), 17; George M. Graham, "Relation of Highway Transportation to Increased

Production—I," *Good Roads,* July 7, 1920, 3; Carlos Schwantes, *Going Places: Transportation Redefines the Twentieth-Century West* (Bloomington: Indiana University Press, 2003), 221.

26. Charles A. Taff, *Commercial Motor Transportation,* 4th ed. (Homewood, Ill.: Irwin, 1969), 91, 99; Karolevitz, *This Was Trucking,* 90, 93, 96; Fred B. Lautzenhiser, "Highway Trailer Operation," *Highway Engineer and Contractor* (June 1929): 50; "The Trailer—Its Design, Application, and Economy," *Power Wagon Reference Book, 1920* (Chicago: Power Wagon, 1920), 474.

27. James J. Flink, *The Automobile Age* (Cambridge: MIT Press, 1988), 171.

28. "Heavy Traffic for Roads and Roads for Heavy Traffic," *Good Roads,* October 6, 1917, 181–82.

29. *Twin Trailer Trucks: Effects on Highways and Highway Safety* (Washington, D.C.: Transportation Research Board, National Research Council, 1986), 3.

30. Harry Wilkin Perry, "Trailers and Trucks for Highway Hauling," *Good Roads,* July 23, 1919, 44.

31. Childs, *Trucking and the Public Interest,* 168–69.

32. Ibid., 34–35.

33. Ibid., 57.

34. Ibid., 39; "Wages and Hours of Labor," *Monthly Labor Review* 38 (June 1934): 1440.

35. Childs, *Trucking and the Public Interest,* 36; "Eastern Hauls Are Short Ones, So Shippers Find Trucks Faster," *Business Week,* May 20, 1931, 28.

36. Childs, *Trucking and the Public Interest,* 53.

37. Ibid., 34–35.

38. For example, see T. R. Dahl, "The Correlation of Transportation Facilities," *Good Roads,* February 1926, 67–69; "Mistaken Railway Arguments against Highway 'Carriers,'" *Roads and Streets* 75 (October 1932): 435.

39. Taff, *Operating Rights of Motor Carriers,* 24–25; Childs, *Trucking and the Public Interest,* 52; J. T. Sharpensteen, "Control of Highway Loading," *Roads and Streets* 70 (May 1930): 182; *Monthly Labor Review* 38 (June 1934): 1432.

40. Taff, *Operating Rights of Motor Carriers,* 24.

41. Ibid., 24–25.

42. Childs, *Trucking and the Public Interest,* 12.

43. Ibid., 19; John Richard Felton and Dale G. Anderson, eds., *Regulation and Deregulation of the Motor Carrier Industry* (Ames: Iowa State University Press, 1989), 16.

44. U.S. President's Research Committee on Social Trends, *Recent Social Trends in the United States* (New York: McGraw-Hill, 1933), 460.

45. Jerome Donald Fellman, "Truck Transportation Patterns of Chicago" (Ph.D. diss., University of Chicago, 1950), 19–20, 29.

46. Michael L. Berger, *The Devil Wagon in God's Country: The Automobile and Social Change in Rural America, 1893–1929* (Hamden, Conn.: Archon, 1979), 42, 43, 110–12.

47. David Witwer, *Corruption and Reform in the Teamsters Union* (Urbana: University of Illinois Press, 2003), 65.

48. John Hess, *The Mobile Society: A History of the Moving and Storage Industry* (New York: McGraw-Hill, 1973), 23.

49. *1963 American Trucking Trends* (Washington, D.C.: American Trucking Associations, n.d.), 3.

50. Childs, *Trucking and the Public Interest,* 163–66.

51. Dorothy Robyn, *Braking the Special Interests: Trucking Deregulation and the Politics of Policy Reform* (Chicago: University of Chicago Press, 1987), 234–35; Felton and Anderson, *Regulation and Deregulation*, 38.

52. Robyn, *Braking the Special Interests*, 15, 23–25; John V. Lawrence, "The Growth of an Industry," *Highway User* 28 (December 1963): 13; *American Trucking: Trends, 1970–71* (Washington, D.C.: American Trucking Associations, n.d.), [3].

53. Felton and Anderson, *Regulation and Deregulation*, 145.

54. Ibid., 146–48, 152.

55. Ibid., 145–46; Marvin Schwartz, *J. B. Hunt: The Long Haul to Success* (Fayetteville: University of Arkansas Press, 1992), 35; *Twin Trailer Trucks*, 10–11, 220.

56. Ben H. Petty, "Those Trucks and Buses!" *Highway Magazine* 43 (April 1952): 78.

57. John B. Rae, *Road and the Car*, 116, 118.

58. Evan McLeod Wylie, "By Piggyback across America," *American Magazine*, February 1956, 24; Ilya Ilf and Eugene Petrov, *Little Golden America: Two Famous Soviet Humorists Survey the United States* (London: Routledge, 1944), 64.

59. Ron Berler, "The Brotherhood of the Dixie Truckers Home in McLean, Ill.," *Chicago Tribune Magazine*, March 10, 1974, 19.

60. *Twin Trailer Trucks*, 19.

61. See, for example, J. C. Young, "Truck Turns," *California Highways and Public Works* 29 (March–April 1950): 14–16.

62. E. J. Raich, "Checking Axle Loads in Illinois," *Highway Magazine* 43 (April 1952): 91.

63. Cullison Cady, "Pennsylvania's Inspection System," *Highway User*, June 1966, 16–19.

64. Petty, "Those Trucks and Buses!" 77–79.

65. *Twin Trailer Trucks*, 4–5, 201; Schwartz, *J. B. Hunt*, 32–33.

66. Fellman, "Truck Transportation Patterns," 46–47, 49, 51, 99; Taff, *Commercial Motor Transportation*, 252–54, 256.

67. Jessica Rowecroft, "The Truck Stops Here! The History and Physical Development of the Truck Stop Industry," paper presented at the Vernacular Architecture Forum, Columbus, Georgia, 1999; Berler, "Brotherhood," 21; Martin A. Wyckoff and Greg Koos, eds., *The Illustrated History of McLean County* (Bloomington, Ill.: McLean County Historical Society, 1982), 369; Jack N. Westsmith, "A Station Built to Service Trucks," *National Petroleum News* 28 (July 1, 1936): 45–46; "Highway Cargo," *Texaco Star*, Midwinter 1947, 8.

68. Cullison Cady, "Truck Stop," *Highway User*, September 1966, 27.

69. Ibid.; Rowecroft, "The Truck Stops Here!"; George Schultz, "Truckstops: An Industry for Sale?" *National Petroleum News* 84 (October 1992): 73, 78; "Truckers to Travelers," *National Petroleum News* 94 (August 2002): 37; "Dad's Family Takes on His Dream of Museum," *Omaha World-Herald*, December 29, 2002, 3D; Renee Barnack, "The Truckstop Transformation," *National Petroleum News* 90 (April 1998): 40–41.

70. Witwer, *Corruption and Reform*, 74.

71. Marc F. Wise and Bryan Di Salvatore, *Truck Stop* (Jackson: University Press of Mississippi, 1995), 19–20, 23–24, 27–28. See also Schwartz, *J. B. Hunt*, 62–76.

72. Ibid., 33.

73. D. Daryl Wyckoff, *Truck Drivers in America* (Lexington, Mass.: Lexington Books, 1979), 51, 53, 128. Also see Edwin G. Flittie and Zane P. Nelson, "The Truck Driver: A Sociological Analysis of an Occupational Role," *Sociology and Social Research* 52 (April 1968): 207; Thorp McClusky, "Truckers Are Human, Too," *Christian Science Monitor*, August 9, 1947, 13.

74. Flittie and Nelson, "Truck Driver," 208.

75. Wise and Di Salvatore, *Truck Stop,* 33.

76. Alfred Maund, "Peons on Wheels: The Long-Haul Trucker," *Nation* 177 (November 14, 1953): 393.

77. Robert E. McCord, "Today's Pirates Sail the Highways," *Popular Science,* November 1953, 115–17, 262.

78. McClusky, "Truckers Are Human, Too," 3.

79. D. Daryl Wyckoff, *Truck Drivers in America,* 1.

80. Witwer, *Corruption and Reform,* 75.

81. See, for example, Malcolm P. McLean, "Opportunity Begins at Home," *American Magazine,* May 1950, 21.

82. McClusky, "Truckers Are Human, Too," 13.

83. Flittie and Nelson, "Truck Driver," 206–8.

84. Witwer, *Corruption and Reform,* 39; Maund, "Peons on Wheels," 394; D. Daryl Wyckoff, *Truck Drivers in America,* 59, 113.

85. Wise and Di Salvatore, *Truck Stop,* 28.

86. McClusky, "Truckers Are Human, Too," 3.

87. Ibid.; Wylie, "By Piggyback across America," 24; Wise and Di Salvatore, *Truck Stop,* 24.

88. Witwer, *Corruption and Reform,* 77; Kenneth C. Crow, *How the Rank and File Took Back the Teamsters* (New York: Scribner's, 1993), 18, 37, 84.

89. Jan Stern, *Trucker: A Portrait of the Last American Cowboy* (New York: McGraw-Hill, 1975); Lawrence Ouelett, *Pedal to the Metal: The Work Lives of Truckers* (Philadelphia: Temple University Press, 1994), 109, 169–72, 175–80; Durr and Cantelon, *Never Stand Still,* 98; Lloyd Klein, "Sex Solicitation by Short Wave Radio," *Free Inquiry in Creative Sociology* 9 (May 1981): 62–63; Jeff Brouws, Wendy Button, Bruce Caron, Mark Frauenfelder, Joel Jensen, M. Mark, Phil Patton, Alan Rapp, Luc Sante, and D. J. Waldie, *Readymades: American Roadside Artifacts* (San Francisco: Chronicle Books, 2003), 99.

90. Wessel Smitter, "Glamour Boys of the Highway," *Saturday Evening Post,* February 23, 1946, 14.

91. Christopher Finch, *Highways to Heaven: The Auto Biography of America* (New York: HarperCollins, 1992), 333–34.

92. H. W. Smith, "The CB Handle: An Announcement of Adult Identity," *Symbolic Interaction* 3 (Fall 1980): 95.

93. James H. Thomas, "Truckstops, Truckers, and Trucks: 1976," *Journal of Popular Culture* 13 (Fall 1979): 227–28.

94. James M. Rubenstein, *Making and Selling Cars: Innovation and Change in the U.S. Automotive Industry* (Baltimore: Johns Hopkins University Press, 2001), 243; Manny Howard, "The Pickup, a Love Story," *New York Times Magazine,* September 28, 2003, 62–63.

95. D. Daryl Wyckoff, *Truck Drivers in America,* 121.

10. Motoring by Bus

1. Alex Roggero, *Go Greyhound: A Pictorial Tribute to an American Icon* (New York: Barnes and Noble, 1996), 18.

2. Burton B. Crandall, *The Growth of the Intercity Bus Industry* (Syracuse: Crandall, 1954), 7.

3. Minnesota Railroad and Warehouse Commission, *Biennial Report, 1925–26* (St. Paul: Minnesota Railroad and Warehouse Commission, 1926), 3.

4. Frank H. Warren, "The Battle of the Bus and the Street Car," *Bus Transportation* 1 (February 11, 1922): 86.

5. Roy Hauer and Geo[rge] H. Scragg, *Bus Operating Practice* (New York: International Motor, 1925), 6.

6. Warren, "Battle of the Bus and the Street Car," 86–87.

7. "Building a Bus Business," *Bus Transportation* 1 (September 1922): 467–69.

8. "Buses Thrive in Florida," *Bus Transportation* 2 (February 1923): 65.

9. "Detroit Railway Bus Lines Acquired by Organization of Bondholders," *Bus Transportation* 7 (November 1928): 642.

10. "Parlor Body Seats Twelve," *Bus Transportation* 7 (January 1928): 41.

11. "Analysis of 1927 Body Production," *Bus Transportation* 7 (February 1928): 93.

12. "Rapid Advance in Stage Design in Washington," *Bus Transportation* 1 (October 1922): 527.

13. "Staggered Passenger Level Finds Favor on Pacific Northwest Lines," *Bus Transportation* 8 (June 1926): 302.

14. "Pacific Coast Has Interurban Scenic Bus Service," *Bus Transportation* 1 (January 1922): 44.

15. C. Arnold, "First Motor Sleeper Completed," *Highway Engineer and Contractor* 19 (September 1928): 66–68.

16. "Lakes to Sea Air-Conditioned Bus 20 Degrees Cooler Inside," *Bus Transportation* 13 (July 1934): 248.

17. "The Growth of the Motor Bus Compared with Other Transportation Factors," in *Bus Facts for 1929* (Washington, D.C.: American Automobile Association, 1929), 5.

18. J. E. Slater, "Motor Transportation in the United States," *American Economic Review* 17 (March 1927): 143.

19. Hauer and Scragg, *Bus Operating Practice,* 30.

20. "Lexington, Ky. Is Important Motor Bus Center," *Reo Review* 1 (May 1922): 12.

21. F. J. Scarr, "The Motorcoach and the Steam Railroad," *Bus Transportation* 6 (July 1927): 381.

22. Slater, "Motor Transportation," 148.

23. Scarr, "Motorcoach and the Steam Railroad," 380.

24. "Trend in Railroad Bus Use Increasing," *Bus Transportation* 9 (June 1930): 120.

25. "Major Cross-Country Bus Systems Form $30 Million Merger," *Bus Transportation* 7 (February 1928): 81.

26. "Motor Transit Takes over Insull Long Distance Lines," *Bus Transportation* 8 (February 1928): 81.

27. "Pennsylvania and Greyhound Lines Form New Bus Combine," *Bus Transportation* 10 (February 1930): 100.

28. "Summary of Greyhound Operations," *Bus Transportation* 12 (November 1933): 428.

29. Crandall, *Growth of the Intercity Bus Industry,* 174.

30. Ibid., 227.

31. "2,500 Buses Used in Sightseeing, Tourist, and Contract Service," *Bus Transportation* 5 (January 1926): 27.

32. Jack Rhodes, *Intercity Bus Lines of the Southwest: A Photographic History* (College Station: Texas A & M University Press, 1988), 118.

33. "Santa Fe Finds Buses of Value in New Service," *Bus Transportation* 6 (January 1927): 8.

34. Lewis R. Freeman, "Cross-Continent Trip by Common Carrier Lines Reveals Need for More and Better Terminals," *Bus Transportation* 5 (March 1926): 140.

35. Lewis R. Freeman, "The Comfortless Comfort Stop," *Bus Transportation* 9 (January 1930): 18.

36. "Los Angeles Union Stage Depot Used by 350 Cars Daily," *Bus Transportation* 1 (May 1922): 275.

37. John C. Fistere, "Bus Terminal Planning," *Architectural Forum* 1 (December 1930): 748.

38. "One Man Controls Bus and Passenger Movement," *Bus Transportation* 10 (August 1931): 412.

39. "The Industry's Finest Terminal Opened in Kansas City," *Bus Transportation* 9 (August 1930): 434.

40. Greyhound, *Annual Report* (Chicago: Greyhound, 1955), 16.

41. "A Special Report: The Suit against GM and What It Means to the Bus Industry," *Bus Transportation* 35 (August 1956): 43, 48.

42. Roggero, *Go Greyhound,* 48.

43. Greyhound, *Annual Report* (Chicago: Greyhound Corporation, 1953), 27.

44. Evan McLeod Wylie, "For a Carefree Holiday, I Rode the Super-Bus," *American Magazine,* January 1955, 32.

45. Greyhound, *Annual Report* (Chicago: Greyhound, 1960), 5.

46. Roggero, *Go Greyhound,* 78.

47. Patricia Brooks, "Leave the Driving to Them," *SRWorld,* March 23, 1974, 27.

48. Kathleen Jonah, "Traveling by Bus: What to Look for, What to Avoid," *Retirement Living* 17 (October 1977): 33.

49. Brooks, "Leave the Driving to Them," 30.

50. Jack Kerouac, "The Great Western Bus Ride," *Esquire,* March 1970, 136–37.

51. Lewis R. Freeman, "From Chicago to Los Angeles on Common Carrier Lines," *Bus Transportation* 5 (June 1926): 297.

52. Bertram B. Fowler, "The Night Bus," *Christian Science Monitor,* July 3, 1935, 10.

53. Mary Day Winn, *The Macadam Trail: Ten Thousand Miles by Motor Coach* (New York: Knopf, 1931), 14.

54. Nathan Asch, "Cross-Country Bus," *New Republic,* April 25, 1934, 301.

55. Don Eddy, "I'm a Vacation Bus Rider," *American Magazine,* July 1958, 31.

56. Jack Kerouac, "On the Road with Memere," *Holiday* 37 (May 1965): 74.

57. *Bus Facts: A Summary of Facts and Figures on the Intercity Bus Industry* (Washington, D.C.: National Association of Motor Bus Operators, 1956), 6.

58. *Bus Facts: A Summary of Facts and Figures on the Intercity Bus Industry* (Washington, D.C.: National Association of Motor Bus Operators, 1964), 4, 10.

11. Convenience in Store

1. Wilbur Zelinsky, *The Cultural Geography of the United States* (Englewood Cliffs, N.J.: Prentice Hall, 1992), 36–64.

2. For convenience as an analytical concept, see Kenneth C. Gerhrt, "The Dimensionality of the Convenience Phenomenon: A Qualitative Reexamination," *Journal of Business and Psychology* 8 (Winter 1993): 163–80.

3. Steve Graves, "The Landscape of Convenience" (unpublished paper, Department of Geography, University of Illinois at Champaign-Urbana, 1995), 1.

4. For modernism's architectural implications, see Edward Relph, *The Modern Urban Landscape* (Baltimore: Johns Hopkins University Press, 1987), 98–118.

5. For the idea of capitalism's creative destruction, see Douglas W. Rae, *City Urbanism and Its End* (New Haven: Yale University Press, 2003), 7–8.

6. Dwayne Jones and Roni Morales, "Pig Stands: The Beginning of the Drive-In Restaurant," *SCA News Journal* 2 (Winter 1991): 1–5. For an overview of the fast food restaurant, see John A. Jakle and Keith A. Sculle, *Fast Food: Roadside Restaurants in the Automobile Age* (Baltimore: Johns Hopkins University Press, 1999).

7. For an assessment of franchising in the quick-service food industry, see Stan Luxenberg, *Roadside Empires: How the Chains Franchised America* (New York: Penguin, 1985). For a detailed look at drive-in architecture, see Philip Langdon, *Orange Roofs, Golden Arches: The Architecture of American Chain Restaurants* (New York: Knopf, 1986).

8. Dave Carpenter, "McDonald's Arching Empire Not So Golden," *Champaign-Urbana News-Gazette,* November 3, 2002, C-1.

9. Eric Schlosser, "Fast Food Nation: Part One—The True Cost of America's Diet," *Rolling Stone,* September 3, 1998, 62.

10. Bruce Horovitz, "What's Next: Fast-Food Giants Hunt for New Products to Tempt Customers," *USA Today,* July 3–4, 2002, 1.

11. Carpenter, "McDonald's Arching Empire," C-1.

12. Dave Carpenter, "McDonald's Gives Hints of Restaurant Vision for Future," *Chicago Tribune,* August 5, 2003, sec. 3, p. 14.

13. For parking and its impact on retailing, see John A. Jakle and Keith A. Sculle, *Lots of Parking: Land Use in a Car Culture* (Charlottesville: University of Virginia Press, 2004).

14. "Banking by Automobile," *Scientific American,* September 1937, 151–52.

15. Beckie Kelly, "ATM's: More than Meets the Eye," *National Petroleum News* 90 (December 1998): 27–28.

16. Chester H. Liebs, *Main Street to Miracle Mile: American Roadside Architecture* (Boston: Little, Brown, 1985), 153.

17. For detailed discussion of the drive-in movie theater, see Joe Bob Briggs, *Joe Bob Goes to the Drive-In* (New York: Delacorte, 1987); Kerry Segrave, *Drive-In Theaters: A History from Their Inception in 1933* (Jefferson, N.C.: McFarland, 1992).

18. Peter Marsh and Peter Collett, *Driving Passion: The Psychology of the Car* (Boston: Faber and Faber, 1986), 7.

19. Ibid.

20. Peter Blake, *Philip Johnson* (Basel: Birkhauser, 1996), 160.

21. Isabel Wilkerson, "New Funeral Option for Those in a Rush," *New York Times,* February 23, 1989, A-16.

22. See Warren J. Belasco, *Americans on the Road: From Autocamp to Motel, 1910–1945* (Cambridge: MIT Press, 1979); John A. Jakle, Keith A. Sculle, and Jefferson S. Rogers, *The Motel in America* (Baltimore: Johns Hopkins University Press, 1996).

23. See John A. Jakle and Keith A. Sculle, *The Gas Station in America* (Baltimore: Johns Hopkins University Press, 1994).

24. "Census Shows Stations Are 40 Percent of Total Gas Sales Places," *National Petroleum News* 24 (June 29, 1932): 44.

25. "Three Gasoline Pumps Every Mile of State of Highway in United States," *Stanolind Record* 21 (February 1940): 7.

26. "Gas Stations a Fading Piece of Americana," *Toledo Blade,* July 4, 1993, 1.

27. "Gasoline Stations Scramble to Meet EPA Regulations," *St. Louis Post-Dispatch,* December 22, 1998, A-14.

28. "History of Convenience Stores Linked to American Mobility," *National Petroleum News* 82 (September 1990): 63.

29. Ibid., 65.

30. "Gasoline and C-Store Derby: Why Circle K Is Gaining in the Home Stretch," *National Petroleum News* 80 (August 1988): 44.

31. Claudia H. Deutsch, "Rethinking the Convenience Store," *New York Times,* October 8, 1989, sec. 3, p. 1.

32. "Major Oil Company Annual Reports, 2001," *National Petroleum News* 94 (Mid-July 2002): 106.

33. Ibid., 107.

34. Jakle and Sculle, *Gas Station in America,* 130.

35. Mark Edmond, "What Marketers Need to Know about C-Store Design Layout," *National Petroleum News* 83 (July 1991): 28.

36. Beckie Kelly, "Designed to Make a Difference," *National Petroleum News* 90 (September 1998): 42.

37. Lisa DuShane, "The Twenty-first Century Store Just Opened in L.A.," *National Petroleum News* 89 (October 1997): 36.

38. Marvin Reid, "How the Self-Service Revolution Bred Price Wars and C-Stores," *National Petroleum News* 76 (October 1997): 36.

39. James Naughton, "QSRs on the Horizon," *National Petroleum News* 93 (October 2001): 48.

40. Peter Blake, *God's Own Junkyard: The Planned Deterioration of the American Landscape* (New York: Holt, Rinehart, and Winston, 1964), 188.

41. Peirce F. Lewis, "The Geographer as Landscape Critic," in *Visual Blight in America,* ed. Peirce F. Lewis, David Lowenthal, and Yi-Fu Tuan (Washington, D.C.: Association of American Geographers, 1973), 3.

12. The Highway Experience: A Conclusion

1. Kris Lackey, *Road Frames: The American Highway Narrative* (Lincoln: University of Nebraska Press, 1997), 16.

2. Mitchell Schwarzer, "The Moving Landscape," in *Monuments and Memory, Made and Unmade,* ed. Robert S. Nelson and Margaret Olin (Chicago: University of Chicago Press, 2003), 84.

3. Paul C. Adams, "Peripatetic Imagery and Peripatetic Sense of Place," in *Textures of Place: Exploring Humanist Geographies,* ed. Paul C. Adams, Steven Hoelscher, and Karen E. Till (Minneapolis: University of Minnesota Press, 2001), 187.

4. Ibid., 189.

5. Julius H. Parmelee and Earl R. Feldman, "The Relation of the Highway to Rail Transportation," in *Highways in Our National Life: A Symposium,* ed. Jean Labatut and Wheaton J. Kane (Princeton: Princeton University Press, 1950), 238.

6. Julius Weinberger, "Economic Aspects of Recreation," *Harvard Business Review* 15 (Summer 1937): 456.

7. Carlton S. Van Doren and Sam A. Lollar, "The Consequences of Forty Years of Tourism Growth," *Annals of Tourism Research* 12 (special issue 1985): 473.

8. [Arthur J. Eddy], *2,000 Miles on an Automobile—By Chauffeur* (Philadelphia: Lippincott, 1902), 9, 40.

9. Myron M. Stearns, "Notes on Changes in Motoring," *Harper's,* September 1936, 441.

10. See John A. Jakle and Keith A. Sculle, *Signs in America's Auto Age: Signatures of Landscape and Place* (Iowa City: University of Iowa Press, 2004).

11. Lord Kinross, *The Innocents at Home* (New York: Morrow, 1959), 74; all ellipses in original except the final set.

12. Guillermo X. Garcia, "I-35 through Texas Is a Brutal Drive," *USA Today,* February 2, 2002, A-3.

13. Randy Kennedy, "I-95, a River of Commerce Overflowing with Traffic," *New York Times,* December 29, 2000, A-21.

14. Peter T. Kilborn, "In Rural Areas, Interstates Build Their Own Economies," *New York Times,* July 14, 2001, A-1.

15. Scott Armstrong, "Size of Tandem Rigs Sparks Debate in Congress and in West," *Christian Science Monitor,* June 19, 1966, 5.

16. Todd S. Purdum, "A Game of Nerves, with No Real Winners," *New York Times,* May 17, 2000, E-13.

17. "Automated Road Is First in Nation," *New York Times,* July 13, 1997, A-15.

18. D. H. Lawrence, *Studies in Classic Literature* (New York: Viking, 1923), 172.

19. See Michael Bernick and Robert Cervero, *Transit Villages in the Twenty-first Century* (New York: McGraw-Hill, 1997), 43.

20. Sandra Rosenbloom, "Why Working Families Need a Car," in *The Car and the City: The Automobile, the Built Environment, and Daily Life,* ed. Martin Wachs and Margaret Crawford (Ann Arbor: University of Michigan Press, 1992), 39.

21. Ibid., 40.

22. James Rubenstein, *Making and Selling Cars: Innovation and Change in the U.S. Automotive Industry* (Baltimore: Johns Hopkins University Press, 2001), 296.

23. Richard Moe, "Adding Up to No Place: How Transportation Policy Shapes Communities," *Historic Preservation News* 34 (June–July 1994): 14.

24. James J. Flink, *America Adopts the Automobile, 1895–1910* (Cambridge: MIT Press, 1970), 64. See also Michael L. Berger, *The Devil Wagon in God's Country: The Automobile and Social Change in Rural America, 1893–1929* (Hamden, Conn.: Archon, 1979).

25. See Lewis Mumford, *The Highway and the City* (New York: Harcourt, Brace, 1963).

26. See Robert A. Caro, *The Power Broker: Robert Moses and the Fall of New York* (New York: Vintage, 1975).

27. "Who'll Get Helped or Hurt by Auto Freeways," *U.S. News and World Report,* December 21, 1956, 90.

28. Polly Praeger, "Extinction by Thruway: The Fight to Save a Town," *Harper's,* December 1958, 64–66, 69–71.

29. "The Revolt against the Big-City Freeways," *U.S. News and World Report,* January 1, 1962, 48.

30. See Helen Leavitt, *Superhighway, Superhoax* (New York: Ballantine, 1970); Jane Holtz Kay, *Asphalt Nation* (New York: Crown, 1997); Andre Duany, Elizabeth Plater-Zyberk, and

Jeff Speck, *Suburban Nation: The Rise of Sprawl and the Decline of the American Dream* (New York: North Point, 2000).

31. Phil Patton uses the term *Parkinson's Law* (*Open Road: A Celebration of the American Highway* [New York: Simon and Schuster, 1986], 109). Bruce Radde uses the term *Murphy's Law* in reaching the same conclusion (*The Merritt Parkway* [New Haven: Yale University Press, 1993], 11).

32. Quoted in Fred W. Failey, "American Highways: Going to Pot," *U.S. News and World Report*, July 24, 1978, 36.

33. Cindy Skrzykcki, "The Rush to Rebuild Crumbling U.S. Highways," *U.S. News and World Report*, July 5, 1999, 51.

34. Warren Cohen and Mike Tharp, "Roadblock Ahead: A Record Highway Repair Spree Is Also Snarling Traffic," *U.S. News and World Report*, July 5, 1999, 19.

35. "Diamonds Are Forever," *Time*, May 17, 1976, 86.

36. Andrew Ferguson, "Road Rage," *Time*, January 12, 1998, 64.

37. Brian Ireland, "American Highways: Recurring Images and Themes of the Road Genre," *Journal of Popular Culture* 26 (December 2003): 483.

38. Peter Freund and George Martin, *The Ecology of the Automobile* (Montreal: Black Rose, 1993), 3.

39. Mark Williams, *Road Movies: The Complete Guide to Cinema on Wheels* (New York: Proteus, 1982), 6.

40. Roland Barthes, "The New Citroen," in *Autopia: Cars and Culture*, ed. Peter Wollen and Joe Kerr (London: Reaktion, 2002), 340.

41. Peter Marsh and Peter Collett, *Driving Passion: The Psychology of the Car* (Boston: Faber and Faber, 1986), 10.

42. Edward Hungerford, "The Traveling of Lydia," *Collier's*, January 3, 1920, 64.

43. Jean Baudrillard, *America*, trans. Chris Turner (London: Verso, 1989), 8.

44. Least Heat Moon, *Blue Highways: A Journey into America* (New York: Ballantine, 1982).

45. See, for example, Jack D. Rittenhouse, *A Guide Book to Highway 66* (Los Angeles: Rittenhouse, 1946); Ethel Bennercoff, *Travel Guide along Route 66* (San Francisco: Crocker, 1965); Quinta Scott and Susan C. Kelly, *Route 66: The Highway and Its People* (Norman: University of Oklahoma Press, 1988); Gerd Kittel, Alexander Bloom, and Freddy Langer, *Route 66* (New York: Thames and Hudson, 2002).

46. Dorothy R. L. Seratt, "Preserving Route 66," *Historic Illinois* 21 (June 1998): 7.

47. See Drake Hokanson, *The Lincoln Highway: Main Street across America* (Iowa City: University of Iowa Press, 1988).

48. Brian Butko, *The Lincoln Highway: Pennsylvania's Traveler's Guide* (Mechanicsburg, Pa.: Stackpole, 1996).

INDEX

References to illustrations are italicized.